Teachers' Career Trajectories and Work Lives

Professional Learning and Development in Schools and Higher Education

Volume 3

Professional Learning and Development in Schools and Higher Education disseminates original, research informed writing on the connections between teacher learning and professionalism in schools and higher education. Global in their coverage, the texts deal with the problems and practices of the field in different national and international cultural, policy and practice contexts. The methodology employed encompasses a broad spectrum of conceptual, theoretical, philosophical and empirical research activities. The series explicitly encompasses both the fields of schools and higher education.

The subject areas covered by the series are: professional learning in schools; contexts for professional learning; professional learning in higher education; change; the (new) meanings of professionalism in schools and higher education; training and development in schools and higher education; the 'well-being' agenda in schools and higher education; autonomy, compliance and effectiveness in schools and higher education; principal leadership in schools and higher education; middle-level leadership in schools and higher education.

For other titles published in this series, go to
www.springer.com/series/7908

Martin Bayer · Ulf Brinkkjær
Helle Plauborg · Simon Rolls
Editors

Teachers' Career Trajectories and Work Lives

 Springer

Editors

Martin Bayer
Danish School of Education
University of Aarhus
Department of Curriculum Research
Copenhagen
Denmark

Ulf Brinkkjær
Danish School of Education
University of Aarhus
Department of Curriculum Research
Copenhagen
Denmark

Helle Plauborg
Danish School of Education
University of Aarhus
Department of Curriculum Research
Copenhagen
Denmark

Simon Rolls
Danish School of Education
University of Aarhus
Department of Curriculum Research
Copenhagen
Denmark

ISBN: 978-90-481-2357-5   e-ISBN: 978-90-481-2358-2
DOI: 10.1007/978-90-481-2358-2
Springer Dordrecht Heidelberg London New York

Library of Congress Control Number: 2009928833

Springer is part of Springer Science+Business Media (www.springer.com)

Contents

Introduction to Teachers' Career Trajectories 1
Martin Bayer, Ulf Brinkkjær, Helle Plauborg, and Simon Rolls

1 Teachers' Career Trajectories: An Examination of Research 9
   Simon Rolls and Helle Plauborg

2 Career Stories as Gateway to Understanding
   Teacher Development... 29
   Geert Kelchtermans

3 Committed for Life? Variations in Teachers' Work,
   Lives and Effectiveness... 49
   Christopher Day, Pam Sammons, Qing Gu, Alison Kington,
   and Gordon Stobart

4 On the Unacknowledged Significance of Teachers'
   Habitus and Dispositions.. 71
   Jette Steensen

5 Teachers' Professional Learning
   and the Workplace Curriculum... 93
   Martin Bayer and Ulf Brinkkjær

6 Careers Under Stress: Teacher Adaptations at a Time
   of Intensive Reform.. 117
   Geoff Troman and Peter Woods

7 The Careers of Urban Teachers: A Synthesis of Findings
   from UCLA's Longitudinal Study of Urban Educators 143
   Karen Hunter Quartz

8 Teacher Gender and Career Patterns 159
   Mary Thornton and Patricia Bricheno

9   Regenerating Teachers 179
Corrie Stone-Johnson

**10   Listening to Professional Life Stories: Some
Cross-Professional Perspectives**.. 203
Ivor Goodson

Epilogue: Teaching Professions in Restructuring Contexts.......................... 211
Sverker Lindblad

Author Index... 225

Subject Index... 229

Introduction to Teachers' Career Trajectories

Martin Bayer, Ulf Brinkkjær, Helle Plauborg, and Simon Rolls

Teachers' career trajectories and work lives are at the centre of this anthology, with the contributions exploring a variety of aspects related to choosing and having a career in teaching. Whilst the focus is therefore primarily on teachers themselves and not so much on the schools or the educational systems in which they are employed, there can be little doubt that extensive reforms of the organization of schooling during recent years have had a significant impact on the teaching profession.

The comprehensive studies of teachers' careers by Lortie (1975), Sikes et al. (1985), Huberman (1993), and Fessler & Christensen (1992) provided new knowledge which remains influential to this day. However, since these results were published, innumerable studies have documented that teachers' work has changed dramatically. We therefore feel that the time is ripe for a book which can provide the reader with an overview of current leading research into teachers' career trajectories and work lives.

The various contributions collected here offer different perspectives on teachers' career trajectories and work lives both regarding the methodological approaches used in the empirical studies described and concerning the themes discussed. By presenting different perspectives, the anthology not only provides insight into many of the issues facing educational policymakers, but, perhaps more importantly, the challenges teachers deal with in their everyday working lives. Despite considerable differences in both the organization, and the pedagogical traditions at the centre of their national educational systems, many countries would appear to be facing similar problems and challenges concerning teachers' careers, professional development, recruitment and retention, etc. This may explain why, even though the various contributors present different national contexts, the issues described resonate far beyond national boundaries.

In this introduction, we will begin by examining the concepts of teachers' career trajectories and work lives and by outlining what characterizes this field of study. Thereafter we will describe the key issues affecting the teaching profession, presenting the various chapters along the way.

M. Bayer et al. (eds.), *Teachers' Career Trajectories and Work Lives,*
Professional Learning and Development in Schools and Higher Education 3,
© Springer Science + Business Media B.V. 2009

Teachers Career Trajectories as a Field of Study

In Chapter 1 'Teachers' Career Trajectories: An Examination of Research' Simon Rolls and Helle Plauborg present an overview of some of the most important contributions to the field of research on teachers' career trajectories and work lives.

As will be apparent from this anthology, studies of teachers' career trajectories and work lives are characterized by diversity in the use of terms and methodological approaches. Among other aspects, this is also due to different understandings of what constitutes a career and how it can be examined.

In everyday conversation the term 'career' usually refers to positions and to rising through the ranks of some form of formal hierarchical order, and is often reserved for specific fields of work. Career is therefore frequently ascribed positive value, which entails the acquisition of material or symbolic benefits such as a higher wage, greater influence or higher social status. It has often been pointed out (Lortie, 1975) that teaching has a relatively flat career structure with few possibilities to make oneself a career in this traditional sense of the word. In as much as teachers climb upward in the occupational hierarchy, this often involves spending fewer hours in the classroom and more time on administrative tasks. It is therefore difficult to identify career trajectories within the classroom, i.e. for teachers performing their key task, although it is possible to register career trajectories within the educational sector.

Research within the field of teachers' career trajectories, however, usually operates with a broader spectrum of definitions of the term 'career'. At one end of this spectrum one finds research where career is understood as the professional and personal development of the teacher over the course of their working life. In these studies teachers' careers are approached as a phenomenon which can be observed progressing through a number of stages or phases. Such an approach shares a linear developmental understanding of career with the everyday definition outlined above. However, instead of advancing through a set of professional positions, the hypothesis is that teachers progress through a number of more or less predetermined phases in the course of their professional lives. In this respect, research adopting such an approach is concerned with mapping general patterns in teachers' ways of handling their working lives, and to this end, it also seeks to predict typical pathways within the profession.

At the other end of the spectrum one finds approaches which operate with an 'empty' concept of career in the sense that career only refers to the period of time the teacher spends within the profession. These studies are often comprised of biographical narratives seeking to understand teachers' work lives in relation to other aspects of their lives. The central role afforded narrative is apparent in the preference for terms such as 'professional biography' or 'career story' instead of career trajectory. The focus here is on teachers' subjective, retrospective reconstruction as narrative of their 'formal career', understood as a 'chronological chain of positions, roles and so on, a teacher is involved in during his or her teaching years' (Kelchtermans, 1993: 445). In other words, the focus is on teachers' interpretations and reinterpretations of their career. In Chapter 2 'Career Stories as Gateway to

Understanding Teacher Development' Geert Kelchtermans offers a biographical approach to investigating teachers' career trajectories and work lives.

Between these two ends of the spectrum, one finds a number of approaches to studying teachers' career trajectories and work lives which, as will be apparent from the various chapters presented in this anthology, combine the two in various ways. What these contributions have in common (besides the fact that they all focus on aspects of teachers' career trajectories and work lives) is an underlying ambition to establish and develop understandings of the unique characteristics of teachers' work and the conditions that affect teachers' careers and work lives. Each in their own way seeks to point the way towards a future with improved possibilities for the performance of teaching.

Teacher Professionalism and Effectiveness

The peculiar characteristics and circumstances of different national contexts mean that it is impossible to provide an overview of all relevant educational reforms here. However, certain common themes can be tentatively identified across national boundaries as common to most, if not all, such reforms including stronger ties between education and economy; greater focus on the skills and competences which young people are equipped with when leaving school, especially in relation to the perceived needs of the labour market; a greater degree of political interference in curriculum goals and processes; a growing focus on evaluation; and parents and pupils regarded as educational consumers (Carney, 2005: 81). Stephen Ball sums up these changes in stating that teaching has to all intents and purposes been transformed into a commodity (Ball, 1998). These changes and tendencies have had, and continue to have, wide-reaching implications for teachers' everyday lives and for what is understood as constituting teacher professionalism.

The matter of what constitutes teacher professionalism and, indeed, whether or not teaching should be considered a profession has been the subject of considerable debate during recent years. Andy Hargreaves argues that the view of the teacher as an autonomous professional is a thing of the past and that we stand at a crossroads with one path leading towards a new flexible post-modern professionalism and the other towards a post-professional age (Hargreaves, 2000). Certainly, it is possible to view many of the educational reforms implemented in recent years as evidence that teachers' professional status is under threat. The tendency in many countries has been towards a more centralized control over curriculum. Providing an increasingly detailed programme stipulating the content of lessons removes one of the cornerstones of teacher professionalism, i.e. teachers exerting a considerable degree of control over *what* they teach. In addition, various national curricula, along with the growth in evaluations of teaching frequently involving surveillance of teachers' classroom practice, often attempt to determine not only the content of lessons, but also the form, thereby infringing upon teachers' ability to decide for themselves *how* they teach. Gill Helsby, for example, describes the effects of a series of structural changes to the educational system in the UK on teaching, concluding that they 'would seem to suggest a transformation of teachers' work and a mutation of their role from semi-autonomous professional to managed and expendable employee' (Helsby, 1999: 172). Such erosions of teacher autonomy have been accompanied by growing accountability demands. In many countries, new procedures have been introduced for testing pupils from an early age with the results, in some cases, used to compile league tables enabling comparisons between schools. As such, teachers are increasingly held responsible for the performance of their pupils despite the fact that a growing proportion of the actual performance of teaching is prescribed. It is perhaps to be expected that such changes can leave many teachers scratching their heads and wondering *why* they teach.

In Chapter 3 'Committed for Life? Variations in Teachers' Work, Lives and Effectiveness', Christopher Day, Pam Sammons, Qing Gu, Alison Kington and Gordon Stobart describe variations in teachers' work, lives and effectiveness in the context of precisely such reforms as described above. The chapter is based upon data from the VITAE project (Variations In Teachers' work, lives And Effectiveness) – a large study of teachers' careers conducted in England from 2001 to 2006. Although the empirical material stems from the UK, an increasing focus on accountability and effectiveness is far from unique to the UK educational sector, with reforms being introduced in many countries enabling the monitoring of pupil performance. Combining data on pupil achievement and factors relating to teachers' work lives and careers differentiates the VITAE study from other comprehensive studies of teachers' career trajectories.

Teacher Recruitment and Retention

One of the most debated issues facing the teacher profession is the recruitment and retention of adequate numbers of well-qualified teachers. Young people considering a future within the teaching profession may seek other fields in a time where work is often viewed as a source of not only income, but also self-fulfilment and personal development. This is especially problematic as teaching in most Western countries is currently in the process of a changing of the guard, with the generation which has dominated the profession for several decades reaching retirement age (OECD, 2005). Indeed, many countries are already facing a teacher shortage leading to an increasing focus on recruitment and retention. Hargreaves suggests that this does not only constitute a problem, but also provides a unique opportunity for renewal:

> Teaching is becoming a young person's profession again. Whoever enters teaching and however they approach their work will shape the profession and what it is able to achieve with our children for the next thirty years (Hargreaves, 2003: xvii).

An understanding of what motivates new entrants to the profession and the challenges they face, as well as the career pathways and changing work lives of their more senior colleagues, is essential if this opportunity is to be exploited. This is one of Jette Steensen's conclusions in Chapter 4 'On the Unacknowledged Significance of Teachers' Habitus and Dispositions', where she compares American and Danish student teachers' reasons for choosing a career as a teacher.

In Chapter 5 'Teachers' Professional Learning and the Workplace Curriculum', Martin Bayer and Ulf Brinkkjær present some results from a case study following two teachers' different career strategies during their first 8 years within the profession. By introducing the concept 'workplace curriculum' they illuminate an understanding of professional learning which involves both the development of classroom teaching skills and learning how to tackle the unwritten rules which apply within the workplace.

The rise of international comparisons of educational attainment, such as PISA, as well as the demands of an international labour market for a highly educated workforce, has led to an increasing focus not only on teacher recruitment and retention, but also on attracting and hanging on to *better* teachers. One field of study relating to the retention of teachers is stress and burnout, which became established as a field of research towards the end of the 1970s and was particularly widespread during the 1980s (see for instance Maslach, 1982a, b; Kyriacou & Sutcliffe, 1977a, b, 1978a, b, 1979; Woods, 1989). However, few studies have focused on those teachers who choose to leave the profession early and begin a new career away from teaching. Such a perspective is addressed by Geoff Troman and Peter Woods in Chapter 6 'Careers Under Stress: Teacher Adaptation at a Time of Intensive Reform', which describes the consequences of stress for teacher careers, and teachers' own strategies and adaptations in adjusting their careers. With a dramatic increase in recent years in the number of teachers receiving breakdown pensions and leaving the profession long before the pensionable age, combined with a growing global teacher shortage, it is glaringly obvious that far more attention needs to be paid to the conditions that contribute to career satisfaction within teaching.

As was evident from the above discussion of teacher professionalism, the criteria for what constitutes good teachers or good teaching, as well as who defines these criteria, are contested fields. Nevertheless, no matter how the 'good teacher' is defined, the goal of improving the quality of teaching at a time with a shortage of qualified teachers results in something of a conundrum. Schools are often forced to rely on staff without professional training in order to make up the numbers, with governments compelled to establish new short-course programmes resulting in a qualification as, for example, teaching assistant, or designed to quickly qualify individuals from other fields to enter teaching. In Troman's postscript he discusses the trajectories of 'career changers', i.e. individuals entering teaching from a background within a private sector occupation.

Recruiting teachers without a full teacher qualification may address short-term recruitment problems; however, reducing the qualification requirements for entering the profession can further undermine teacher professionalism, as it can be seen as giving credence to a belief that 'anyone can teach', thereby doing little to address the long-term problems of recruiting and retaining a quantity and quality of teachers able to provide an education to future generations.

Whilst recruitment and retention as such constitute major challenges in many countries, the extent of these challenges is related to various demographic factors. In Chapter 7 'The Careers of Urban Teachers: A Synthesis of Findings from

UCLA's Longitudinal Study of Urban Educators', Karen Hunter Quartz focuses on recruitment and retention of teachers in high-poverty, urban school districts. In Los Angeles, the University of California Los Angeles (UCLA) has established Center X which takes an experimental approach to the provision of pre- and in-service training of teachers and school leaders with the stated aim of preparing and retaining teachers in Los Angeles' most challenging schools. The overall focus in the chapter is on the effect of the teacher education programme on recruitment and retention of teachers within these high-poverty schools in Los Angeles.

A Gender Perspective on Teachers' Careers

Teaching, and especially primary teaching, has long been female dominated, with male teachers generally teaching older pupils – and this is certainly no less true today than in the past (Acker, 1996: 125). However, men continue to fill a disproportionate number of management and headteacher positions (Riddell & Tett, 2006). As Thornton and Bricheno point out in their book *Missing Men in Education*, '[t]eaching and the division of labour within it cannot be understood in isolation from the complex and changing social world in which it is located' (Thornton & Bricheno, 2006: 141). As such, the teaching profession reflects the general tendencies that women dominate what are considered the caring professions while men in the vast majority of fields are relatively well represented in positions of authority.

Despite the fact that there are clearly considerable differences in the career trajectories of male and female teachers, much of the classic literature on teachers' career trajectories and work lives pays little attention to the gender perspective. In her critical discussion of research on gender and teachers' work, Acker (1996) finds that, while a body of feminist work on teachers' work lives exists, this remains largely ghettoized. Meanwhile, most mainstream studies either disregard gender entirely or rely on stereotypical concepts of gender difference. When gender is incorporated, it is often briefly noted, but considered peripheral to the issue at hand. In Chapter 8 'Teacher Gender and Career Patterns', Mary Thornton and Patricia Bricheno go some way towards remedying this situation in presenting an overview of research into the relationship between gender and teachers' career trajectories, incorporating many recent studies. Here they consider the influence of political, economic and social factors in gendering teachers' careers.

Looking to the Future

In Chapter 9 'Regenerating Teachers', Corrie Stone-Johnson considers the role played by the specific historical context and conditions in determining teachers' career trajectories by introducing the concept of generation. Here she concentrates in particular on teachers belonging to what is commonly referred to as

'Generation X'. These teachers are of particular interest as the so-called baby boom generation, who have long dominated the teaching workforce, move into retirement and their younger colleagues begin to take up positions of authority and increasingly assume responsibility for shaping the future of the teaching profession. As previously noted, many of the most influential studies of career trajectories were conducted during a relatively short period stretching from the mid-1980s to the beginning of the 1990s. To what extent do the various career stages and trajectories identified in these studies apply to younger generations of teachers and how can we expect the careers of this group of teachers to develop over the coming years? It is these questions which lie at the centre of Stone-Johnson's chapter.

Few studies exist offering a cross-professional perspective on career trajectories. However, one such study is the Profknow project undertaken by a consortium of researchers from seven European nations. This extensive study compares professional knowledge and work lives of teachers and nurses. The final chapter and the Epilogue deal with issues relating to the Profknow study from different perspectives. In Chapter 10 'Listening to Professional Life Stories: Some Cross Professional Perspectives', Ivor Goodson provides examples comparing the life histories of teachers and nurses which can provide insight into careers within the teaching profession: both its unique characteristics and properties shared with careers within other so-called caring professions.

In the Epilogue 'Teaching Professions in Restructuring Contexts', Sverker Lindblad, on the basis of his work as part of the Profknow study, focuses on the intersection of the teaching profession and educational restructuring. By reviewing recent currents within research into the teaching profession, Lindblad's Epilogue can place the research presented in the preceding chapters on teachers' career trajectories and work lives within a broader perspective. In doing so, this can help to identify areas where further research could be fruitful. Further research into teachers' career trajectories and work lives is encouraged in a recent Organisation for Economic Co-operation and Development (OECD) report dealing with the issues of 'attracting, developing and retaining effective teachers': 'In many countries there are extensive research gaps concerning teachers, their preparation, work and careers' (OECD, 2005: 15).

Hopefully this anthology can be a step towards bridging that gap and can serve to inspire others to help build a body of knowledge which can inform educational policy and debates on the future of the teaching profession.

Acknowledgements We would like to thank everyone who over the years has inspired us in our work on teachers' careers and lives and thereby in some way contributed to the genesis of this anthology. First and foremost we thank all the contributors in the anthology for their cooperation, their belief in the project and all their hard work. We are particularly grateful to series editor Christopher Day who patiently believed in the idea of this anthology and made it possible. We would also like to thank Bernadette Ohmer at Springer for encouragement and quick responses which made us determined to finish the project. Our colleagues at The Danish School of Education, Marianne Brodersen and Leif Glud Holm, must be thanked respectively for critical response and moral support; and for tackling the technical and practical elements involved in compiling the manuscript. As editors, we take full responsibility for all errors, omissions and misinterpretations.

This anthology is part of a larger research project undertaken by Martin Bayer and Ulf Brinkkjær. The work of contacting and responding to the contributors and the publisher was undertaken by Helle Plauborg and Simon Rolls but without the commitment of Martin and Ulf, the anthology would have never come about.

References

Acker, S. (1996). Gender and teachers' work. *Review of Research in Education*, 21, 99–162.

Ball, S. (1998). Big policies/small world: An introduction to international -perspectives in education policy. *Comparative Education*, 34(2), 119–130.

Carney, S. (2005). Læreres Professionelle Udvikling. Mellem Politik, magt og Præstation. In T. Rask Eriksen & A.M. Jørgensen (Eds.), *Professionsidentitet i forandring*. Copenhagen: Akademisk Forlag.

Fessler, R. & Christensen, J. (1992). *The teacher career cycle: Understanding and guiding the professional development of teachers*. Boston, MA: Allyn & Bacon.

Hargreaves, A. (2000). Four ages of professionalism and professional learning, *Teachers and teaching: History and Practice*, 6(2), 151–182.

Hargreaves, A. (2003). *Teaching in the knowledge society: Education in the age of insecurity*. Maidenhead: Open University Press.

Helsby, G. (1999). *Changing teachers' work: The 'reform' of secondary schooling*. Buckingham: Open University Press.

Huberman, A. M. (1993). *The lives of teachers*. New York: Cassell.

Kelchtermans, G. (1993). Getting the story, understanding the lives: From career to teachers' professional development. *Teaching and Teacher Education*, 9, 443–456.

Kyriacou, C. & Sutcliffe, J. (1977a). Teacher stress: A review. *Educational Review*, 29, 299–306.

Kyriacou, C. & Sutcliffe, J. (1977b). The prevalence of stress among teachers in medium-sized mixed comprehensive schools. *Research in Education*, 18, 75–79.

Kyriacou, C. & Sutcliffe, J. (1978a). A model of teacher stress. *Educational Studies*, 4, 1–6.

Kyriacou, C. & Sutcliffe, J. (1978b). Teacher stress: Prevalence, sources and symptoms. *British Journal of Educational Psychology*, 48, 159–167.

Kyriacou, C. & Sutcliffe, J. (1979). Teacher stress and satisfaction. *Educational Research*, 21, 89–96.

Lortie, D. (1975). *Schoolteacher – A sociological study*. Chicago, IL: University of Chicago Press.

Maslach, C. (1982a). *Burnout: The cost of caring*. Englewood Cliffs, NJ: Prentice-Hall.

Maslach, C. (1982b). Understanding burnout: Definitional issues in analyzing a complex phenomenon. In W. S. Paine (Ed.), *Job stress and burnout* (pp. 29–40). Beverly Hills, CA: Sage.

OECD (2005). *Teachers matter – attracting, developing and retaining effective teachers*. Paris: Organisation for Economic Co-operation and Development.

Riddell, S. & Tett, L. (2006). *Gender and teaching: Where have all the men gone?* Edinburgh: Dunedin Academic Press.

Sikes, P. J., Measor, L., & Woods, P. (1985). *Teacher careers: Crises and continuities*. London: Falmer.

Thornton, M. & Bricheno, P. (2006). *Missing men in education*. Stoke-on-Trent: Trentham Books.

Woods, P. (1989). Stress and the teacher role. In M. Cole & S. Walker (Eds.), *Teaching and stress*. Buckingham: Open University Press.

Chapter 1
Teachers' Career Trajectories:
An Examination of Research

Simon Rolls and Helle Plauborg

During the 1980s, teachers' career trajectories were subject to significant interest among educational researchers. Three major contributions, undertaken by Michael Huberman in Switzerland, Ralph Fessler in the US and Patricia Sikes in the UK, saw the light of day. All three presented models dividing teachers' career trajectories as a whole, from graduation to retirement, into various phases or stages. As such, they sought to identify generally valid patterns in the ways in which teachers' work lives developed. Since then, most studies of teachers' work lives have either concentrated on particular issues such as teacher retention and classroom effectiveness, or taken a biographical approach presenting the career histories of a single or a small number of teachers. One exception is the extensive investigation of variations in teachers' professional lives in England undertaken by Day et al. (2006). Today, these four studies constitute the most comprehensive investigations of the career paths of teachers and, in this chapter considerable attention is therefore paid to the work of Huberman, Fessler, Sikes and Day, supplemented by insights contributed by other recent research dealing with particular aspects and periods of teachers' professional lives in greater detail.

The question at the centre of this chapter is 'What do we know about teachers' career trajectories?' Initially, our ambition was to categorize the research within the field. We envisaged that it would be possible to identify patterns which would enable us to perform such a categorization, for example in the methodological approach to studying teachers' career trajectories or in the conclusions drawn from these studies. However, we found that such a categorization was somewhat arbitrary and became more a constraint than a support with regard to our intention of examining the research within the field. That is not to say that the attempt by Huberman et al. (1997) to divide studies of teachers' career trajectories into a paradigmatic and a narrative category is without value, but like most categorizations, focusing on differences and similarities concerning one particular aspect often leads to a neglect of differences and similarities concerning other aspects.

In the following sections, we will therefore map the main contributions to research within this area available in English. As such, the objective of this chapter is to summarize and discuss the findings and approaches of research within the field of teachers' careers.

M. Bayer et al. (eds.), *Teachers' Career Trajectories and Work Lives*,
Professional Learning and Development in Schools and Higher Education 3,
© Springer Science + Business Media B.V. 2009

Introduction to the Work of Huberman, Fessler, Sikes and Day

In his highly influential work *The Lives of Teachers* (Huberman, 1993[1]), Michael Huberman presented a study of career phases as experienced by middle school and high school teachers in Geneva. This presentation builds upon extensive qualitative research involving lengthy interviews with 160 teachers and provides a highly detailed account of the differences and similarities in their career trajectories.

Inspired by developmental psychology and social psychological perspectives represented by the 'Chicago school' (Park, Mead, Cooley, Thomas, Blumer), Huberman seeks to apply and test more wide-reaching theories and models of the human life cycle in relation to teachers and their careers. As such, on the basis of existing literature, he identifies seven phases which he groups under the heading "General trends in the professional life cycle of teachers" (Huberman, 1993: 3).

Central to the work of Ralph Fessler is the Teacher Career Cycle Model which he first developed in 1984 and has since regularly returned to and reassessed. The most comprehensive description of the model is to be found in the book *The Teacher Career Cycle – Understanding and Guiding the Professional Development of Teachers*, written in collaboration with a number of colleagues and with Fessler and Judith C. Christensen as lead authors and editors (Fessler & Christensen, 1992). The foundations for the Teacher Career Cycle Model were formed by extensive empirical studies, utilizing workplace observations, interviews, case studies and literature review (Fessler & Christensen, 1992: 31). The model is intended to help understand the dynamic nature of teachers' work lives, taking into account the effects of various factors, both inside and outside of the workplace environment, on teachers' motivation, commitment and enthusiasm at different stages of their careers. Fessler identifies eight career stages, but stresses that these are not to be understood as comprising a straightforward linear development, but rather that the range of influences exerted by what he terms *external environmental factors*, which he splits into the broad categories of *personal and organizational environment*, means that the individual teacher will drift up and down between the stages (Fessler & Christensen, 1992).

Patricia Sikes outlines five phases of teachers' career trajectories which correspond with their broader life cycles. Her conception of the human life cycle references the work of Levinson and his broad social-psychological understanding of adult development (Sikes, 1985). In identifying the age at which teachers enter and leave the various phases, Sikes differs somewhat from Huberman and Fessler which, as we will see, also results in certain differences with regard to how the phases of teacher career trajectories are perceived. The research which forms the foundation for Sikes' articulation of 'the life cycle of the teacher' was conducted with 48 secondary school teachers using the life history method. These teachers represent a wide range of ages, career stages and subjects, and the various phases are described on the basis of the descriptions of both teachers describing their current situations, and those reflecting upon earlier stages of their careers.

Day et al. conducted the VITAE project (Variations in Teachers' Work, Lives and Their Effects on Pupils) between 2001 and 2005, commissioned by the UK

Department for Education and Skills. At the centre of this project is a longitudinal study of the lives and careers of 300 teachers from 100 different schools representing a broad range of socio-economic contexts and pupil attainment levels (Day et al., 2007: 2). The study utilized both qualitative and quantitative data encompassing interviews, teacher and pupil questionnaires and pupil assessment data. As suggested by the inclusion of pupil assessment data, as well as the project's title, VITAE, unlike the studies carried out by Huberman, Sikes and Fessler, explicitly addresses the question of teacher effectiveness and how this changes over the course of teachers' careers and lives. The study identifies six professional life phases, grouped according to the number of years a teacher has spent within the profession.

We will now explore in more detail the various models of career trajectories presented in these four major studies, supplemented by insights provided by other relevant research concerning the professional lives of teachers.

Entering the Profession and the First Years

The path to becoming a teacher varies due to a wide range of both national and institutional approaches to teacher training and education. Furthermore, such approaches are subject to constant change. For example, the overwhelming majority of teachers in Denmark have completed a 4-year education at a teacher training college. An alternative path has only existed since 2002 for people with another educational background to complete a shorter teacher training course and enter the profession. Currently, discussions are ongoing with regard to establishing full teacher training courses placed within universities. This goes to show the variations in the possible paths to becoming a teacher – and that is just looking at Denmark over the last 7 years! It is clear that such differences in the educational backgrounds of teachers will be of significance in determining their future career trajectories.[2] However, in this examination of research we have chosen to concentrate on studies of teachers' career trajectories after they have finished their education. Whilst Fessler includes what he terms the preservice phase, which is the period of training and education prior to a career as a teacher, in keeping with his emphasis on the cyclical nature of teachers' careers, he also allows for the possibility that teachers can find themselves at the preservice stage later in their careers. This possibility arises when a significant change of role necessitates retraining.

Newly Qualified

Huberman, Sikes, Fessler and Day all describe a phase concerning the newly qualified teacher's first steps upon entering the profession. Huberman refers to this phase as career entry, which is characterized as a period of survival and discovery and can therefore be regarded as representing the often contradictory emotions experienced by newly qualified teachers. On the one hand, the teacher is faced with the challenge of meeting a reality which their training has seldom fully prepared them for, often resulting in a lack of self-confidence or a feeling of inadequacy. On the other hand, precisely these challenges and the opportunity to utilize the training they have received lead to an eagerness to learn and develop as a teacher (Huberman, 1993: 5).

Following Levinson (1978) Sikes et al. term this phase, wherein teachers between the ages of 21 and 28 are situated, *entering the adult world*. A lot of teachers in this age group have not yet made a conscious decision of a long-term future within the profession, and only a few have what could be considered a career plan. In common with Huberman, Sikes describes how on entering the profession the majority of teachers experience a reality shock, where they struggle to tackle disciplinary problems at the same time as dealing with the problems of acquiring knowledge of a subject and communicating this knowledge to pupils. However, Sikes finds that during this phase disciplinary problems become less important to the teachers in her study, who instead begin to prioritize subject-related expertise as their most important competence. Similarly, promotional ambitions are to a large extent related to becoming the head of a subject department as opposed to positions of pastoral care (Sikes et al., 1985: 25ff.).

Fessler likewise describes an induction phase during which teachers, having qualified and begun their first job, spend a few years being socialized into the system and adjusting to the gulf between the theory acquired during their preservice training and the realities of classroom practice they are now faced with. The main priorities for teachers during this phase are gaining the respect of pupils and colleagues, and becoming comfortable in dealing with everyday classroom practice. Once again, Fessler stresses that teachers may re-enter the induction phase later in their careers in conjunction with a significant change in their working lives, such as moving to a new workplace (Fessler & Christensen, 1992: 41).

Day found that the vast majority of teachers had a high level of commitment to the profession during their first 3 years of teaching. Day divides this cohort of teachers into two subgroups, one with a developing sense of efficacy and another with a diminishing sense of efficacy (Day et al., 2006: 89). Common for both groups are difficulties in learning to deal with pupil behaviour. What proved decisive in determining whether the newly qualified teachers had an easy or difficult beginning to their careers was the amount of support they received from school or departmental leaders (Day et al., 2006: 91).

Whilst there is clearly a great deal of common ground to be found within these accounts, all of which stress a, at times, complicated acclimatization to the realities of everyday classroom practice, it is already possible to identify a few vital differences between the work of Huberman, Sikes, Fessler and Day. Day divides the teachers into groups according to number of years spent within the profession. Within these seniority groups, Day identifies subgroups according to the teachers' self-efficacy. Due to her division of teacher career trajectories according to age groups, Sikes allows for a significant degree of development and change in teachers' concerns and priorities within a particular stage. Huberman and Fessler, on the other hand, tend to regard significant changes in teachers' needs, attitudes and situations as constituting a transition between phases, as it is these very attributes which form the basis for the various stages they identify, as opposed to the fixed boundaries in the models developed by Sikes and Day. Indeed Fessler emphasizes the possibility that teachers can re-enter the same phase at various points in their career, which, naturally, is not possible with age-determined phases as used by Sikes or phases based on professional seniority as found in the VITAE project. However, they all agree that teachers during their first years in the profession are especially vulnerable. Incidents and experiences during this phase can prove decisive in determining their further career trajectories – or indeed, whether or not they remain within teaching.

The terms *critical incidents* or *critical phases* are widely used within research on teachers' work lives. Lynda Measor studied the role of critical incidents in determining the career trajectories and identities of teachers (Measor, 1985; Sikes et al., 1985). 'I want to argue that there are "critical incidents" which are key events in the individual's life, and around which pivotal decisions revolve. These events provoke the individual into selecting particular kinds of actions, they in turn lead them in particular directions, and they end up having implications for identity' (Measor, 1985: 61). Measor identifies three types of critical phases during which critical incidents are most likely to occur: extrinsic, personal and intrinsic. Extrinsic critical phases can be brought about by historical events, such as wars, which dramatically alter individuals' life conditions, or, for example, by changes more directly related to the workplace, such as policy changes significantly altering practice within schools. Personal critical phases are, unsurprisingly, related to major upheavals in individuals' personal lives, such as marriage, divorce, childbirth or the death of a family member. Intrinsic critical phases are specific periods during an individual's career where he or she is faced with important decisions. Measor pinpoints six such periods:

1. 'Choosing to enter the teaching profession
2. The first teaching practice
3. The first eighteen months of teaching
4. Three years after taking the first job
5. Mid-career moves and promotion
6. Pre-retirement.' (Measor, 1985: 62)

Her study focuses on the third of these intrinsic critical phases, the period of the first 18 months of teaching, and is based on interviews with English secondary school teachers at various career stages, from 5 years of teaching experience to retirement, looking back upon the early stages of their careers. The majority describe their initial problems in controlling their pupils. The critical incident in this case takes the form of an often violent confrontation between the teacher and the pupils, and forces the teacher to seriously consider his or her approach to pupil discipline. It is the ability of a particular event to bring about self-reflection regarding the individual's identity as a teacher – sometimes through a change in direction, sometimes through a newfound clarity in relation to an existing direction involving the articulation of a coherent set of values – that marks it out as a critical incident. 'It is not that the critical incident necessarily introduces anything totally new into the ideology or framework of practices of the teacher, rather it probably acts to crystallize, and set ideas, attitudes and actions that the teacher has more generally been considering' (Measor, 1985: 68). Other critical incidents, identified by teachers as constituting defining moments, take place at various stages of the teacher's career, comprising key elements in the construction of the self and forming crossroads in relation to career trajectories.

David Tripp operates with a broader understanding of critical incidents. Unlike Measor, Tripp's definition allows for less dramatic situations, for example where a particular lesson results in an unexpectedly positive reaction from pupils. For Tripp '[s]uch incidents are rendered critical by the author by being seen as indicative of underlying trends, motives, and structures, and are often presented to teachers in the form of a dilemma in which they have a choice of at least two mutually exclusive courses of action' (Tripp, 1994: 69). As such, incidents are assigned critical status retrospectively when identified by the teacher as being of significance for later practice. The early stages of a teacher's career can be of particular importance in this regard, presenting the newly qualified teacher with a series of dilemmas such as Tripp describes, and often helping to form approaches to teaching which are maintained throughout the career.

The significance attached to the early years within the profession is evident from the amount of research which, whilst not explicitly dealing with teachers' career trajectories, investigates the transition from teacher training to the workplace. The work of Les Tickle looks more closely at some of the dilemmas and challenges related to the induction of new teachers into the profession. Like Huberman, Tickle found the widely referred to reality shock encountered by new teachers on entering the profession, and the resulting feelings of frustration and anxiety, to be countered by excitement at the challenges they faced and joy and satisfaction when a lesson or teaching strategy was a success (Tickle, 1994: 148). These contradictory emotions reflect the complex web of factors described by Tickle as impacting upon the newly qualified teacher's entry into the profession: '[Induction is] a process of becoming a teacher in a system of mass schooling, which is increasingly buffeted by structural economic, technological, political, and social changes, resulting commonly in contradictory pressures and increased role expectations' (Tickle, 2000: 6ff.). Moreover, Tickle's study of teachers entering the profession shows that the individual teacher is often largely left to his or her own devices in dealing with the challenges of the profession, receiving little formal support or guidance from colleagues. Those frameworks for support and guidance which do exist commonly have the simultaneous function of assessing the performance of the newly qualified teacher. The potentially damaging consequences a negative assessment can have for their careers do little to encourage an open dialogue regarding problems and possibilities for improvement in relation to professional practice. As such, new teachers are frequently left to make informal approaches to staffroom colleagues when seeking advice or just in need of someone to listen to their thoughts and anxieties – something which many are reluctant to do due to a fear of appearing vulnerable or incompetent to more experienced colleagues (Tickle, 1994).

Tickle argues that the common view of teacher induction as a bridge between initial training and a professional career, during which time the newly qualified teacher is gradually socialized into the world of teaching, is neither accurate nor desirable. Indeed, such a view, according to Tickle, suggests the reproduction of existing practice, neglecting the opportunity for entrants to the teaching profession to provide the renewal and innovation which can help equip schools to tackle the constantly changing challenges of teaching: '[T]his image of professional growth and development is not entirely appropriate, given the problematic and changing nature, and dynamic contexts, of professional practice which induction might help teachers to enter' (Tickle, 2000: 1ff.). Tickle also prescribes possible solutions and suggests that an environment where greater value is placed on the ability of new teachers to contribute to professional practice may have the advantage of lessening the anxiety described above when seeking advice from experienced colleagues.

The Swedish researchers Fransson and Morberg (2001) have likewise examined some of the problems faced by newly qualified teachers in their encounter with practice. On the basis of existing research, the following tendencies are identified:

1. Compared to experienced teachers, newly qualified teachers find it difficult to adapt lesson plans, whether in terms of content or teaching strategy, when the situation demands it. Among other things this has to do with the fact that they have yet to develop a repertoire for dealing with unpredictable situations.
2. Newly qualified teachers explain the learning difficulties of pupils with reference to these pupils' personal and social circumstances, whereas experienced teachers look for explanations within the specific learning situations, enabling a more solution-oriented approach.
3. Newly qualified teachers are not prepared for many of the challenges that the teaching profession presents, such as problems with regard to classroom management and tackling disciplinary problems.
4. Finally, newly qualified teachers have problems exercising leadership and handling conflicts. (Fransson, 2001: 190ff.)

McCormack et al. (2006) find that teachers in the initial stages of their career struggle to develop a professional identity. 'Many came to the end of their first year of teaching questioning their position in the school and their success as a teacher, still needing and wanting some form of feedback and confirmation as to their value within the school' (McCormack et al., 2006: 110).

The results of Bayer and Brinkkjær's study suggest the role played by colleagues in the attempts by newly qualified teachers to develop an identity as a teacher. Shortly after being employed in their first teaching post, a group of newly qualified Danish teachers were asked to order their relationships with their pupils, colleagues, pupils' parents and school management according to their importance in their everyday working lives. More than 15% pointed to their relationships with colleagues as more important than even their relationships with their pupils. The teachers were asked similar questions after approximately 1 and 2 years of employment, and the proportion of teachers who stated that their relationships with colleagues were the most important remained more or less the same (Bayer & Brinkkjær, 2005: 125). Here, it is worth bearing in mind that, particularly among lower primary teachers in Denmark, it is not uncommon for a considerable amount of their teaching to be conducted in cooperation with a support teacher. In Bayer and Brinkkjær's (2005) study, 19% state that they primarily perform their daily tasks in collaboration with colleagues. Although a correspondence is not clear from the results, one might expect these teachers to be more likely to ascribe importance to their relationships with colleagues.

To summarize, when entering the profession, newly educated teachers face a reality shock. However, at the same time, the potential exists for a high degree of satisfaction when a lesson goes well. The newly educated teachers focus on gaining the respect of pupils and colleagues, although the latter can seem difficult as the teachers are to a large extent left to their own devices with little contact or formal support from their fellow teachers.

Established Within the Profession: The Mid-Career

Following the often turbulent period immediately after entering the profession, research on teachers' careers is somewhat scant. It would almost seem as though mid-career teachers are only of interest when they are considering leaving the profession, or when in the middle of some or other form of crisis. However, this might be expected to change in the near future, what with the growing focus on teachers' continuing professional development (see, e.g., Day & Sachs, 2004), and on the challenges of teacher retention demanding a greater understanding of the ups and downs experienced by teachers during the course of their careers. Especially studies dealing with what teachers consider the positive aspects of their job, what inspires teachers to continue to strive to improve their classroom practice, or studies of incidents with considerable positive impact on the further career trajectories of teachers are rare and may present fertile ground for future research. As such studies are not yet common, in the following sections we focus on teachers' decisions to stay within the profession, their mid-career crises and teacher dropout.

Making a Commitment

Huberman's second phase is termed the stabilization phase. It is during this period that the teacher commits himself or herself to a career in teaching. Stabilization also refers to pedagogical mastery insofar as the teacher achieves a greater degree of comfort within the classroom and confidence in his or her abilities.

According to Day, teachers who have spent between 4 and 7 years within the profession are concerned with gaining confidence within the classroom and establishing an identity as a good and effective teacher (Day et al., 2006: 93). Promotion and additional responsibilities beyond the classroom are likewise identified as key factors influencing the professional lives of teachers during this phase. As such Day, in contrast to Huberman, identifies this phase as one which for many teachers is not characterized by stabilization, but rather by experimentation and diversification – a phase which Huberman identifies at a later point in the teacher's professional life. Day attributes this difference in findings to changes in the structure of the teaching profession, with a tendency towards teachers receiving promotion and greater responsibility at an earlier stage in their careers. Again Day operates with subgroups, in this case teachers who are classified as growing, coping or declining in relation to their sense of identity, self-efficacy and perceived effectiveness. Of particular importance in determining these subgroups is the teachers' ability to manage their workload and events in their personal lives (Day et al., 2007: 75ff.).

For Sikes, the *age 30 transition* phase (28–33 years) is characterized by teachers feeling that they either have to fully commit themselves to teaching or change careers. As such, unlike Huberman, she includes those teachers who decide to leave the profession in her account and there is therefore not talk of a period of unequivocal stabilization. According to Sikes, those who decide to make the commitment to teaching consider themselves sufficiently experienced to take on tasks that require a greater degree of responsibility, and this, combined with the fact that many start a family and therefore need a higher income, means that the desire for promotion plays an increasingly prominent role. Teachers maintain a higher degree of relational distance to their pupils than was the case in the previous phase where they felt closer to their pupils, both emotionally and in terms of age. Some of the teachers begin, during this period, to have a more relaxed attitude towards preparation and classroom activities, whilst others become increasingly concerned with pedagogical development rather than their subject (Sikes et al., 1985: 41ff.).

During Fessler's third *competency building* stage, the teacher seeks to further hone his or her skills, attempting to develop new teaching methods and strategies. Fessler characterizes the teacher at the competency building stage as highly motivated and receptive to new ideas (Fessler & Christensen, 1992: 41). Similar to Sikes' identification of the phase teachers enter after a few years within the profession as one where a decision is made to either fully commit to a teaching career or attempt to pursue other possible lines of work, Fessler identifies the degree of success in getting to grips with the job during this period as central in determining whether the teacher will continue to grow into the job or experience frustration and instability.

Whilst Fessler's competency building stage would seem to include a certain degree of stabilization, at least if the teacher is successful in his or her attempts to master pedagogical skills, the emphasis on trying out new ideas also has much in common with the phase Huberman terms *experimentation and diversification*. As the name suggests, teachers are here likely to take a more experimental approach and to seek new challenges, both inside and outside the classroom.

Becoming Established Within the Profession

According to Day, a critical phase in a teacher's professional life is situated between 8 and 15 years of seniority (Day et al., 2006: 101). He refers to this period as a crossroads where teachers decide upon the direction of their remaining careers: Should they dedicate themselves to classroom teaching? Or should they prioritize climbing the rungs of the career ladder? However, not all teachers within this phase have such a positive view of their future professional lives. For the teachers within this more pessimistic subgroup, it is rather a question of whether or not to remain within the profession due to declining motivation levels and an increasing disillusionment with teaching.

In Fessler's account, teachers at the *enthusiastic and growing* stage are now experienced and good at their jobs, but nevertheless continue to strive to improve. This stage is dependent upon high levels of motivation and enthusiasm and a workplace environment providing encouragement and opportunities for continued development. Here we see an example of the importance Fessler attaches to external environmental factors in determining the individual teacher's route through the teacher career cycle. As mentioned previously, he operates with two broad categories: personal and organizational environment factors, with the above providing an example of a factor relating to the organizational environment.

Another example of an organizational environment factor is public trust. Teachers' commitment to their profession can be either reinforced or undermined by the level of public trust, whether at national, local or school level. Cutbacks, a perceived increase in the burden of administrative work and bureaucratic control mechanisms, or the regular expression of highly critical opinions of schools and teachers within the media and the political sphere are likely to lead to a degree of disillusionment or in extreme cases even career exit. Investments in facilities and professional development, meanwhile, can ignite renewed enthusiasm and growth in teachers.

Among the examples of personal environment factors Fessler identifies is family. The level of support provided by partner and offspring is likely to be reflected in the teacher's professional motivation and commitment. In addition, the birth of a child, a divorce or the loss of a parent are just three examples of family matters whose impact is likely to reach beyond the home and into the classroom, whether positively or negatively.

Individual disposition is likewise an important personal environment factor. The goals, experiences and values of an individual teacher will have a great significance in relation to his or her career cycle. For example, the importance of achieving promotion will be dependent upon the individual's level of ambition, so, in the case of a teacher with the goal of becoming headmistress, a failure to reach the level of head of department by her mid-30s may lead to disillusionment and career frustration. Over time, the individual's disposition can develop, resulting in changing priorities, with a greater or lesser degree of commitment as a result (Fessler & Christensen, 1992: 35ff.).

Sikes' third phase (30–40 years) is a period of *settling down* and is the point at which energy, commitment, ambitions and self-confidence are at their highest. Two challenges are evident during this phase, especially for men. Firstly, they attempt to establish themselves professionally, to be recognized by their colleagues and by the local society. Secondly, they put a lot of effort into achieving promotion if they have not already done so. A number of these male teachers assume positions as scout leaders, football coaches, etc. For female teachers, it is common that, by now, they have children of their own, and that the job as a teacher has consequently become second priority. Women who have been on maternity leave come back as 'mothers', in the sense that their relationship to the pupils becomes more maternal (Sikes et al., 1985: 45ff.).

Whilst Sikes' use of the phrase 'settling down' may give associations to Huberman's stabilization phase, her description of male teachers seeking new challenges both inside and outside the classroom and high levels of energy and commitment is undoubtedly reminiscent of both Huberman's account of the experimentation and diversification phase and Fessler's enthusiastic and growing stage. Here it is important to note that Sikes, unlike the other studies mentioned here, highlights common differences between the sexes. Nowhere are such differences more conspicuous than during this period, where Sikes found that many female teachers put their careers on hold for several years in order to concentrate on caring for their families, whilst their male counterparts find achieving promotion all the more important, often becoming the family's primary breadwinner as their wives stay home to look after the children. While Fessler includes family situation as an example of an external environmental factor, he does not explore how the impact of parenthood can vary considerably in relation to the career trajectories of male and female teachers. Sikes' account, on the other hand, once again reflects the foundation of her approach upon the general life stages of individuals, where there are considerable differences between the stage of early motherhood and that of early fatherhood. It is worth noting that Sikes' study was first published in 1985, when it was far more common for women to play the roles of mother and housewife until their children started school. In a contemporary context, in particular in countries with a highly developed system of childcare institutions such as one finds in Scandinavia, it may be suggested that the differences in the career trajectories of male and female teachers would be less significant, although societal expectations that women put their career ambitions to one side and prioritize the welfare of their children undoubtedly still play a role. A contemporary exploration of gender differences in relation to teachers' career trajectories can be found in Chapter 8 by Thornton and Bricheno in this book.

The fourth phase outlined by Sikes (40–50/55 years) is a period where those teachers who have successfully come through the previous phases now often occupy positions as school leaders, vice-principals or leaders on other levels. Most teachers in this phase therefore spend relatively few hours in the classroom. Sikes' study thus incorporates teachers who, for all intents and purposes, no longer perform teaching work, in contrast with Huberman and Fessler who both concentrate on the career trajectories of teachers who continue to work as teachers. Once again, gender is also a significant factor in Sikes' study of the career trajectories of teachers during this period. The male teachers who are yet to be promoted have by now given up this ambition, whilst the female teachers within this age group have increasing promotional ambitions, as their children are now of an age that makes this possible. As such, the career aspirations of female teachers at this point often mirror those of their male counterparts some years previously (Sikes et al., 1985: 50ff.).

For teachers who had spent 16 to 23 years within the profession, Day describes that events in their personal lives, as well as professional duties outside the classroom, had a greater impact on their commitment than previously. As a consequence Day divided these teachers into three subgroups: those who continue to advance to higher positions within the educational hierarchy and, as a result, display increasing motivation and commitment; those who cope with the challenges of both their professional and personal lives and maintain more or less the same level of commitment; and those who, due to career stagnation, no longer find satisfaction in their work (Day et al., 2006: 108).

Should I Stay or Should I Go?

According to Sikes, it is common for teachers between 37 and 45 to experience a crisis, with those who feel they have not fulfilled their professional ambitions naturally being especially vulnerable. However, despite the fact that many teachers experience a crisis during this phase, Sikes finds that it is also a period where teachers have a high work morale. Teachers are also by now often regarded as staffroom authorities, acting as role models and setting the standards for how the job as teacher should be performed (Sikes et al., 1985: 50).

One can find a parallel to these descriptions of mid-career crises in the phase Fessler terms *career frustration*. This is described as a period of disillusionment with the teaching profession often located at the midpoint of a teacher's career, but which can be found earlier, particularly among those who have struggled during the competency building stage or those who find themselves unable to transform their ideals into practice. During this stage, teachers find themselves stuck in a job they find unsatisfying, unable to see perspectives for future development. Therefore, teachers can either rediscover enthusiasm or gradually withdraw from the profession (Fessler & Christensen, 1992: 257).

Huberman's *reassessment* phase is likewise characterized by varying degrees of self-doubt, ranging from a sense of stagnation, where teaching practice is felt to have become routine and uninspiring, to complete disillusionment brought about, for example, by a perceived lack of career opportunities within the profession, or a series of educational reforms which the teacher is unable to align with his or her personal ideals and beliefs. As a result, the teacher may reassess his or her future career, attempting to regain previous commitment through a break with established routines; seeking pastures anew, inside or outside of the profession; or alternatively accepting the status quo and deciding to soldier on. However, despite the common appearance of such a phase in the literature, Huberman does not find many examples of teachers going through a period of self-doubt and reassessment.

The next phase identified by Huberman is one of *serenity and affective distance*. This is a state of mind prevalent amongst teachers well established within the profession. The teacher feels self-sufficient, confident in her ability to deal with the challenges of classroom practice and with little to prove to herself or others. At the same time, the close bond often felt by younger teachers in relation to their pupils is replaced by a greater degree of distance and less emotional investment.

The question of teachers leaving the profession is also dealt with in the VITAE project. Among these teachers, only a very small number regarded it as likely that they would work outside the school or change their career completely (Day et al., 2006: 183). This contradicts Bayer and Brinkkjær's study of newly qualified teachers' job satisfaction, as here the proportion of teachers who did not wish to remain in the teaching profession in the long run was 34% – a figure that increased during their second year of employment to 44%. In other words, it appears as if the teachers' dissatisfaction with the profession increases after a couple of years of employment (Bayer & Brinkkjær, 2005: 134). However, available statistics detailing the proportion of teachers completing their training between 1992 and 2001 working within schools during this period show that few actually leave teaching (Statistics Denmark, 2004).

A number of studies explore the reasons behind teacher dropout. In a longitudinal study following 156 individuals since their participation in a postgraduate teaching diploma at the Sydney Teachers' College in 1978, the differences between those who leave the profession and those who stay are investigated (Wilhelm et al., 2000). After 15 years, 87 of the graduates remained within the profession. Of those who had left, the great majority (74%) did so within 5 years of graduating, with the behaviour of pupils, conflict with colleagues, a lack of feedback from students and a poor salary among the reasons most often cited. Interestingly, salary is also cited, alongside holiday and leave conditions, making a difference in relation to pupils, feedback from students and a good social network within the school among the common reasons for teachers remaining within the profession. At the same time, the study found that those who went on to leave often had a more negative image of the profession prior to entry than those who stayed and were less likely to envisage themselves teaching after graduation. This leads the authors to conclude: 'It appears that decisions regarding teaching and not teaching were often made prior to entering into the profession' (Wilhelm et al., 2000: 301). As such, it is suggested that factors relating to professional working conditions and work-related stress are of less importance than individuals' perceptions in this regard prior to entering the profession. Indeed, many undertake teacher training with a view of their future career path as outside of the profession.

In surveying available studies, Kyriacou et al. (2003) conclude that four reasons for leaving the teaching profession appear to be particularly common:

> Firstly, workload: the workload is too heavy, the work is too pressurised and stressful, and there is too much administration to do. Secondly, salary: the salary level does not provide them with the type of lifestyle they want and the associated career prospects are poor. Thirdly, disruptive pupils: some pupils' constant misbehaviour makes the work too difficult. Fourthly, low status: the status of the teaching profession is perceived to be low. (Kyriacou et al., 2003: 256).

As they point out, these characteristics of the teaching profession should come as little surprise, and, as was the case with the study conducted by Wilhelm et al., they underline that in such cases a long-term career in teaching may never have been the intention. The fact that such large numbers either never enter the profession or leave within the first few years would seem to support this.[3]

As such, leaving the profession prior to retirement would seem to be less common amongst teachers at later stages of their careers. However, their careers can still be subject to major upheaval, even if they are more likely to continue teaching in some or other capacity. In their study of stress among mid- to late-career UK primary school teachers, reprinted in this volume, Geoff Troman and Peter Woods identify three strategies for dealing with stress: retreatism, downshifting and self-actualization (Troman & Woods, 2000: 260). In the first case, the teacher feels forced to leave the profession for good, no longer feeling able to cope, whether through early retirement or a move to a new and unrelated area of work. Downshifting refers to teachers, again feeling unable to deal with the demands of their current positions, taking a voluntary step down the career ladder, relinquishing posts of responsibility, or even moving to part-time or supply teaching and thereby effectively giving up any ambitions of future career advancement and instead seeking ways of coping until retirement. Finally, self-actualization refers to teachers who are able take a more active approach in overcoming career-related stress. Whilst this can involve leaving the profession in order to pursue unfulfilled ambitions, it can also sometimes be achieved through a move to a different school better aligned with the individual's values, or through participation in leisure-time activities outside the workplace. Overall, the picture painted by Troman and Woods is of a profession where teachers are exposed to increasingly stressful working conditions leading to a realignment of career trajectories.

In a survey carried out amongst over 70,000 UK teachers, the General Teaching Council found that 56% of those questioned reported a lower morale than when they first began teaching, with only 11% reporting an increase. The most common reasons appear to be too heavy a workload and a seemingly endless and constantly expanding stream of administrative tasks (Kyriacou et al., 2003: 261). The results of Day's study (see Chapter 3 by Day in this book) likewise show that recent reforms lead to an increase in the stress experienced by teachers.

To summarize, there would seem to be broad agreement among researchers that teachers in their mid-career period are at their peak. Thus, the mid-career is characterized by teachers that are focused on pedagogical and curricular development as well as their own career development. In particular, male teachers seek promotion whilst their female counterparts are often described as being primarily committed to raising a family. However, it is also during this period that a considerable number of teachers experience career frustration and even crisis which for some leads to serious considerations regarding their future within the profession.

The Final Years

As was seen earlier when looking at research into teachers' mid-career, there is a tendency to concentrate on 'problem' teachers, e.g. those who leave the profession early. As such it will come as little surprise that research on teachers approaching retirement is sparse. After all, these teachers are on their way out of the profession anyway and therefore there is little incentive to fund and conduct research into the professional lives of these teachers. In recent years, life-history research has mined the wealth of experience and information offered by teachers in the latter stages of their careers, able as they are to provide a retrospective account of an entire career trajectory. However, the focus here is predominantly on the career as a whole, with particular attention often paid to the important transition phases and critical incidents earlier in their careers and with detail rarely provided concerning the teacher's work life as he or she approaches retirement.

Disengagement

Fessler describes a phase he terms *career stability* which bears little resemblance to Huberman's stabilization phase. During this career stability phase, teachers no longer exhibit the same degree of commitment and job satisfaction as earlier in their careers. They may well still perform a perfectly adequate job, but are no longer motivated to seek new teaching practices and are 'in the process of disengaging from their commitment to teaching' (Fessler, 1995: 186). Whilst the acceptance of one's lot and dampening of ambitions is reminiscent of Huberman's account of a serenity and relational distance phase as well as of Sikes' account of middle-aged male teachers who had failed to fulfil their ambitions regarding promotion, the serenity and high work morale present in their accounts is nowhere to be found, replaced by a disinterested detachment.

Dissatisfaction is, however, apparent in the phase Huberman refers to as one of *conservatism and complaints* where teachers feel aggrieved at current developments. Ideals for creating a better future are replaced by the impetus to protect the present from degeneration and a harkening back to a perceived golden age. Huberman did not find evidence that the majority of teachers become more conservative and dissatisfied as they get older. On the contrary, he identified a large group of elder teachers who remained open, energetic and optimistic (Huberman, 1993: 246).

The final phase identified by Huberman is *disengagement*. This is a phase where the teacher gradually withdraws from professional commitments, prioritizing matters unrelated to his or her career and taking a more selective approach to professional activities.

The results of the VITAE project indicate that teachers with 24 to 30 years of experience, as is the case with those with 16 to 23 years within the profession, are negatively impacted by external policies and initiatives. Again Day identifies two subgroups: teachers who remain satisfied and committed to the profession; and teachers who continue to lose their motivation, often resulting in early retirement (Day et al., 2006: 111). During the final phase, comprised of teachers with more than 30 years of experience, relationships with pupils and pupil attainment are the key factors in determining levels of job satisfaction. For one subgroup of teachers motivation and commitment remained high, whilst the other subgroup consisted of teachers in whom declining levels of motivation and increasing disillusionment lead to career exit.

Sikes' fifth and final phase (50/55 years – retirement) has preparing for retirement as its most significant challenge. Although teachers still display high work morale, they sense a decline in energy and enthusiasm for the job. During this final phase, teachers are less concerned with disciplinary problems and become increasingly occupied with what their pupils get out of their teaching. Teachers have authority and, due to their experience within the profession, are no longer willing to waste time on matters they consider trivial (Sikes et al., 1985: 52ff.).

Fessler also describes a phase he terms *career wind-down*, during which the teacher prepares to leave the profession, whether due to retirement or a career change, voluntary or not. The period can be marked by either pleasant reminiscing or bitter recriminations and can last anything from a month or two to several years. Often this period will be characterized by mixed emotions on the part of the teacher, a mixture of excitement and uncertainty as to what the future after teaching holds.

As was the case with Fessler's preservice phase, he is also alone in detailing a post-service phase which he terms *career exit*. This phase is, naturally, the period immediately after leaving the profession, whether due to retirement, unemployment, maternity leave, beginning work in a new profession or taking up an administrative post within education.

To sum up, during the final years of their career, teachers are on the one hand confident in their abilities as a teacher and on the other hand preparing to withdraw from the profession. As they approach retirement, teachers are described as having falling levels of motivation and commitment. This is often accompanied by an appraisal of their careers, whether this takes the form of a nostalgic trip down memory lane or a series of bitter regrets.

Research into Teachers' Career Trajectories – What Next?

So what does the future hold for research into teachers' career trajectories? The first question one must pose in this respect is to what extent the term career trajectory is relevant and useful in the study of teachers' work lives. Despite Fessler's attempts to underline the cyclical nature of the various stages identified in his career model, the very concept of a career trajectory and of a series of career stages or phases seems unable to escape a certain linearity, proposing a limited number of established pathways which the individual can follow and giving the impression of a unified movement in one particular, implicitly forward, direction. Their general nature means that the individual teacher will seldom be able to recognize himself or herself within the broad brushstrokes of such models. Additionally, one could argue that the picture painted does not necessarily only apply to teachers but to career trajectories within a variety of professions. For example, it does not seem specific to the teaching profession that one can become frustrated in one's career when ambitions of promotion are not fulfilled or that levels of motivation and commitment can decline as one approaches retirement. There is a lack of research on what is particular to *teachers'* careers and one way of gaining insight into this field could be to compare with careers within other professions. At the same time, such studies can enable a cross-pollination of ideas between related but previously separate fields of research. The pan-European PROFKNOW study, which compares and contracts the professional lives of teachers and nurses, is one of the few examples of such a cross professional perspective (see Chapter 10 by Goodson in this book).

Chapter 6 by Troman and Woods in this book suggests that the idea of a personal career trajectory carved out by the individual teacher does not accurately describe the experiences of many teachers. At the same time, they conclude that traditional views of a career within teaching are disintegrating and point towards discontinuous and fragmentary careers as a tendency that will continue to become increasingly common. Indeed, recent reforms in Denmark making it easier for teachers to supplement their training with further degrees seem likely to increase the frequency of teachers leaving the profession or using it as a springboard for an entirely different career. As mentioned at the beginning of this chapter, there is now also easier access to the teaching profession via untraditional routes. Are we witnessing the beginning of the end of the idea of teaching as a vocation populated by individuals who dedicate their working lives to the classroom? Certainly, the tendencies outlined would seem to suggest teaching will increasingly comprise but one part of a career, and that the teaching corps will become far more heterogeneous with regard to educational and professional background.

The very fact that four separate studies, undertaken within three different national contexts, resulted in the identification of a broadly similar set of career stages suggests that they are not without foundation, with the generality of the descriptions comprising both the greatest strengths and primary weakness of the models presented by Day, Huberman, Fessler and Sikes. Studies tracing individuals' paths in and out of the profession are increasingly common. Research charting, for example, how the various stages and phases are manifested among those entering teaching later in life or the significance of different backgrounds for teachers' work lives helps to add greater complexity and nuance to these general models. Likewise, studies focusing on particular aspects of the teaching profession contribute with more detailed descriptions. Teaching practice, that is to say how teachers' preparation and execution of lessons develop during the course of their careers, has for instance been largely neglected in studies of teachers' career trajectories. This is somewhat surprising bearing in mind that classroom-based teaching is usually considered teachers' primary task. Focusing greater attention on this central element of teachers' work lives would further pinpoint the particularity of teachers' career trajectories in relation to more general tendencies applicable to careers within a variety of professions. Such studies could aid in targeting continuing professional development (CPD) initiatives by providing insight into the challenges and problems commonly faced by teachers in the classroom at various points in their careers. Teachers' knowledge is often described as tacit, segmental, intuitive and individual (see, e.g., Elbaz, 1983; Lortie, 1975). Studying the development of teachers' practice within the classroom in a longitudinal perspective could generate opportunities for verbalizing the knowledge teachers draw upon in the course of their everyday working lives.

Conclusion

At the beginning of this chapter we asked the question: What do we know about teachers' career trajectories? To answer this question, we have examined the models presented by Huberman, Fessler, Sikes and Day, as well as introducing the results of other studies concerning particular aspects or stages of teachers' work lives.

The difficult transition from teacher training to entering the profession in the form of a first job is often described as a 'reality shock'. It can be argued that such transitions will always be difficult, regardless of profession. However, the lack of contact with colleagues that still characterizes the vast majority of time spent performing the job's primary task would seem to exaggerate this shock. Despite attempts to establish more collaborative forms of teaching, teachers are often left feeling alone and isolated, with little support in dealing with the problems they face. However, entering the teaching profession is not without its rewards, as teachers express that a great deal of satisfaction is gained when a lesson goes well. For much of this early part of their careers, teachers are concerned with gaining the respect of both colleagues and pupils, and learning some basic tools for planning and conducting lessons. Those teachers who successfully tackle the difficult first period continue to grow in self-confidence, motivation and ability during their mid-career, but throughout teachers' careers critical incidents can result in periods of crisis and fluctuations in levels of job satisfaction. Factors such as ambitions of promotion, fulfilled or not, and family life can likewise have a significant impact on teachers' work lives during this period. As teachers approach retirement, their motivation often declines. Time is spent looking back over their careers and reflecting upon whether they have achieved what they set out to. Such reminiscing can lead to a positive appraisal of their achievements or regrets of missed opportunities as there is no longer the possibility to do anything about them.

Since the 1980s, when Huberman, Fessler and Sikes conducted their respective studies, there seems to have been a movement within the field of research into teachers' careers and work lives away from the sort of general models they presented. This examination of research indicates, despite one significant exception, namely the VITAE project (Day et al., 2006), that studies of teachers' careers are becoming less comprehensive, focusing instead on particular aspects of teachers' careers or on individual teachers' life histories. These changes in approach may reflect changes in the ways teachers' careers are conceived towards a less linear, more individual understanding. The challenge for future research within the field is to rethink the ways in which teachers' careers are investigated and to re-conceptualize the term career trajectories in such a way that it reflects the complexity of contemporary career patterns.

Notes

1. Originally published in his native French in 1989.
2. For further exploration of the significance of teacher training, see, for example, Darling-Hammond and Bransford (2005).
3. In England, approximately 40% of those who begin a teacher training course never enter the profession, while of those who do approximately 40% have left again within 5 years (Kyriacou et al., 2003: 256).

References

Bayer, M. & Brinkkjær, U. (2005). *Professional Learning in Practice: Newly Qualified Teachers' and Educators' Encounter with Practice*. Copenhagen: Danish University of Education Press.

Darling-Hammond, L. & Bransford, J. (Eds.) (2005). *Preparing Teachers for a Changing World*. San Francisco, CA: Jossey-Bass.

Day, C. & Sachs, J. (Eds.) (2004). *International Handbook on the Continuing Professional Development of Teachers*. Maidenhead: Open University Press.

Day, C., Stobart, G., Sammons, P., Kington, A., Gu, Q., Smees, R., & Mujtaba, T. (2006). *Variations in Teachers' Work, Lives and Effectiveness*. London: Department for Education and Skills, Research Report No. 743.

Day, C., Sammons, P., Stobart, G., Kington, A., & Gu, Q. (2007). *Teachers Matter: Connecting Work, Lives and Effectiveness*. Maidenhead: Open University Press.

Statistics Denmark (2004). *Lærerflugt?* News, May 2004, UVM.

Elbaz, F. (1983). *Teacher Thinking – A Study of Practical Knowledge*. London: Croom Helm & Nichols.

Fessler, R. & Christensen, J. (1992). *The Teacher Career Cycle: Understanding and Guiding the Professional Development of Teachers*. Needham Heights/Boston, MA: Allyn and Bacon.

Fessler, R. (1995). Dynamics of Teacher Career Stages. In T. Guskey & M. Huberman (Eds.), *Professional Development in Education: New Paradigms and Practices* (pp. 171–192). New York: Teachers College Press.

Fransson, G. & Morberg, Å. (Eds.) (2001). *De första ljuva åren: lärares första tid i yrket*. Lund: Studentlitteratur.

Fransson, G. (2001). Den första tiden – en forskningsöversikt med fördjupningar. In G. Fransson & A. Morberg (Eds.), *De första ljuva åren: lärares första tid i yrket* (pp. 186–215). Lund: Studentlitteratur.

Huberman, M. (1993). *The Lives of Teachers*. London: Cassell.

Huberman, M., Thomson, C. L., & Weiland, S. (1997). Perspectives on the Teaching Career. In *International Handbook of Teachers and Teaching* (pp. 11–77). Dordrecht: Kluwer.

Kyriacou, C., Kunc, R., Stephens, P., & Hultgren, Å. (2003). Student Teachers' Expectations of Teaching as a Career in England and Norway. In *Educational Review* Vol. 55, No. 3, pp. 255–263. Routledge.

Lortie, D. (1975). *Schoolteacher – A Sociological Study*. Chicago, CA: University of Chicago Press.

McCormack, A., Gore, J., & Thomas, K. (2006). Early Career Teacher Professional Learning. In *Asia-Pacific Journal of Teacher Education* Vol. 34, No. 1, pp. 95–113. Routledge.

Measor, L. (1985). Critical Incidents in the Classroom: Identities, Choices and Careers. In S. Ball & I. Goodson (Eds.), *Teachers' Lives and Careers* (pp. 61–77). Lewes: Falmer.

Sikes, P. J. (1985). The Life Cycle of the Teacher. In S. Ball & I. Goodson (Eds.), *Teachers' Lives and Careers* (pp. 27–60). Lewes: Falmer.

Sikes, P. J., Measor, L., & Woods, P. (1985). *Teacher Careers: Crises and Continuities*. Lewes: Falmer.

Tickle, L. (1994). *The Induction of New Teachers*. London: Cassell.

Tickle, L. (2000). *Teacher Induction: The Way Ahead*. Maidenhead: Open University Press.

Tripp, D. (1994). Teachers' Lives, Critical Incidents, and Professional Practice. In *International Journal of Qualitative Studies in Education* Vol. 7, No. 1, pp. 65–76. Taylor & Francis.

Troman, G., & Woods, P. (2000). Careers Under Stress: Teacher Adaptations at a Time of Intensive Reform. In *Journal of Educational Change* Vol. 1, No. 3, pp. 253–275. Kluwer.

Wilhelm, K., Dewhurst-Savellis, J., & Parker, G. (2000). Teacher Stress? An Analysis of Why Teachers Leave and Why They Stay. In *Teachers and Teaching: Theory and Practice* Vol. 6, No. 3, pp. 291–304. Routledge.

Chapter 2
Career Stories as Gateway to Understanding Teacher Development

Geert Kelchtermans

Talking about a teacher's 'career' may sound to some like a contradictio in terminis. Since most often teachers work with some status of civil servant, once they have obtained a tenure contract, most of them remain a classroom teacher for the rest of their professional lives. Possibilities for vertical promotion (and thus for 'making a career' in that particular sense) are scarce. This remains true in spite of the different initiatives to create positions for so-called teacher leaders, where teachers take up other responsibilities within a school besides (or instead of) being a classroom teacher (see e.g. Smylie, 1994; Harris, 2003). One example is the use of experienced teachers as mentors or coaches of beginning colleagues. Another is the involvement of teachers as administrative staff to support the principal in developing the local school policy. Teachers, however, tend to think of these jobs not so much in terms of a career promotion as a teacher, but rather as taking on a new and different job, which implies a (temporary) farewell to the core business of being a classroom teacher. That core business entails teaching one's own group of students (in primary schools) or one's own subjects to a specific number of class groups (in secondary schools). Smylie's review of research on teacher leaders (Smylie, 1994) also confirmed this central focus on the teacher–student interaction: teacher leaders valued their (temporary or part-time) role outside the classroom more positively if they saw immediate benefits from it for their own students.

The traditional concept of 'career' as the chain of the possible and actually acquired hierarchical positions within a particular professional occupation has limited analytical value with regard to teaching. Yet, – as I argue in this chapter – it might remain meaningful to talk about a 'career' in teaching if one conceives of 'career' in terms of one's learning processes 'on the job'. In my work I have approached the teaching career in these terms, focusing on the process of professional development as the lifelong learning and development processes teachers find themselves in during their professional lives in the job. From that perspective, career promotion is not so much a 'moving up' in the hierarchy of positions (since the position most often remains more or less the same), but rather a 'growing' of one's professionalism. In that case, the focus of attention shifts towards the experiences of the person in the job and therefore the teachers' experiences in their working lives over time. Or in other words, the concept of career is approached from its subjective meaning for the person involved. In order to explain and illustrate this approach to teachers' careers or work lives, I will draw on my research on teacher development from a narrative–biographical perspective (Kelchtermans, 1993, 1994, 1996, 1999; Kelchtermans & Ballet, 2002a, b; Kelchtermans & Vandenberghe, 1994).

After presenting the theoretical assumptions underlying the narrative–biographical perspective, I will discuss in more detail the phenomena of critical incidents, phases and persons and their role in teachers' career stories. Next I will elaborate the idea of professional development as a process of career-long learning, resulting in changes in teachers' actions as well as in their thinking. To conceptualize this thinking I have introduced the notion of the personal interpretative framework, which encompasses both an understanding of one's self as a teacher (professional self-understanding) and the professional know-how that is used in the enactment of the job. In the final paragraph I use the concept of 'parallel careers' to illustrate how the narrative–biographical perspective allows us to acknowledge the idiosyncratic nature of teachers' work lives as well as to move beyond the individual teacher and his or her career story into a more general, yet grounded, understanding of teachers' careers.

The Teacher Career from a Narrative–Biographical Perspective

In the narrative–biographical perspective on teachers' work lives, one is less interested in teachers' formal career (the chronological list of positions a teacher takes up over the years), but rather looks at the so-called subjective career, i.e. teachers' personal experiences in their professional lives over time (Kelchtermans, 1993). *Biographical* refers to the fact that teachers – like all human beings – live their lives between birth and death (e.g. see Goodson, 1984, 1992; Krüger & Marotzki, 1996). Human existence is fundamentally characterized by temporality. Interpretations, thoughts and actions in the present are influenced by experiences from the past, and expectations for the future. This influence, however, is not to be thought of in a deterministic or objective and causal sense, but rather rests on complex processes of interpretation and sense-making. From a biographical perspective, we are thus not so much interested in teachers' experiences as historical facts, but rather in the meaning these events have for the people who live them. In other words, 'the work from this perspective is centred on the practical understandings that teachers develop as they enter into and begin to teach and on the ways in which beginning and/or experienced teachers come to frame their understandings within their life stories or life experiences' (Carter & Doyle, 1996, p. 129). The subjective career thus encompasses the personal meaning teachers attribute to job experiences over time.

The *narrative* aspect in the perspective refers to the central role of stories and story-telling in the way teachers deal with their career experiences. Since the mid-1980s, research on teachers and teaching has become strongly influenced by the developments in cognitive psychology and, in particular, by the growing understanding of how people's actions are influenced by their cognitions.

In order to understand (but also to influence or train) teachers' actions, one needs to identify and analyse their 'thinking' (cognitive processes and representations) (e.g. see Clark & Peterson, 1986; Richardson & Placier, 2001; Wideen et al., 1998; Cochran-Smith & Lytle, 1999). This 'teacher thinking' research developed into different strands of research and methodologies. One of them was the narrative approach (e.g. see Carter & Doyle, 1996; Casey, 1995–1996; Clandinin, 2006; Gudmundsdottir, 2001). Teachers – again like other human beings (Polkinghorne, 1988) – spontaneously tend to use narrative language to represent their sense-making of job experiences. Since 'narrative is the discourse structure in which human action receives its form and through which it is meaningful' (Polkinghorne, 1988, p. 135), narratives are considered to be a powerful way to unravel and understand the complex processes of sense-making that constitute teaching. 'Humans are storytelling organisms who, individually and socially, lead storied lives. The study of narrative, therefore, is the study of the ways humans experience the world' (Connelly & Clandinin, 1990, p. 2; see also Clandinin, 2006). In other words, teachers' 'subjective careers' are reflected in, and represented through, their narrative accounts of those experiences.

This narrative–biographical perspective has guided my research on teachers' work lives and careers over the past 2 decades. In my understanding this perspective is characterized by five theoretical assumptions: narrative, contextualized, interactionist, constructivist and dynamic (Kelchtermans, 1993). It draws on collecting and analysing the narrative accounts (stories, anecdotes, metaphors, etc.) through which teachers reconstruct their job experiences and make sense of them by organizing them in a meaningful narrative structure. I refer to these accounts (representing teachers' subjective careers) as 'career stories' or 'professional biographies'.

The approach thus is also in line with *constructivist* thinking: teachers actively (re)construct their experiences into a narrative that makes sense to them (e.g. see Berger & Luckmann, 1985; Gergen & Gergen, 1987; Markus & Wurf, 1987). Career stories are constructed in the act of telling: they are told and can be retold. Their importance and relevance lies not so much in their historical truth, but rather in their power to reveal the particular meaning events had for the teacher.

This sense-making does not happen in a vacuum, but always takes place in particular *contexts*. From this perspective, however, context is understood both in a temporal and a spatial sense. Stories inevitably situate experiences in both time and space. There is always a when and a where. The 'when' refers to a particular moment or period in time. The 'where' includes the organizational, institutional, political, social, cultural and material environments and conditions teachers work in (e.g. the school with its particular staff, school population, infrastructure, embedded in particular ways in the local communities and in a particular prevailing policy environment – see e.g. Kelchtermans, 2007b).

It is clear that the perspective also implies an *interactionist* stance (Blumer, 1969; Mead, 1974). Human behaviour is understood as resulting from a meaningful interaction with the environment or context, in which other social actors as well as shared patterns of sense-making (e.g. organisational culture – Schein, 1985) play a prominent role. Both the interactionist and the constructivist characteristics help to avoid a conception of human action that is too cognitivistic as well as too subjectivist (e.g. only considering what happens 'inside' the teacher).

Finally, the interactionist, constructivist and contextualized characteristics imply that the narrative–biographical perspective takes a largely anti-deterministic stance: the person is the story of his or her life as he or she tells it. The meaning of (career) experiences for a person thus may change over time. This *dynamic* aspect acknowledges that we don't need to look for stories as the one (historically) true representation of one's experiences, but that stories are acts of sense-making and thus may be re-storied over time. This implies that the 'subjective career', as represented in career stories, can change as time passes.

Before elaborating on the particular outcomes of this approach, it is important to stress that the narrative–biographical perspective on teachers' work lives and careers is particularly relevant from an *educational research interest*. Different from a developmental psychological interest (e.g. aiming at identifying development phases in adult life) or a sociological research interest (e.g. the fluctuations in the social status of the teaching job over time), an educational research interest focuses on what happens with the protagonist of the story as a particular person. More specifically, the narrative–biographical perspective allows reconstruction and analysis of teachers' professional learning and development based on the experiences during their career. This interest in teacher development over time has been the focus of my own work: Career stories reveal how teachers make sense of career experiences and what they learn and take with them in their future perceptions, deliberations and actions.

In the rest of this chapter I will illustrate this potential of the narrative–biographical approach to teachers' work lives to deepen our understanding of teachers' professional learning over time.

Critical Incidents, Phases and Persons

Unlike the work on teachers' careers by Sikes et al. (1985) or Huberman et al. (1989, 1993), my goal was not to develop a model of career phases, but rather to reconstruct teachers' professional learning over time.[1]

In the professional biographies, I found that certain events, phases or people operated as key experiences or turning points for the narrator. Those experiences had created a problem, a new situation, a challenge to the self-evidence of one's normal routines or actions. They created a kind of rupture in the smooth development of one's work life (see also Sikes et al., 1985; Measor, 1985). They forced the teacher to rethink and reassess particular ideas or beliefs or to reconsider taken-for-granted actions or practices. Because of their compelling character I called them – following Sikes et al. (1985) – 'critical incidents' or 'critical phases', being 'key events in an individual's life, ... around which pivotal decisions revolve. They provoke the individual into selecting particular kinds of actions which lead in particular directions' (Sikes et al., 1985, p. 57). Because I found that very often the critical character is also linked to meeting or working with a particular person, I added the notion of 'critical persons' (Kelchtermans, 1993, 1996, 1999; Kelchtermans & Vandenberghe, 1994).

'Critical' here thus needs to be understood as distinctive, compelling and challenging, often with a strong emotional connotation. Filipp (1990) has emphasized the 'emotional non-indifference' which characterizes these experiences. Because of their emotional pervasiveness, these experiences actually force teachers to stop and reconsider their taken for granted courses of action. They feel compelled to do so as if they didn't have a choice. Denzin uses the concept of 'epiphany' in a similar way, to refer to 'those life experiences that radically alter and change the meanings persons give to themselves and their experiences' (Denzin, 1989, p. 125). Epiphanies, he argues, alter the fundamental meaning structures in a person's life. Their effects may be both positive and negative (Denzin, 1989, p. 141).

It is important to stress, however, that the critical character of these incidents, persons and phases lies not so much in the incident, person or phase as such, but rather in the meaning they had and have for the narrator. Critical incidents, phases and persons are only identified in retrospect and are as such 'constructed' by the storyteller. The same experience (e.g. participating in in-service training or the encounter with a particular inspector during a school audit) can become a critical incident for one teacher, yet not for his or her colleague who was involved as well. As such the definition of critical incidents, phases and persons remains a formal one: events and people that are remembered as having had a particularly significant meaning for the narrator. The specific content of the events or the relation to the people can be very different and also differ between teachers.

A Fragment from Leo's Career Story (Kelchtermans, 1993)

During the interview, Leo, an experienced primary school teacher, recalls the three years that he had worked as a remedial teacher. Because at that time the job of remedial teacher in primary schools in Flanders was relatively new and because he soon realised that his knowledge on learning problems and remedial teaching interventions was rather limited, he had decided to enrol in a three-year intensive training on remedial teaching. Thanks to that course as well as to the many informal meetings with colleagues, he got acquainted with remedial teachers from other schools in a climate of collegiality, commitment and dynamism. Leo is enthusiastic when recalling those years of trying, studying, and exchanging with colleagues. ... It was "a wonderful period" and "a heroic period" too. Those times gave him great personal satisfaction and stimulated him in his job. At the same time it gave him a new perspective for his career as a teacher: "I was determined to be a remedial teacher for the rest of my life". He was prepared to do whatever it took in terms of study and specialisation to achieve this career ambition. The authenticity of his commitment becomes evident from the fact that the training took place every Wednesday afternoon and Saturday morning for three years and as such cost him a lot of his leisure time. Not to mention his personal study time. But Leo was really 'fascinated by the domain of learning problems and ... I was prepared to deeply engage and commit myself'.

This euphoric period, however, was abruptly ended when the school board decided to put Leo in Grade 3. The role of remedial teacher was assigned to a colleague, who had been on sick leave and was still struggling with health problems. Therefore it was difficult for her to manage a full class group. For 'reasons of humanity and compassion', the school board had judged that working with small numbers of pupils would be more feasible and appropriate for that teacher. The board's autocratic decision ruined Leo's prospects as a remedial teacher. Fortunately the pupils in Grade 3 were a motivated and pleasant group to work with. The classroom, however, was an old, ugly and unpleasant room and Leo absolutely detested it ('I couldn't work in such a place'). Because the school board had led him to believe that he would stay in that grade and that classroom as a teacher in the future, Leo decided to thoroughly renovate the room. With a few 'artistic friends' he spent a couple of weeks renovating the entire classroom, painting the ceiling in blue with white clouds and rainbows, etc., turning it into a colourful environment and made it 'his' room. But two years later, Leo was once more moved by the school board to teach a class in the Boys School, a few blocks down the road. In this way, Leo not only lost his favourite classroom, but he also found himself forced to work in a room that was even worse than the last one had been. 'I arrived in a real pigsty … that made things even worse. It was unbelievable'. Yet, because Leo at that time still didn't have his tenure contract, he was in too weak a position to challenge that decision (at the risk of losing his job). The eight years of his career in Boys School are described by Leo as his 'career breakdown': he taught without any commitment or enthusiasm and tried to cope with the disillusion by developing activities outside school, like training to become a librarian (in line with his love for books and literature) and working as a freelance journalist.

Leo's past as a remedial teacher continued to influence his professional judgements and opinions. Especially when his oldest daughter turned out to have learning problems … 'I've often said – since K. (daughter) was in Grade 1 – in fact, every teacher should have a son or daughter with learning problems. I know it sounds a bit crude … but only then did I fully realise what I was actually doing to the children as a teacher. What a threat or burden it could be to them, having to do homework and having lessons to learn. … How exhausted children can be when coming home after a full day in school. I didn't have any idea of all that before then…or how depressed children can be because of school. I didn't have the slightest idea … how could I? Well, and if one has kids who are doing well at school, one will never get to understand that. But, yes, the experience of K. definitely influenced my teaching, it certainly made me change the way I use homework, the way I handle tests … yes, absolutely.'

This fragment clearly illustrates the notions of critical incident, person and phase. Leo's period as a remedial teacher and the one in the Boys School are examples of critical phases for Leo. They respectively had a deeply positive and a negative impact on his career, his professional commitment and job satisfaction. At the same time the school board, and in particular its chair, obviously acted as negative critical persons. Their decisions had a devastating influence on Leo's working conditions, his expectations for the future as well as his idea about himself as a teacher. First they ruined his future as a remedial teacher and then they took away the renovated classroom. Especially the latter is interesting, since the classroom becomes a strong symbol in Leo's story: renovating it was part of his emotional coping strategy to deal with the decisions of the board. It was his way of trying to get over it in a positive way and rediscover his job motivation and a sense of commitment. A metaphorical reading of this story fragment shows that even the hardly recovered feeling of 'being at home' in the classroom (and thus in the job as a teacher) is destroyed by literally putting him 'out of the house' (equal to the cherished and creatively decorated 'own' classroom). Only from this biographical background can the pervasive emotional meaning of what – from a distance – may look like a trivial organizational issue be properly understood.

The fragment also shows how the narrative approach is able to grasp and unravel the complex interplay of personal experiences and expectations of an individual teacher, his professional behaviour as well as the organisational context he works in. It further illustrates how fatal and devastating certain formal decisions on these organisational working conditions can be for the teacher's professional development and job commitment, even if those decisions seem evident from a view of rational organization planning.

Fragments from Anita's Career Story (Kelchtermans & Vandenberghe, 1994)

When Anita, a first grade teacher, returned to work after having been on maternity leave, she discovered that the pupils in her class had made very little progress in reading during her absence.

> She explains 'The principal had taken a Kindergarten teacher as a substitute for me ... and then ... the kids just couldn't read. Absolutely nothing. On the second day of my return, the principal came into my classroom and complained about the poor reading results of my pupils. And he blamed me for it! And I – I hadn't completely recovered from pregnancy and the birth of my child yet ... because that had been quite a difficult time ... and I started to cry. Oh, I felt so miserable! If this would happen now, I would just frankly tell him what I think ... but ... I never forgot this. It was so unfair! How could I help it ... I just hadn't been there'.

The intonation, the vehemence with which she recalls this small incident after more than 10 years reflect the deep indignation and humiliation she had felt at the time about this unfair treatment: being personally blamed for failing students who she hadn't been teaching for several months.

> In another fragment Anita also recalls the pupils in her class three years before [the interview]. That class had been very difficult to handle. It was a rather large class and some of the pupils struggled with learning and behavioural problems. One of them was Peter. Anita tells how the experiences with that class had really made her doubt her capacities as a teacher and almost made her quit teaching. One incident illustrates the conflict, but also its resolution.
>
> 'One day I had to fight with Peter. Really fight him, you know. Afterwards I stood there ... trembling all over. I was handing out papers to do a writing exercise. Peter took the sheet of paper, crumpled it up, and threw it on the floor. I ordered him to pick it up. He refused, laid his head on his arms and did not move. I again ordered him to pick it up. No movement. Then I said: "Listen, you will not go home until you've picked up the paper". And then he started to fight. Took his school bag and started to hit me. I really had to use force to make him stop and sit down again. I said: "Peter, pick up that sheet of paper". Finally, he did it ... and that was the turning point ... I had broken his resistance. From that day onwards, I had few problems with him. You know, that is exactly what makes it so difficult in this job: you have to stick to your guns. It's much easier to give in, but then you'll always have the same problems coming up again and again.'

This fragment illustrates also what Sikes et al. (1985) have called 'counter incidents': incidents that look like critical incidents in their constellation, but the way people cope with them is different. A counter-incident is successfully mastered. It usually follows a critical incident or it can mark the end of a critical phase. The counter-incident shows that the new situation, challenge, task or problem is successfully 'countered'. The fight with Peter showed Anita that she was (still) able to handle difficult class groups and thus do a good job as a teacher, after she'd been having doubts about herself.

A Fragment from Marc's Career Story (Kelchtermans, 1999)

In his career story, Marc, a fourth grade teacher in mid career, recalls a 'nervous breakdown' when he was in his early 30s. This experience marked the end of the first phase in his career, which he labelled as 'searching, experimenting and working hard to get external recognition'. During these first 10 years he had worked hard to build a feeling of professional competence that was publicly acknowledged by the principal, colleagues and parents.

> His own experiences in primary and secondary school had not provided him with a positive sense of self. On the contrary. During his years in secondary school, he became aware of the reality of differences in social class and how they were apparent in the arrogant attitude and behaviour of some classmates (the 'sons of lawyers and doctors'), as well as in teachers explicitly alluding to his working class background and 'pushing him aside'. 'As a little boy I was completely defenceless to that'. Later on – and in Marc's perception because of those experiences – feelings of self-doubt, fear of failure and insecurity played an important part during his years in teacher training. Only a few of the teacher educators are remembered by him as positively contributing to his building of a self-esteem: 'They made me feel like I was somebody, that I counted and was valued as a person.'
>
> In his first year of teaching, Marc had interim contracts in ten different schools. Although the lack of job security was not always pleasant to live through, Marc says that the overall experience was a positive and even a reassuring one for him. Working in different schools helped him to develop a more realistic view on what life and work in Flemish primary schools actually could mean. Moreover, his short stays in these schools provided more freedom to experiment with different teaching strategies. He knew that if he 'messed things up', he would be able to leave the school shortly without too much 'damage done'. This attitude made him more relaxed and helped him to concentrate on coping with the day-to-day demands of the job.
>
> For his second year in teaching, Marc got a contract for a full year in one school. That year, however, ended in conflict and misunderstanding with parents, colleagues and the principal. The next year he got a job in the school where he is still working. His first contact with the principal, however, was shocking. The man thought very highly of the educational quality of 'his' school. Marc was asked bluntly how he – being a young, inexperienced teacher- had the gall to apply for a job in a school with such a high standard and reputation. Since the school needed an extra teacher and the school board appreciated Marc's voluntary commitment in the local youth movement, he still got the job. Struggling with the problems of a beginning teacher, increased by his personal and professional uncertainties, as well as by a demanding and critical principal, Marc had a difficult start. However, things improved the following year when the principal asked him to experiment with a new teaching method for mathematics. From then on, he found his principal -although still very demanding- to be a competent supporter. 'That man gave me a whole lot of self-confidence (...and) that

was an enormously stimulating experience.' The principal's judgments of Marc's work were severe, but he was also explicitly valued for his efforts and for the positive results he achieved. 'That was exactly what I needed at that time'. After several years, the principal asked Marc to take over the first grade. 'That again was a very hard change to make. But again I got a lot of support from that man.' From Marc's account, the principal stimulated him and helped with concrete methodological or practical questions. He insisted that Marc would take his time to deal with the challenges of teaching a first grade. That year, Marc spent much time studying learning problems and remedial teaching strategies, dealing with the specific needs of several children. Gradually, his work began to run more smoothly and he got positive feedback and public recognition from the parents. Given Marc's personal and career history until then, this appreciation was of great importance to him.

During his fourth year in the first grade, Marc had a class of 32 pupils, among whom 6 had learning and behavioural problems. Together with other health problems (kidney stones; problems with his back), the stress of working with this difficult group 'finished me off'. He was sent on sick leave and had to stay home for several weeks. In retrospect, this sick leave had become for Marc a time of self-reflection and reconsideration of his work and of his commitments as a teacher. He learned that it is not possible to work like 'driving at 120 kilometres per hour all the time' and that he had to look for other, better balances in his energy and engagement.

The fragment from Marc's story illustrates that teachers' actual behaviours and perceptions are embedded in their personal history (Carter, 1993, p. 7) and this – in turn – implies that teachers' thoughts and actions can only be understood properly as the result of learning processes throughout their career, as subjective histories of learning.

Further, the fragment from Marc's story also exemplifies the particular contextualization that characterizes an analysis from the narrative–biographical perspective: teachers and teaching are approached in their context, both in its spatial and its temporal dimension. For example, Marc's first confrontation with the principal only takes on its full meaning when taking into account Marc's uncertainties from previous experiences during his induction, and even from his own days as a pupil. Thus, actual teacher behaviour is understood as contextualized both in the teacher's personal history and in his or her professional environment (organizational; sociocultural). Or, as Goodson (1984, p. 139) has put it: Biographical research should 'constantly broaden the concern with personal truth to take account of wider socio-historical concerns, even if these are not part of the consciousness of the individual'. Marc's story reveals the pervasive influence of socio-economic (class) differences on pupils' self-esteem, especially if they are not only played out by other pupils, but also by teachers. It exemplifies the actual impact of the hidden curriculum in schools and how that operates to socialize pupils in the values and norms of the middle class and thus possibly alienate – at a considerable emotional cost – pupils with a working-class background from their life worlds and identities. By situating teachers' 'stories of action' in a broader 'theory of context', they become 'life histories' with the potential for a deep understanding of the lived experience of schooling (Goodson, 1995, 2006).

In teachers' career stories, critical incidents, phases and persons constitute moments of *narrative condensation*. They reveal the complex interactions between teachers and their personal goals, norms, values, on the one hand, and contextual demands on the other. In analysing the meaning and impact of potential stress factors, these are useful heuristic tools: '[T]hey reveal, like a flashbulb, the major choice and change times in people's lives' (Sikes et al., 1985, p. 57). Successful coping with those incidents implies not only developing and employing efficient actions and social strategies, but also provokes changes in teachers' conceptions of themselves as well as in their knowledge and beliefs about teaching. Those changes in teachers' 'thinking' are further discussed in the next section.

Personal Interpretative Framework: Self-Understanding and Subjective Educational Theory

My use of the narrative–biographical perspective in research on teachers' lives did not focus on the career stories as a goal in itself. The narrative career accounts served as a vehicle to understand teachers' professional learning as a result of their career experiences over time. In line with the already-mentioned teacher thinking research, I conceive of professional development as the career-long process of learning and development which not only results in more effective professional action, but also in a more sophisticated and valid set of cognitions and understandings about one's job and the way to properly enact it. Based on my research, I have argued that teachers develop a *personal interpretative framework*, a set of cognitions and representations that operates as the lens through which they perceive their practice, make sense of it and act on it (Kelchtermans, 1993, 2007b, in press). This framework thus guides their interpretations and actions in particular situations (context), but is at the same time also modified by, and resulting from, the meaningful interactions (sense-making) with that context. As such it is both a condition for, and a result of, the interaction. It represents the – always preliminary – 'mental sediment' of teachers' learning and developing over time. It is the experience of having to reconsider and possibly change elements of that personal interpretative framework which makes up the 'critical' character of critical incidents, persons and phases.

Within the framework two different domains need to be distinguished: the professional self-understanding and the subjective educational theory.

The Professional Self-Understanding

The first domain in the personal interpretative framework of teachers is their conception of themselves as teachers. Nias was right when she observed and labelled teachers' 'persistent self-referentialism': the fact that when talking about their professional actions and activities, teachers cannot but speak about themselves (Nias, 1989, p. 5). And as such their sense of self is very prominently present in their accounts about their practice (a practice enacted by them as a singular person).

To refer to this sense of self I have deliberately avoided the notion of 'identity', because of its association with a static essence, implicitly ignoring or denying its dynamic and biographical nature (Kelchtermans, 2007a). Instead I have used the term 'self-understanding'. This refers to both the understanding one has of one's 'self' at a certain moment in time (*product*) and the ongoing process of making sense of one's experiences and their impact on the 'self' that produce this outcome. By stressing the narrative nature of self-understanding one can avoid the possible essentialist pitfall in conceptualizing 'identity'. This stance implies that we should not look for a 'deep', 'essential' or 'true' personal core that makes up the 'real' self. The narrative character implies that one's self-understanding only appears in the act of 'telling' (or in the act of explicit self-reflection and as such 'telling oneself').

My analysis of teachers' career stories resulted in the identification of five components that together make up teachers' self-understanding: self-image, self-esteem, job motivation, task perception and future perspective.

The *self-image* is the descriptive component, the way teachers typify themselves as teachers. This image is based on self-perception, but to a large degree also on what others mirror back to the teachers (comments from pupils, parents, colleagues, principals, etc.). The self-image is therefore strongly influenced by the way one is perceived by others. The self-image is at stake in Anita's conflict with her principal: If she as a 'primary school teacher' could be replaced by a 'kindergarten teacher', the principal implicitly questioned her self-image as being someone possessing the necessary and specific expertise required to teach children how to read. Similarly Leo found his self-image as a remedial teacher being redefined into that of a class-room teacher by the board's decision.

Very closely linked to the self-image is the evaluative component of the self-understanding or the *self-esteem*. Self-esteem refers to the teacher's appreciation of his or her actual job performance ('How well am I doing in my job as a teacher?'). Again the feedback from others is important, but that feedback is filtered and interpreted. Feedback from some is considered more relevant, valuable or important than that of others (see also critical persons): The person defines particular individuals or groups as more 'significant' than others (e.g. see Nias, 1985). To most teachers, students are the first and most important source of feedback, since it is only the presence of pupils and students that makes the teacher a teacher. Time and again I also found that this impact of pupils was strongly increased when teachers' own children became pupils, either in their colleagues' classes or in their own class. Because of the obvious emotional bond with their own children, their school experiences deeply affect teachers' ideas of good teaching as well as their self-evaluation as teachers. See, for example, the way his daughter's difficulties in school make Leo reconsider his work as well as his self-appreciation. But also principals, parents, members of the school board, etc. are vital sources of the social recognition that is crucial in building a positive self-esteem. See in the examples from Marc and Anita the possible positive as well as negative impact of the principal on teachers' self-esteem. From all the examples provided, it will be clear that teachers' self-esteem is almost always at stake during a critical incident: One feels questioned or questions oneself on whether or not one is a proper teacher (see also Kelchtermans, 1996). The fact that a positive self-esteem is to a large extent dependent on the social recognition from others and the fact that this recognition can be withdrawn at almost any time, result in the specific sense of vulnerability that characterizes teachers' work lives, as I have argued elsewhere (Kelchtermans, 1996, 2005, 2007b, in press).

The key role of self-esteem in a teacher's self-understanding also reflects the fact that emotions matter a great deal in teaching and teacher development. Positive self-esteem is crucial for feeling at ease in the job, for experiencing job satisfaction and a sense of fulfilment and for one's well-being as a teacher. Those positive self-evaluations, however, are fragile, fluctuate in time and have to be re-established time and again. That is why negative public judgements, which for an outsider look almost trivial, may have a devastating emotional impact on teachers (e.g. see Kelchtermans, 1996, 1999, 2005). This is also why, for example, the issue of having to give up one's classroom can become such a dramatic event in Leo's career.

The self-esteem as the evaluative component has to be understood as intertwined with the normative component of self-understanding: the task perception. This encompasses the teacher's idea of what constitutes his or her professional pro-gramme, his or her tasks and duties in order to do a good job. It reflects a teacher's personal answer to the questions: What must I do to be a proper teacher? What are the essential tasks I have to perform in order to have the justified feeling that I am doing a good job? What do I consider as legitimate duties I have to perform and what do I refuse to accept as part of 'my job'? The task perception reflects the fact that teaching and being a teacher is not a neutral endeavour. It implies value-laden choices, moral considerations (see e.g. Fenstermacher, 1990; Hargreaves, 1995; Oser et al., 1992). The task perception encompasses deeply held beliefs about what constitutes good education, about one's moral duties and responsibilities in order to do justice to students. When these deeply held beliefs are questioned teachers feel that they themselves as a person are called into question and this threatens their self-esteem (Kelchtermans, 1996). Evaluation systems, new policy regulations or imposed educational changes that differ from or contradict teachers' task percep-tion will deeply affect their self-esteem, their job satisfaction, etc. The emotional impact is very strong because teachers feel that their moral integrity as a person and a professional is called into question (vulnerability). Eventually this may even result in turnover, burnout, etc. (see e.g. Achinstein & Ogawa, 2006; Kelchtermans, 1996, 1999; Ballet & Kelchtermans, 2008; Nias, 1996; Hargreaves, 1995).

Marc's effort to treat all pupils in a fair and thoughtful way (partly motivated by his own negative experiences because of his social class background) illustrates how teachers in a personal way define their 'job description' (or add particular emphases to it). Similarly, Leo's self-critical comments on his low commitment during the years when he was teaching grade three also reflect his task perception.

The *job motivation* (or the conative component) refers to the motives that make people choose to become a teacher, to stay in teaching or to give it up for another career. The task perception, as well as the working conditions that allow a teacher to work and act according to that personal normative programme, is a crucial deter-minant for the job motivation. Leo's example presents a clear illustration: his high motivation as a remedial teacher versus the years of low motivation when teaching grade three (and compensating this with a parallel career as a freelance journalist).

Finally, self-understanding also includes a time-related component: The future *perspective* entails a teacher's expectations about his or her future in the job ('How do I see myself as a teacher in the years to come and how do I feel about it?'). See, for example, Leo who builds a strong, future-oriented self-understanding as a remedial teacher at some point or Marc who finds himself forced to rethink, reconsider his personal and emotional commitment during his breakdown in order to develop a feasible 'future' as a teacher. The future perspective further explicitly exemplifies the dynamic character of the self-understanding. This sense of self is not a static, fixed identity, but rather the result of an ongoing interactive process of sense-making and (social) construction. It thus shows how temporality pervades self-understanding: One's actions in the present are influenced by meaningful experiences in the past and expectations about the future. The person of the teacher is always somebody at some particular moment in his or her life, with a particular past and future. This temporality deeply characterizes every human being and therefore needs to be included in an appropriate conception of teachers' professional self-understanding.

These five components of self-understanding can be distinguished analytically, but are all intertwined and refer to each other. Self-understanding thus is both an encompassing (integrative) and an analytical (differentiated) concept. As such it does justice to the dynamic nature and the contextual embeddedness of teachers' sense of self, while still providing an analytical conceptual tool to unravel the way the 'self' pervades all aspects of teaching (Kelchtermans, in press).

Teachers' narrative accounts of their experiences are not just informative about how they think about themselves. Rather they construct that self-understanding in the interactive act of the telling. Thus they at the same time (implicitly or explicitly) acknowledge their 'audience' as well as invite it to recognize, confirm or question and contradict the statement. Narrative accounts revealing one's self-understanding are moments of *interactive sense-making*. The issue at stake is not a neutral statement, but one's sense of self as a teacher and thus the moral choices and emotions it encompasses. Therefore, the career stories always entail an aspect of self-representation and negotiation (seeking recognition or acknowledgement). When shared, the value-laden choices in the task perception, for example, run the risk of being contested, questioned. Yet, at the same time the sharing also offers strong possibilities for negotiating common understandings and for collectively making moral and political choices among colleagues about their professional practice.

The Subjective Educational Theory

By the subjective educational theory I mean the personal system of knowledge and beliefs about education that teachers use when performing their job.[2] It thus encompasses their professional know-how, the basis on which teachers ground their decisions for action. Knowledge refers to more or less formal insights and understandings, as derived from teacher education or in-service training, professional reading, etc. Belief refers to more person-based, idiosyncratic convictions, built up through different career experiences. If juxtaposed like this knowledge and belief suggest two different categories of information. In teachers' thinking, however, they are much more mixed and intertwined and may be better conceived of as the extremes of a continuum. The actual border between knowledge (formalized and grounded in and based on research or collective experiences over time) and more personal beliefs (based on individual experience, single cases, 'hearsay') is not so clear. The subjective educational theory reflects the teacher's personal answer to the questions: 'How should I deal with this particular situation?' (= what to do?) and 'Why should I do it that way?' (= why do I think that action is appropriate now?). 'Using' or 'applying' one's subjective educational theory thus demands first of all a process of judgement and deliberation, an interpretative reading of the situation before deciding on which approach would be most appropriate. See for example the counter-incident in Anita's story showing elements of her subjective educational theory on effective classroom management. 'You know, that is exactly what makes it so difficult in this job: you have to stick to your guns. It's much easier to give in, but then you'll always have the same problems coming up again and again.' Or the rule of thumb in Marc's approach that pupils need to feel accepted and valued for who they are as a person, regardless of their social background. Or Leo's conclusion that when assigning homework as a teacher one should carefully consider whether its possible benefits as a support for students' learning are outweighing the emotional and physical burden they may place on the students (which might dramatically reduce their potential contribution to pupils' actual learning).

The *content* of the subjective educational theory is to some extent idiosyncratic and based on personal experiences of an individual teacher. Formal knowledge (e.g. from the curriculum of teacher education programmes or in-service training) only takes root in the subjective educational theory if (student) teachers have experienced that 'it works for them' or 'is true for their practice'. The same applies to the beliefs, e.g. suggestions or rules of thumb, inherited from more experienced colleagues. The epistemological status of the subjective educational theory is that its content 'holds true' for the teacher involved. Whether or to what extent this claim of truth is justified beyond one's own situation is not the teacher's immediate concern.

Important domains in this subjective theory are on the one hand the concrete subject knowledge, strategies, routines, interventions for enacting teaching and helping students to learn, and on the other hand the complex relational attitudes and skills necessary to effectively position oneself in the job (towards principals, colleagues, parents and pupils). Enacting teaching is clearly about relationships as well as about the individual mastery of knowledge and skills (Kelchtermans, 1993).

The Internal Coherence of the Personal Interpretative Framework

It is important to stress that teachers' self-understanding and subjective theory as the two domains that make up a teacher's personal interpretative framework, need to be conceptualized and treated as closely intertwined. Teachers' 'reading' (perception, interpretation and judgement of appropriate action) of a job situation through the personal interpretative framework always implies both the self-understanding and the subjective educational theory. In the analysis of the situation one implicitly always brings in one's self-understanding. Whatever action is actually taken, its enactment reflects the norms of the task perception, the drives from the job motivation and the emotional meaning in relation to the self-esteem for that particular teacher. Similarly the person of the teacher also shines through in the specific knowledge and beliefs that bring the teacher to take that particular action and enact it in their personal style. For example, if one rule of thumb in teachers' subjective educational theory is that a certain level of authority needs to be and remain established for a teacher to be able to create a learning environment for pupils in schools, the particular actions through which this is achieved can be very different from teacher to teacher, depending on their normative idea about how they want to appear as a teacher in their actual practice. Action in teaching always involves the person one is (or wants to be) (Carter & Doyle, 1996; Richardson & Placier, 2001).

A proper concept of teachers' professional development needs to encompass both a concept of the teacher's self and of his or her professional knowledge. The process of professional learning is never a mere technical process of acquiring knowledge and skills, but always implies the personal integration of the new insights with the knowledge and beliefs that a person already holds. Integration thus can mean extension, refinement or increased sophistication as well as critical rethinking, modifying or giving up previously held beliefs. It is always the person of the teacher in his or her context who 'does' this integration, who 'makes it happen'. And similarly, the idea of a teacher's sense of self only becomes apparent in the actual enactment –the actual use of knowledge and beliefs to act in a particular situation – of a teacher's practice.

Beyond the Idiosyncratic

Throughout this chapter I have argued for the relevance and potential to study teachers' careers and work lives from the so-called narrative-biographical perspective. Conceiving of the career as a life-long learning process of personal and professional growth in different contexts, the narrative accounts of the career experiences can be used to develop an in-depth and situated understanding of this learning. The different examples revealed on the one hand the idiosyncratic and partly unique features of every career story, but on the other hand also how patterns, themes and concepts could be identified and theoretically developed whose relevance moves far beyond the particular individual teachers in a study. The latter can be illustrated by the phenomenon of the 'parallel career' (Nias, 1989; Kelchtermans, 1999). Teachers are often found to engage in skilful and responsible actions (paid or unpaid) parallel to their formal duties as a teacher in the school. Drawing only on the fragments quoted in this chapter, we can already list parallel careers: a mother/housewife (Anita), a freelance journalist and librarian (Leo), a drummer in a jazz-band (Marc), etc. These parallel careers, however, not only can take very different forms, but – more importantly – their meaning and significance for the teachers who enact them may also differ. From the story fragments of Leo it is clear that sometimes the parallel career is a coping strategy to deal with frustrations in the job, looking for possibilities for professional growth as well as for social recognition and self-esteem. The same need for social recognition and/or opportunities for professional growth also motivates teachers, for example, to engage in projects for the development of curriculum materials: collaborating with colleagues from other schools, but using their own classes as a setting to try out the materials (Deketelaere & Kelchtermans, 1996). The analysis of teachers' career stories, however, revealed yet another reason for teachers' choosing a parallel career. Teachers of (very) young children often choose to volunteer as board members of local sport clubs or cultural organizations. These commitments provide opportunities to work, talk and socialize with adults as a counterbalance for their daily and isolated interactions with young children. In all these examples, the teachers' formal career position remained the same: that of the classroom teacher. In that sense 'parallel career' doesn't imply a vertical promotion. But the reasons for the parallel career choices indicate how teachers themselves create a 'relief' in what from the outside appears only as the 'flat' landscape of their career.

The example of the 'parallel career' thus shows how a narrative–biographical analysis of teachers' career experiences provides insight in the dynamics that drive teachers over time and provides more grounded theoretical concepts to understand teachers' work lives. In order to understand these 'careers', prepare teachers for them and create opportunities for support and professional development over time, an in-depth understanding of the complex contextualized patterns in job experiences, sense-making and action is necessary. The narrative–biographical perspective has proven to be a powerful approach in this respect.

Notes

1. In order to collect teachers' career stories I developed a research procedure of 'stimulated autobiographical self-thematisation', in which several research techniques were combined: a questionnaire on the formal career, biographical interviews, classroom and school observations and a reflective log by the researcher. A cycle of three semi-structured biographical interviews constituted the core of the procedure. The interviews stimulated teachers to look back on their career experiences and reconstruct what they had meant to them and possibly still mean to them in the form of a professional biography or career story. The research procedure was cumulative: The different steps of data collection were building on each other. Every interview or observation was preceded by, and based on, an interpretative analysis of the data that had already been collected (see Kelchtermans, 1994 for a more extensive overview).
2. I am aware that the phenomenon I am referring to has been labelled differently by other authors, like 'subjective theory' (Mandl & Huber, 1983), 'implicit theory' (Clark & Peterson, 1986), 'practical knowledge' (Elbaz, 1981), 'personal practical knowledge' (Clandinin, 1986), etc., and that adding another label may contribute to a further proliferation of concepts rather than contributing to synthesis and theory building. Yet, this risk is outweighed by the advantage that

subjective educational theory as a label explicitly includes some of its essential characteristics:
It is an ordered, more or less systematic whole ('theory') of knowledge and beliefs, constructed
by the person involved ('subjective') about education.

References

Achinstein, B. & Ogawa, R. (2006). (In) Fidelity: What the resistance of new teachers reveals
  about professional principles and prescriptive educational policies. *Harvard Educational
  Review*, 26(1), 30–63.
Ballet, K. & Kelchtermans, G. (2008). Workload and willingness to change. Disentangling the
  experience of intensified working conditions. *Journal of Curriculum Studies*, 40, 47–67.
Berger, P. & Luckmann, T. (1985; orig. 1966). *The Social Construction of Reality. A Treatise in
  the Sociology of Knowledge*. Harmondsworth/New York: Pelican Books.
Blumer, H. (1969). *Symbolic Interactionism. Perspective and Method*. Englewood Cliffs, NJ:
  Prentice Hall.
Carter, K. (1993). The place of story in the study of teaching and teacher education. *Educational
  Researcher*, 22, 5–12, 18.
Carter, K. & Doyle, W. (1996). Personal narrative and life history in learning to teach. In J. Sikula,
  Th. J. Buttery, & E. Guyton (Eds.), *Handbook of Research on Teacher Education*, Second edi-
  tion (pp. 120–142). New York: Macmillan.
Casey, K. (1995–1996). The new narrative research in education. *Review of Research in
  Education*, 21, 211–253.
Clandinin, D. (1986). *Classroom Practice: Teacher Images in Action*. London/Philadelphia, PA:
  Falmer.
Clandinin, J. (Ed.) (2006). *Handbook of Narrative Research Methodologies*. Thousand Oaks: Sage.
Clark, C. & Peterson, P. (1986). Teachers' thought processes. In M. Wittrock (Ed.), *Handbook of
  Research on Teaching*, Third Edition (pp. 255–296). New York/London: Macmillan.
Cochran-Smith, M. & Lytle, S. L. (1999). Relationships of knowledge and practice: Teacher learn-
  ing in communities. *Review of Research in Education*, 24, 249–305.
Connelly, F. & Clandinin, D. (1990). Stories of experience and narrative inquiry. *Educational
  Researcher*, 19(4), 2–14.
Deketelaere, A. & Kelchtermans, G. (1996). Collaborative curriculum development. An encounter
  of different professional knowledge systems. *Teachers and Teaching: Theory and Practice*, 2,
  71–85.
Denzin, N. (1989). *Interpretive Interactionism*. Newbury Park/London/New Delhi: Sage.
Elbaz, F. (1981). The Teachers' Practical Knowledge. Report of a Case Study. *Curriculum Inquiry*,
  11(1), 43–71.
Fenstermacher, G. (1990). Some moral considerations on teaching as a profession. In J. Goodlad,
  R. Soder, & K. Sirotnik (Eds.), *The Moral Dimensions of Teaching* (pp. 130–151). San
  Francisco, CA: Jossey-Bass.
Filipp, S.-H. (Ed.) (1990), *Kritische Lebensereignisse* [Critical Life Experiences]. München:
  Psychologie Verlags Union.
Gergen, K. & Gergen, M. (1987). The self in temporal perspective. In R. Abeles (Ed.), *Life Span
  Perspectives and Social Psychology* (pp. 121–137). Hillsdale: Erlbaum.
Goodson, I. (1984). The use of life histories in the study of teaching. In M. Hammersley (Ed.),
  The Ethnography of Schooling (pp. 129–154). Driffield: Nafferton.
Goodson, I. (Ed.) (1992). *Studying Teachers' Lives*. London: Routledge.
Goodson, I. (1995). The story so far: Personal knowledge and the political. *International Journal
  of Qualitative Studies in Education*, 8(1), 89–98.
Goodson, I. (2006). The rise of the life narrative. *Teacher Education Quarterly*, 33, 7–21.

Gudmundsdottir, S. (2001). Narrative research on school practice. In V. Richardson, (Ed.), *Handbook of Research on Teaching*, Fourth edition (pp. 226–240). Washington: AERA.

Hargreaves, A. (1995). Development and desire. A post-modern perspective. In T.R. Guskey & M. Huberman (Eds.), *Professional Development in Education: New Paradigms and Perspectives* (pp. 9–34). New York: Teachers College Press.

Harris, A. (2003). Teacher leadership as distributed leadership: Heresy, fantasy or possibility? *School Leadership and Management*, 23, 313–324.

Huberman, M., Grounauer, M., & Marti, J. (1989). *La vie des enseignants. Evolution et bilan d'une profession*. Neuchâtel Paris: Delachaux et Niestlé.

Huberman, M., Grounauer, M., & Marti, J. (1993). *The Lives of Teachers*. London: Cassell.

Kelchtermans, G. (1993). Getting the story, understanding the lives. From career stories to teachers' professional development. *Teaching and Teacher Education*, 9, 443–456.

Kelchtermans, G. (1994). Biographical methods in the study of teachers' professional development. In I. Carlgren, G. Handal, & S. Vaage (Eds.), *Teachers' Minds and Actions: Research on Teachers' Thinking and Practice* (pp. 93–108). London: Falmer.

Kelchtermans, G. (1996). Teacher vulnerability. Understanding its moral and political roots. *Cambridge Journal of Education*, 26, 307–323.

Kelchtermans, G. (1999). The teaching career: between burnout and fading away? Reflections from a narrative and biographical perspective. In R. Vandenberghe & M. Huberman (Eds.), *Understanding and Preventing Teacher Burnout: A Sourcebook of International Research and Practice* (pp. 176–191). Cambridge: Cambridge University Press.

Kelchtermans, G. (2005). Teachers' emotions in educational reforms: Self-understanding, vulnerable commitment and micropolitical literacy. *Teaching and Teacher Education*, 21, 995–1006.

Kelchtermans, G. (2007a). Professional commitment beyond contract. Teachers' self-understanding, vulnerability and reflection. In J. Butcher & L. McDonald (Eds.), *Making a Difference: Challenges for Teachers, Teaching, and Teacher Education*, (pp. 35–53). Rotterdam: Sense Publishers.

Kelchtermans, G. (2007b). Teachers' self-understanding in times of performativity. In L.F. Deretchin & C.J. Craig (Eds.), *International Research on the Impact of Accountability Systems. Teacher Education Yearbook XV* (pp. 13–30). Lanham, MD: Rowman & Littlefield.

Kelchtermans, G. (2007c). Macropolitics caught up in micropolitics. The case of the policy on quality control in Flanders. *Journal of Education Policy*, 22, 471–491.

Kelchtermans, G. (in press). Who I am in how I teach is the message: Self-understanding, vulnerability and reflection. *Teachers and Teaching: Theory & Praxis*.

Kelchtermans, G. & Ballet, K. (2002a). The micropolitics of teacher induction. A narrative-biographical study on teacher socialisation. *Teaching and Teacher Education*, 18, 105–120.

Kelchtermans, G. & Ballet, K. (2002b). Micropolitical Literacy: Reconstructing a neglected dimension in teacher development. *International Journal of Educational Research*, 37, 755–767.

Kelchtermans, G. & Vandenberghe, R. (1994). Teachers' professional development: A biographical perspective. *Journal of Curriculum Studies*, 26, 45–62.

Krüger, H.-H. & Marotzki, W. (Eds.) (1996). *Erziehungswissenschaftliche Biographieforschung*. [Biographical Research in Education]. Opladen: Leske & Budrich.

Mandl, H. & Huber, G. (1983). Subjektive Theorien von Lehrern [Teachers' subjective theories]. *Psychologie in Erziehung und Unterricht*, 30, 98–112.

Markus, H. & Wurf, E. (1987). The dynamic self concept. A sociological psychological perspective. *Annual Review of Psychology*, 38, 299–337.

Mead, G. (1974). *Mind, Self and Society from the Standpoint of a Social Behaviorist*. Chicago, IL: University of Chicago Press.

Measor, L. (1985). Critical incidents in the classroom: Identities, choices and careers. In S. Ball & I. Goodson (Eds.), *Teachers' Lives and Careers* (pp. 61–77). London/Philadelphia, PA: Falmer.

Nias, J. (1985). Reference groups in primary teaching: Talking, listening and identity. In S. Ball & I. Goodson (Eds.), *Teachers' Lives and Careers* (pp. 105–119). London/Philadelphia, PA: Falmer.

Nias, J. (1989). *Primary Teachers Talking: A Study of Teaching as Work*. London/New York: Routledge.

Nias, J. (1996). Thinking about feeling: The emotions in teaching. *Cambridge Journal of Education*, 26(3), 293–306.

Oser, F., Dick, A., & Patry, J. L. (Eds.) (1992). *Effective and Responsible Teaching*. San Francisco, CA: Jossey-Bass.

Polkinghorne, D. (1988). *Narrative Knowing and the Human Sciences*. Albany, NY: State University of New York Press.

Richardson, V. & Placier, P. (2001). Teacher change. In V. Richardson (Ed.), *Handbook of Research on Teaching*, Fourth edition (pp. 905–947). Washington, DC: American Educational Research Association.

Schein, E. (1985). *Organizational Culture and Leadership: A Dynamic View*. San Francisco, CA: Jossey-Bass.

Sikes, P., Measor, L., & Woods, P. (1985). *Teacher Careers. Crises and Continuities*. London/Philadelphia, PA: Falmer.

Smylie, M. (1994). Redesigning teachers' work: Connections to the classroom. *Review of Research in Education*, 20, 129–177.

Wideen, M., Mayer-Smith, J., & Moon, B. (1998). A critical analysis of the research on learning to teach: Making the case for an ecological perspective on inquiry. *Review of Educational Research*, 68(2), 130–178.

Chapter 3
Committed for Life? Variations in Teachers' Work, Lives and Effectiveness

Christopher Day, Pam Sammons, Qing Gu, Alison Kington, and Gordon Stobart

Introduction

This chapter is based upon a unique mixed methods 4-year research project which focused upon the variations in teachers' work, lives and effectiveness of 300 elementary and secondary school teachers in a range of 100 schools across seven regions of England. Its findings challenge linear conceptions of teacher development and expertise and provide new understandings of the effects of personal, school and broader policy contexts upon professional life phase trajectories and teachers' emotional identities. It finds connections between these and teachers' commitment, resilience and effectiveness. This chapter discusses these in relation to the school standards and teacher retention agendas.

Reform Contexts

When discussing teachers it is important, first, to place their work in the context of increasingly intensive and persistent results-driven national policy interventions into the governance and work of their schools which are intended to raise standards of teaching, learning and achievement, to increase efficiency and effectiveness. Whilst the project on which this chapter is based took place in the context of English schools, the reform scenarios themselves are being played out in many countries across the world as governmental concerns about levels of pupil achievement have caused them to intervene more directly into the curriculum, teaching and assessment of quality in schools (UNESCO, 1998; OECD-PISA, 2003; Tatto, 2007). Such reforms have changed what it means to be a professional (Hargreaves, 2000; Helsby, 1999; Sachs, 2003) as the locus of control has shifted from the individual to the system managers and as contract has replaced covenant (Bernstein, 1996).

Performativity agendas, coupled with the continuing monitoring of the efficiency with which teachers are expected to implement externally generated initiatives have five consequences. They have in the past

M. Bayer et al. (eds.), *Teachers' Career Trajectories and Work Lives,*
Professional Learning and Development in Schools and Higher Education 3,
© Springer Science + Business Media B.V. 2009

1. Implicitly encouraged teachers to comply uncritically, e.g. teach to the test so that teaching becomes more a technical activity and thus more susceptible to control (Gewirtz et al., 2006; Elkins & Elliott, 2004; Ingersoll, 2003)
2. Challenged teachers' substantive identities (Evetts, 2005; Hargreaves, 1993)
3. Reduced the time teachers have to connect with, care for, and attend to, the needs of individual students (Hargreaves, 2001; McNess et al., 2003; Woods et al., 1997)
4. Threatened teachers' sense of agency and resilience (Werner, 1990; Troman & Woods, 2001; Hargreaves, 2000)
5. Challenged teachers' capacities to maintain motivation, efficacy and, thus, commitment (Hodkinson & Hodkinson, 2005; Goss, 2005; Tschannen-Moran et al., 1998)

More recently, reforms in English schools have also

6. Provided additional time and resource to enable teachers to manage their teaching (e.g. through the guarantee for all teachers of 10% time each week out of the classroom and the provision of teaching assistants)
7. Ensured that teachers are rewarded for leadership responsibilities which are directly connected to teaching and learning (through the creation of teaching and learning leadership roles)
8. Continued to demand more of teachers in terms of both academic and social responsibilities (McLaughlin & Talbert, 2006)

Examples of (8) above are the 'Every Child Matters' agenda in which teachers' responsibilities for the socio-emotional education of students are, de facto, extended; emphasis upon 'personalized learning' in which teachers are now expected to collect and analyse data in relation to the academic progress of every student so that they can better meet their learning needs; the continuation of an inclusion policy which has resulted in teachers having to manage a greater range of educational needs in their classrooms, and a steady stream of centrally initiated reforms which include revision of what is taught to students aged 14–19 by the addition of vocational subjects. Perhaps it is not surprising, then, that there is little independent evidence which suggests that the high levels of morale and commitment which teachers need to be at their best have been raised. In fact, surveys consistently suggest the opposite (Guardian, 2003).

Although the reality is that most teachers adapt, at least survive, and do not leave the profession, little is known about variations in their work and lives and how these affect their effectiveness. Such knowledge would not only be useful to teachers themselves, school leaders and all with a stake in quality education, but also to those who are engaged in initial teacher education and training.

There have been over 2 decades of reform a considerable number of small-scale qualitative research studies which have focused upon the negative consequences of reform upon teachers' and teacher educators' work lives and well-being (e.g. Troman & Woods, 2001; Kyriacou, 2000; Nash, 2005; Kelchtermans, 2005). Whilst these have been challenged by school effectiveness and improvement studies, neither the former nor the latter have been able to take a broad and deep longitudinal perspective upon variations in the work and lives of teachers.

The VITAE project (2001–2006) was commissioned by the Department for Education and Skills (DfES) in order to explore variations in teachers' lives, work and effectiveness in different phases of their careers. It involved a nationally representative sample of 300 primary teachers of 7- and 11-year-old students (Key Stage 1 and 2) and secondary teachers of 14-year-old students (Key Stage 3 English and Maths) working in 100 schools across seven local authorities (LAs, which are similar to school districts). The choice of teachers who taught these student age groups meant that 'key stage' (KS) national test results could be used as pupil outcome measures. The schools themselves were selected to be representative in terms of the level of social disadvantage and attainment levels,[1] although schools which served disadvantaged communities were oversampled in view of the high attrition rate among teachers. The project examined influences upon and between teachers' professional and personal lives, identities and school contexts in which they worked; and associations between these and their effectiveness over time.

Key Questions

The aim of VITAE was, 'to assess variations over time in teacher effectiveness, between different teachers and for particular teachers, and to identify factors that contribute to variations'. The department (DfES) wanted to understand how teachers become more effective over time. Key questions were:

1. Does teacher effectiveness vary from one year to another and in terms of different pupil outcomes and do teachers necessarily become more effective over time?
2. What are the roles of biography and identity?
3. How do school and/or department leadership influence teachers' practice and their effectiveness? What particular kinds of influence does continuing professional development (CPD) have on teachers' effectiveness?
4. Are teachers equally effective for different student groups or is there differential effectiveness relating (for example) to gender or socio-economic status?
5. Do the factors which influence effectiveness vary for teachers working in different school cultures contexts, or for different kinds of outcomes?
6. Do factors influencing teachers' effectiveness vary across different sectors (primary and secondary) and different age groups (7, 11 and 14 years)?

The research recognized that effectiveness involves both teachers' perceptions of their own effectiveness and their impact on students' progress and attainments. Each of these dimensions is important in its own right. One relates to recruitment and retention and the other to the 'standards' agenda. However, the research data suggested that there might be a relationship between the two.

1. **Recruitment and retention** (perceived effectiveness): Effectiveness in this sense is the extent to which teachers believe that they are able to do the job to the best of their ability. Effectiveness is perceived in both cognitive and emotional ways. It includes perceptions of the effectiveness of their classroom relationships and student progress and achievement.

2. **The 'standards' agenda** (effectiveness as pupil progress and attainment): Effectiveness in this sense is measured by 'value-added' student attainment data as defined by national tests at KS1 (age 7), KS2 (age 11) and KS3 (age 14). In addition to these results we administered an independent test and pupil attitude surveys at the beginning of each year to students at KS2 and KS3 in order to test progress over the year of students taught by the same teacher.

The data thus provided the possibility of examining both relative effectiveness (one teacher's effectiveness in relation to another who has similar experience and works in similar organizational contexts), i.e. how their 'performance' in terms of student progress and attainment compares and why, and relational effectiveness (how one teacher is and how he or she performs in relation to his or her past history).

VITAE is the most comprehensive, large-scale and extensive study of teachers' work and lives and the first to explore associations between these and effectiveness. The findings from VITAE have much to offer in considering issues of teacher preparation, teaching standards, teacher quality retention, and, in relation to these, the factors that enable (or do not enable) teachers to build and sustain their sense of identity, commitment, agency and effectiveness.

Methods

The main data concerning perceived effectiveness were collected through twice yearly semi-structured, face-to-face interviews with all the teachers. These were supplemented at various stages of the research by document analysis and interviews with school leaders and groups of students.

Measures of teachers' relative effectiveness as expressed through improvements in students' progress and attainment were collected through matching baseline test results at the beginning of the year with students' national curriculum results at the end. This enabled differences in the relative value added to be analysed, using multi-level statistical techniques that included adjustment for individual background factors such as gender and eligibility for free school meals, as well as prior attainment. Student attitude surveys were also conducted each year to gather students' views of their schools and teachers. The data were collected concurrently. In order to ensure both conceptual and methodological synergy regular data analysis, interpretation and hypothesis building meetings were held. This enabled formative integration of the qualitative and quantitative data. Detailed holistic profiles of teachers' work and lives over time were constructed to see whether patterns emerged over a 3-year period in terms of perceived and relative effectiveness and, if so, why (see Day et al., 2006). It is important to note that whilst all teachers participated in all interviews, this was not the case in relation to the student tests.[2]

For the purpose of this chapter, the findings are organized in two parts. The first discusses variations in terms of moderating factors on teachers' effectiveness. These are features of the wider context in which the teachers work (i.e. their personal and professional life phases, scenarios which shape their identities). They are influenced, positively and negatively, by pupils, policies, school leadership and colleagues, socio-economic contexts of their workplaces, school phase, continuing professional development (CPD) and personal events and experiences. The second part discusses associations between the success with which teachers in different professional life phases and scenarios are able to manage the interactions between these influences and their capacity for commitment, resilience and effectiveness.

Moderating Factors

Professional Life Phases

The findings show clearly that teachers' effectiveness is not simply a consequence of age or experience. The results identify teachers who are more, and less, effective in terms of their own perceptions and students' progress and attainment in each phase of their professional lives. The different professional life phases of teachers are core moderating influences upon their effectiveness. Six professional life phases, relating to experience rather than age or responsibilities, were identified. Within each phase the majority of teachers perceived increasing effectiveness, but there were different challenges and concerns. Teachers in each phase were placed into groups, each reflecting the extent to which they were sustaining their commitment. The work built on, but went beyond Huberman's (1993) seminal study of Swiss secondary school teachers' lives.

- Phase 1: 0–3 years – Commitment: Support and challenge. The focus here was a developing sense of efficacy in the classroom. This was a phase of high commitment. A crucial positive factor in this period was the support of school/ department leaders. Poor pupil behaviour was seen as having a negative impact. Teachers in this professional life phase had either a developing (60%) or a reducing (40%) sense of efficacy.
- Phase 2: 4–7 years – Identity and efficacy in the classroom. The key characteristic was an increased sense of confidence in effectiveness. Seventy-eight percent of teachers in this phase had taken on additional leadership responsibilities outside the classroom which further strengthened their emerging identities. The management of heavy workloads had a negative impact on some teachers. Teachers in this professional life phase were grouped as (a) sustaining a strong sense of identity, self-efficacy and effectiveness (49%); (b) sustaining identity, efficacy and effectiveness (31%); or (c) identity, efficacy and effectiveness at risk (20%).
- Phase 3: 8–15 years – Managing changes in role and identity: Growing tensions and transitions. This phase was seen as a watershed in teachers' professional development. 80% had posts of responsibility and for many there were decisions to make about progression in their career. Of the teachers in this professional life phase, 76% were judged to have sustained engagement, with 24% showing detachment/loss of motivation. The portrait of Katie, a teacher in this phase of experience, provides an illustration of this group.

A portrait of Katie: Detachment/loss of motivation

Katie was a Year 6 teacher in a rural high-socio-economic status (FSM1) primary school. She was 49 years old, having taught for 13 years. Support and trust from the headteacher and her colleagues had a positive impact on her sense of efficacy. Katie felt that her sense of effectiveness varied, depending upon the composition of her class. 'Sometimes I feel I can be more effective simply because I have less children in the class, but then I've got this one extra child who does make life difficult.' Her students' test scores were below expectation. Student behaviour had been a detrimental influence upon her motivation and commitment – 'There is nothing more demotivating than a class that doesn't want to be taught. It's a constant drip of minor misbehavior that builds up and wears you down.' She also felt demotivated and less committed when the parents questioned and complained about her methods of teaching.

The target-driven culture was another negative influence on her decreased motivation in the profession. She was extremely negative about the excessive workload generated by the National Curriculum and the pressure from OFSTED inspections: 'This time last year ... we were in the throws of OFSTED which was the most stressful experience I had ever been through, with the worst class in the school.'

She also struggled with a lack of work-life balance: 'I have to be very careful how I balance the support I give my own children, as I've got a pile of books to mark. Everything has to be planned like a military operation. If my husband wants us to go somewhere, like on Saturday, then I have to know. He can't tell me on Saturday morning that he wants to go out. He has to tell me the week before, so I can get my marking done, so that my Saturday can be free.'

Katie felt that there was a slim chance of promotion for her in her current professional life phase.

- Phase 4: 16–23 years – Work–life tensions: Challenges to motivation and commitment. As well as managing heavy workloads, many were facing additional demands outside school, *making work–life balance a key concern*. The struggle for balance was often reported as having a negative impact. The risk at this stage was a feeling of career stagnation linked to a lack of support in school and negative perceptions of student behaviour. The three subgroups of teachers in this professional life phase were: (a) further career advancement and good results leading to increased motivation/commitment (52%); (b) sustained motivation, commitment and effectiveness (34%); or (c) heavy workload/competing tensions/career stagnation leading to decreased motivation, commitment and effectiveness (14%). The portrait of Cathy, a teacher in this phase of experience, provides an illustration of a teacher who was sustaining her commitment and relative effectiveness in the face of new challenges.

A portrait of Cathy: Continuing to cope

Cathy was 44 years old when the project began and had been teaching English for 22 years, almost all in this FSM 3, 11–16 years, suburban secondary school (High School and Arts College) with 1,000 pupils. Prior to this, she taught in one other over a period of 2 years. She had responsibility for the library and had recently been appointed as the KS3 co-ordinator and Deputy Head of Department. She regularly attended professional development events, all connected directly with her role. Her motivation over the 3 years prior to the project was high and she had been attracted to teaching because she wanted 'to help pupils of all abilities achieve their full potential'. This was still the case. She worked 46–55 hours per week and experienced high levels of stress. This only occasionally affected her work. She felt that the changing nature of society characterized by a loss of community and deterioration in pupil behaviour was having an impact on teaching. A significant change occurred in 1999 when the student intake to the school changed. Students' behaviour deteriorated and the senior leadership team (SLT) did not provide leadership to combat this, being 'over tolerant'.

A newly appointed Head had, however, 'done a lot for the school … new facilities, decorating the corridors', and, 'the ethos of the school has changed'. 'The children are more valued'. Members of the Department supported each other with 'difficult' pupils in order to minimize disruption to others: 'We're very positive … we want to do our best for children … we don't give up on them.' Cathy was generally content with the job, though felt that having a large gap between the birth of her two children had curtailed her career ambitions. Because she had one school age son who needed her to sit with him when he did his homework, Cathy often did not start work on school-related tasks until 9:00 pm. Cathy had considerable home support from her husband and mother. Without this, she said, it was doubtful as to whether she could have maintained her commitment to, and effectiveness in, teaching – particularly when her own children were of school age.

She now spent significant 'teaching' time in managing student behaviour. Whilst her self-efficacy, commitment and motivation remained high, her job satisfaction was declining. Her recent promotion, however, had renewed her motivation and interest in her career which, prior to this had become 'a little stagnant'. Cathy had not really changed other than 'more hours working at home' because of her new responsibility. She was established in the school, having taught parents of present pupils and was comfortable with her 'kind' approach with pupils. She spent more time now in 'training for the tests': 'They are having lessons before school, at break, after school as well as booster lessons. They're being overwhelmed.' Her students' test scores were as expected and in the final year of the project an unfavourable OFSTED had dented the morale of the department.

- Phase 5: 24–30 years – Challenges to sustaining motivation. Maintaining motivation in the face of external policies and initiatives, which were viewed negatively, and declining pupil behaviour were the core struggles for teachers in this phase. While 60% of the primary teachers were judged to have retained a strong sense of motivation, over half the secondary teachers were rated as losing motivation. Teachers in this phase were categorized as either sustaining a strong sense of motivation and commitment (54%), or holding on but losing motivation (46%).
- Phase 6: 31 + years – Sustaining/declining motivation, coping with change and looking to retire. For the majority of teachers this was a phase of high commitment. Of the small group of teachers in this phase (22), almost two thirds were judged to have high motivation and commitment. Positive teacher–pupil relationships and pupil progress were the basis of this. Government policy, health issues and pupil behaviour were often perceived as the most negative factors for this group. Teachers in this phase were seen as either maintaining commitment (64%), or 'tired and trapped' (36%).

When the perceptions of teachers in each phase over 3 years were matched to the progress and 'value added' attainment scores of their students, it was clear that those in their later years of teaching were more 'at risk' in terms of their effectiveness than those in early and middle phases.

Figure 3.1 illustrates the relationship between 'value added' student progress and attainment scores of students of teachers in early (0–7), mid (8–23) and late (24+) years of experience in one year of the project. The pattern was repeated. It should not be interpreted as applying to all teachers in each of these experience groupings. However, in terms of the standards agenda it might be seen to suggest that attention needs to be focused upon experienced teachers.

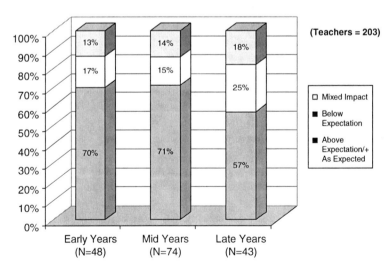

Fig. 3.1 The impact of professional life phase on student value-added progress and attainment

Professional Identities: The Emotional Contexts of Teaching

The second moderating influence relates to teachers' sense of identity – the emotional context of their work. In teacher education, much research literature demonstrates that knowledge of the self is a critical element in the way teachers construe and construct the nature of their work (Kelchtermans & Vandenberghe, 1994) and that events and experiences in the personal lives of teachers are intimately linked to the performance of their professional roles (Acker, 1999; Goodson & Hargreaves, 1996).

There are unavoidable interrelationships between professional and personal identities, if only because the overwhelming evidence is that teaching demands significant personal investment.

> The ways in which teachers form their professional identities are influenced by both how they feel about themselves and how they feel about their students. This professional identity helps them to position or situate themselves in relation to their students and to make appropriate and effective adjustments in their practice and their beliefs about, and engagement with students. (James-Wilson, 2001, p. 29)

In his study of the career stories of ten experienced Belgian primary school teachers, Kelchtermans (1996) found two recurring themes:

- *Stability in the job*: A need to maintain the status quo, having achieved ambition, led to job satisfaction.
- *Vulnerability*: The teachers felt vulnerable to the judgements of colleagues, the headteacher and those outside the school gates, e.g. parents, inspectors, media, which might be based exclusively on measurable student achievements. As vulnerability increased, so they tended towards passivity and conservatism in teaching.

Thus, a positive sense of identity with subject, relationships and roles is important to maintaining self-esteem or self-efficacy, commitment to, and a passion for, teaching (Day, 2004).

> Identity must be distinguished from what, traditionally, sociologists have called roles, and role sets. Roles ... are defined by norms structured by the institutions and organisations of society. Their relative weight in influencing people's behavior depends upon negotiations and arrangements between individuals and those institutions and organisations. Identities are sources of meaning for the actors themselves, and by themselves, constructed through the process of individuation. (Castells, 1997, pp. 6–7).

The VITAE research revealed that teacher identity itself is a composite of the interactions between professional, situated and personal dimensions (Day et al., 2005). Professional identity reflects social and policy expectations of what a good teacher is and the educational ideals of the teacher. The situated dimension is located in a specific school and context and is affected by local conditions (i.e. pupil behaviour, level of disadvantage), leadership, support and feedback. The personal dimension is based on life outside school and is linked to family and social roles. The majority of teachers (67%) had a positive sense of identity and associated this with self-efficacy and agency – their belief that they could 'make a difference' to the learning and achievement of their pupils. However, one in three teachers did not have a positive sense of identity.

Four scenarios were identified which reflected different relationships between these dimensions of identity:

- The first was holding the three in balance. Over a third (35%) of teachers were in this group, with over half coming from primary schools and the majority coming from more advantaged schools. The dominant characteristics of this group of teachers included being highly motivated, committed and self-efficacious.
- In the second scenario, one dimension was dominant, for example, immediate school demands dominating and impacting on the other two. This was the largest group (44% teachers), predominantly from the 4–15 years professional life phases and more likely to be female (82%). Most were highly committed and saw themselves as effective. A third of these teachers were rated as vulnerable in terms of resilience, while less than a quarter reported positive well-being. Coping strategies included accepting the imbalance, subjugating one dimension ('life on hold') or tolerating it for the present.
- In the third scenario, consisting of 44 teachers (15%), two dimensions dominated and impacted on the third. Over half of this smaller group were secondary teachers. While their motivation levels generally remained high, they were more negative about their well-being and work–life balance.
- The fourth scenario represents a state of extreme fluctuation within and between each dimension. Of the 6% of teachers in this small but vulnerable group nearly three quarters (72%) taught in socially disadvantaged schools (FSM 3 and 4).

A portrait of Scarlett: Vulnerable/declining

Scarlett's experience illustrates a decline in motivation and commitment to teaching because of a perceived lack of support in the school culture and her heavy workload. She was 27 years old and had taught English for 5 years, 4 of which had been at this urban, FSM 4 school. She had wanted to be a journalist on completion of her first degree, but because she could not afford the course, she undertook a teaching qualification and enjoyed it. She came from a teaching family who tried to change her mind on becoming a teacher, but she ignored their advice. At the beginning of the Project, she had grown to love teaching.

Scarlett viewed the senior leadership team in the school positively, but felt much less positive about the leadership in her department where she lamented a lack of sharing of good practice. Nevertheless, the staff at her current school were 'incredibly supportive and friendly' and she enjoyed the pleasant environment in the school. Scarlett had established a good relationship with her students, but found that, overall, student behaviour had become more challenging.

Her growing professional experience had increased her perceived effectiveness as a teacher. Her self-efficacy and confidence in managing the

(continued)

(continued)

classroom had improved since she began teaching. At the beginning of the project she was highly committed and was very pleased to see that she could make a difference to students both academically and personally. She saw teaching as 'a life as well as a job'. Not surprisingly, she enjoyed an extremely high level of job satisfaction. Scarlett suggested that three critical incidents had improved her effectiveness as a teacher in her initial 4 years in teaching – gaining a permanent contract, recovering from a broken relationship, and taking on new responsibilities after OFSTED. Her students' test results for the first 2 years of the study were as expected.

However, in her fifth year Scarlett's motivation had decreased because of increased workload and ill-health. She had nearly 3 months off school and believed that her illness was work-related. Although Scarlett had previously aimed to apply for promotion as second in her department, she now felt that she was 'not utterly convinced' that she wanted to stay in teaching.

Self-efficacy and a sense of agency are fundamental to motivation and commitment. It is clear that these can be adversely affected not only by external change demands but also personal and school-specific factors. Professional identity depends upon the capacity of teachers to manage different scenarios.

Comments relating to their professional, situated and personal scenarios suggested that many teachers were working under considerable persistent and negative pressures and that, depending upon professional life phase and school context; these were largely connected to relationships with school leadership and colleagues, deteriorating pupil behaviour and attitudes, lack of parental support, the effects of government policies and unanticipated life events. For some, negative pressures from outside the school were moderated by strong educational values (internal), support from within the school and/or department (situated) and personal support from family or friends (Table 3.1).

It was interesting, also, to find that, whereas all teachers spoke about their heavy workloads, it was those who taught in schools, especially secondary schools, which served disadvantaged communities, who were more negative.

In all, 198 (67%) of teachers who expressed a positive sense of agency, resilience and commitment in all scenarios spoke of in-school and personal support. The supporting factors mentioned most frequently were:

- **Leadership (76%)**

  It's good to know that we have strong leadership who has a clear vision for the school. (Larissa, Year 6)

- **Colleagues (63%)**

  We have such supportive team here. Everyone works together and we have a common goal to work towards. (Hermione, Year 2)

  We all socialize together and have become friends over time. I don't know what we'd do if someone left. (Leon, Year 9)

Table 3.1 Negative and positive (mediating) factors affecting teachers' commitment

Negative factors	Positive factors
Professional factors	**Personal factors**
• Workload	• Workload
• Policies/initiatives – demoralising, no support	• Policies/initiatives – supported by SMT
Situated factors	**Situated factors**
• Pupils – disaffected, challenging behaviour	• Pupils – positive relationships, few behaviour problems
• Parents – unmotivated, unsupportive	• Parents
• Leadership – inconsistent leadership	• Leadership – support of the head teacher
Personal factors	• Colleagues – support of other staff, feeling of being in a team
• Health – health problems that affect family	**Professional factors**
• Values	• Health – no major health worries
	• Values – confident about making a difference

- **Personal (95%)**

  It helps having a supportive family who don't get frustrated when I'm sat working on a Sunday afternoon and they want to go to the park. (Shaun, Year 9)

Ninety seven (33%) of teachers whose effectiveness was judged to be at risk spoke of negative pressures. Those mentioned most frequently were:

- **Workload (68%)**

  It never stops, there's always something more to do and it eats away at your life until you have no social life and no time for anything but work. (Jarvis, Year 6)

  Your life has to go on hold – there's not enough time in the school day to do everything. (Hermione, Year 2)

- **Student behaviour (64%)**

  Over the years, pupils have got worse. They have no respect for themselves or the teachers. (Jenny, Year 6)

  Pupil behaviour is one of the biggest problems in schools today. They know their rights and there's nothing you can do. (Kathryn, Year 9)

- **Leadership (58%)**

  Unless the leadership supports the staff, you're on your own. They need to be visible and need to appreciate what teachers are doing. (Carmelle, Year 2)

  I feel as if I'm constantly being picked on and told I'm doing something wrong. (Jude, Year 9)

The Influence of School Context

An analysis of teachers' perceptions of effectiveness in different work contexts was made in order to discover whether there were differences between primary and secondary teachers and between those in schools in different socio-economic

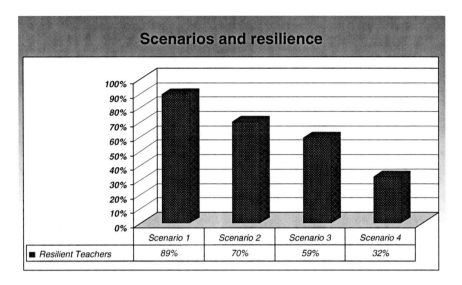

Fig. 3.2 Scenarios and resilience

contexts. Whilst almost all teachers referred to deteriorating student behaviour and the negative impact of central government initiatives on workload and class composition, it was those in schools in areas of social and economic deprivation who referred more frequently to these, to lack of parental support and to associated problems of demoralization, failing energy and ill-health. It is this group of teachers, working in especially challenging circumstances and more likely to work in secondary than primary schools, that may be said to be at greater risk of sooner or later losing their motivation and commitment to their work. Figure 3.2 indicates the associations between scenarios and resilience.

Further analysis of the data also revealed that (a) teachers in secondary schools experience these more keenly than those in primary schools; and that (b) the more complex the scenarios, the more likelihood of the threat to resilience.

Commitment, Resilience and Effectiveness

Commitment

Teacher commitment has been identified as one of the most critical factors in the success of education (Huberman, 1997; Nias, 1981). If you talk to any teacher, teacher educator, schools inspector or superintendent, administrator, principal or parent about reform or raising standards or the quality of education, it will not be very long before the word 'commitment' enters into the conversation. They 'know' that whilst the headteachers' commitment to change is essential to its success, so too is that of their staff. Without commitment, change efforts – those within and especially those which are initiated from outside the school or other organization – will be limited in their success.

Commitment has been defined as a predictor of teachers' performance, burn-out, attrition as well as having an important influence on students' cognitive, social, behavioural and affective outcomes (Firestone, 1996; Louis, 1998; Day et al., 2005). It is a term often used by teachers to describe themselves and each other (Nias, 1981), is a part of their professional identity (Elliott & Crosswell, 2001), and may be enhanced or diminished by factors such as student behaviour, collegial and administrative support, parental demands, and national educational policies (Day, 2000; Louis, 1998; Riehl & Sipple, 1996; Tsui & Cheng, 1999). Teachers who are committed have an enduring belief that they can make a difference to the learning lives and achievements of students (efficacy and agency) through *who* they are (their identity); *what* they know (knowledge, strategies, skills); and *how* they teach (their beliefs, attitudes, personal and professional values embedded in, and expressed through, their behaviours in practice settings).

Ebmeier and Nicklaus (1999) connected the concepts of commitment and emotion, defining commitment as part of a teacher's affective or emotional reaction to their experience in a school setting and part of the process which determines the level of per-sonal investment which teachers make to a particular school or group of students. This connection is central to understanding teachers' perceptions of their work, colleagues, school leadership, and the interaction between these and their personal lives.

In a recent report of empirical research on teachers' commitment in Australia, Crosswell (2006, p. 109) suggests that there are six dimensions of commitment:

Commitment as passion
Commitment as investment of extra time
Commitment as a focus on the well being and achievement of the student
Commitment as a responsibility to maintain professional knowledge
Commitment as transmitting knowledge and/or values
Commitment as engagement with the school community

There seems to be little doubt, therefore, that commitment (or lack of it) is a key influencing factor in the performance effectiveness levels of teachers (Bryk et al., 1993; Kushman, 1992). Initial commitment, however, may rise, be sustained or decline depending on their management of life and work experiences. Commitment, for VITAE teachers, was both a condition for teaching and an outcome of their experience. The research revealed, also, a clear association between teacher com-mitment and their professional life phase.

It would seem from Fig. 3.3 that the commitment of teachers in late professional life phase is more likely to decline than those in early and middle years. Given the nature of teaching, particularly in inimical reform contexts, this is, perhaps unsurprising. However, an association was also found between teachers' commit-ment and student progress and attainment as measured by contextual, value-added national test scores at age 11 and 14. It seems that, at least for some teachers, where effectiveness declines over time, this is associated with their ability to sustain their commitment, i.e. be resilient.

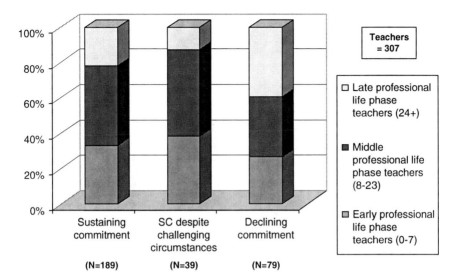

Fig. 3.3 Teachers' commitment by professional life phase

Resilience

Resilience, i.e. enduring commitment, is both a product of personal and professional dispositions and values and socially constructed. Henderson and Milstein (1996) compare characteristics of *resilient children*, as described by Benard (1991), and those of *resilient adults* as noted by Higgins (1994), and claim that the process of resilience building is remarkably similar for children and for adults. The characteristics of both resilient children and resilient adults include being able to form and sustain socially positive relationships, being adept in problem solving, having a sense of purpose and motivation for self-improvement, and having the capacity to 'bounce back' in adverse circumstances.

The need to understand, acknowledge and attend to teachers' sense of resilience is twofold. First, it is unrealistic to expect students to be resilient if their teachers, who constitute a primary source of their role models, do not demonstrate resilient qualities (Henderson & Milstein, 1996). Second, an understanding of teacher resilience in the process of meeting prescribed targets and managing work–life tensions over the course of a career and in different contexts will contribute to the existing knowledge of how teachers sustain their commitment and effectiveness.

Challenges to positive, stable identities may affect teachers' resilience, and such threats are more likely to occur in schools with higher levels of social disadvantage, and for teachers in the later phases of their careers. Teachers' effectiveness in these circumstances is likely to be more at risk. For example, VITAE found that whereas 78% of teachers in early career (0–7 years) and 76% of teachers in mid-career (8–23 years) were resilient, this applied to only 56% of teachers with 23+ years of

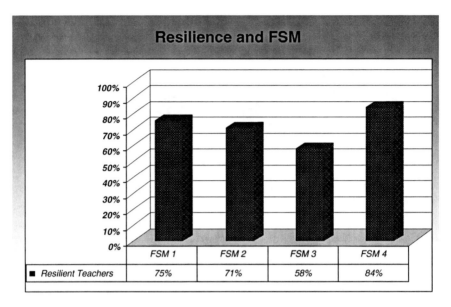

Fig. 3.4 Resilience

experience. Fig. 3.4 indicates how the teachers' resilience in schools which serve more highly disadvantaged communities is more at risk.

Interestingly, there is also a difference between those in the most disadvantaged communities and those in communities which were disadvantaged but less so. It may be the case that FSM4 schools, which receive more advantageous resourcing than others, also attract more teachers who are more vocationally and ideologically oriented to working in areas of extreme socio-economic deprivation than others.

This evidence about variations in teacher resilience provides a new perspective on teacher quality, effectiveness and retention issues. Research on teacher retention tends to focus on factors affecting teachers' decision to leave the teaching profession. Instead, what is required is a better understanding of the factors that have enabled the majority of teachers to sustain their motivation, commitment and, therefore, effectiveness in the profession.

Pupil Progress and Attainment

The VITAE research confirmed findings of previous research that differences in the characteristics of pupils do not fully account for the differences in levels of students' attainment or progress between classes and teaching groups. However, for the first time statistically significant associations were found between teachers' commitment and students' progress and levels of performance in value-added attainments in national tests at age 7 (KS1), 11 (KS2) and 14 (English and Maths, KS3) (Fig. 3.5).

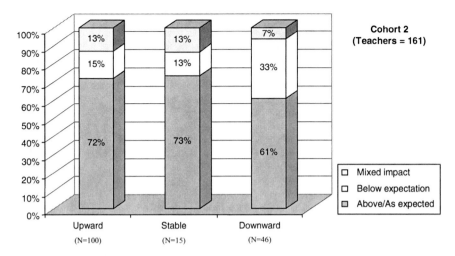

Fig. 3.5 Associations between teacher commitment and effectiveness as defined by student value-added progress and attainment

Students of teachers in each professional life phase who were sustaining or continuing to build their commitment and resilience (74%) were more likely to attain results at or above the level expected, regardless of school context. Students of the minority of teachers who were not sustaining their commitment and resilience (26%) were more likely to attain results below the level expected, regardless of school context. How well teachers managed their work–life balance also appeared to relate to their sense of effectiveness. The qualitative data revealed no systematic links between relative effectiveness and age, professional life phase or gender, although teachers in later years of experience were more at risk of being less effective in terms of student attainment than their younger colleagues, and those working in more complex scenarios were more at risk of declining commitment and resilience.

Relatively less effective 'vulnerable' teachers were also more likely to report personal factors, student behaviours or policy initiatives which were impacting negatively on their work.

Conclusions

The research has highlighted the important moderating influences on teacher effectiveness of professional life phases, emotional identities, school contexts and the interplay between personal and professional lives; and it has revealed the ways in which variations in these and the influences upon them affect teachers' capacities to be effective and to sustain teaching effectiveness. If teachers are to manage the tensions they face within and across both, and sustain and, where appropriate, increase their commitment, resilience and effectiveness, they and those responsible for their training, education and leadership must be encouraged to build understandings of the cognitive and emotional contexts in which they work in order to increase their capacities to manage these. This in turn is likely to foster their perceived and relative effectiveness.

There are five core findings, each with messages for policy and practice.

Five Core Findings

1. Pupils of teachers who are committed and resilient are likely to attain more than pupils whose teachers are not. An implication of this finding is that policymakers, national organizations and headteachers concerned with raising standards in schools need to address the associations between teachers' well-being, commitment, resilience and effectiveness, by providing more robust, comprehensive personnel support structures.
2. Teachers' sense of positive professional identity is associated with well-being and job satisfaction and is a key factor in their effectiveness. An implication of this finding is that strategies for sustaining commitment in initial and continuing professional development programmes should differentiate between the needs of teachers in different phases of their professional lives.
3. The commitment and resilience of teachers in schools serving more disadvantaged communities are more persistently challenged than others. An implication of this finding is that schools, especially those which serve disadvantaged communities, need to ensure that their CPD provision is relevant to the commitment, resilience and health needs of teachers in each of their professional life phases.
4. The majority of teachers maintain their effectiveness but teachers do not necessarily become more effective over time. Teachers in later years are at greater risk of becoming less effective though these are still a minority. An implication of this finding is that national organizations and schools need to target strategies for professional learning and development to support teachers in the later stages of their careers.
5. Sustaining and enhancing teachers' commitment and resilience is a key quality and retention issue. An implication of this finding is that efforts to support and enhance teacher quality should focus upon building, sustaining and retaining their commitment and resilience, as well as on more usual aspects such as curriculum-related, teaching and role matters.

There is much previous research which suggests, like VITAE, that teacher commitment is important because it is a significant factor in teaching quality, teachers' capacities to adapt successfully to change, retention and student attitudes and learning outcomes. At present English schools may be witnessing the first signs of a sea change in the way policymakers think about change. Whilst the reform bandwagon shows little sign of slowing, it does seem as though teachers are being invited to adapt to working in a less prescriptively imitative environment than has been the case over the last 20 years. For some, already battered by many years of difficult imposed adaptation and perhaps now cynical about the benefits of more change, it may be too late. However, for many who remain committed to their students, their school, their profession and their own learning, it is not. As the importance of student engagement in learning is being once again acknowledged, and as personalized learning (the worth of individually oriented teaching and learning) is once again emphasized in policy documents, it is clear that, to be successful, teachers themselves must be passionately motivated and committed.

It may be then, that for the first time in many years, the needs and concerns of policymakers and classroom teachers are coinciding. However, for commitment to flourish and for teachers to be resilient and effective, they need a strong and enduring sense of efficacy – the ability to handle new situations confidently, believing that they will make a difference – and they need to work in an external environment which is less alienating, less bureaucratically managerial, less reliant on crude measures of performativity – for we know from countless studies that this saps rather than builds morale. And they need to work in schools in which leadership is supportive, clear, strong, emotionally and socially intelligent and passionate about sustaining the quality of their commitment.

Teachers in all countries need support for their commitment, energy and skill over their careers if they are to grapple with the immense emotional, intellectual and social demands as they work towards building the internal and external relationships demanded by ongoing government reforms and social movements. The picture of teachers in English schools involved in the VITAE project gives cause for concern and hope – concern because it is clear that the variations in perceived effectiveness which relate to life events, age, experience, phase of schools and their socio-economic status do not yet seem to be acknowledged in the school effectiveness, improvement and CPD agendas of policymakers and school leaders; concern because of the high levels of professional stress which, for many, are having negative effects upon their personal lives; concern also as to whether such levels can be sustained without the physical loss of some of the best teachers or loss of their energy, commitment and sense of purpose. Yet there is hope, too, because of the high levels commitment and agency, often against the odds, which many teachers' accounts reveal, regardless of experience, phase or context.

Reforms of school standards in all countries tend to focus on increasing pedagogical skills, content knowledge and forms of quality control and assurance and factors which affect teachers' decisions to leave the profession. This research provides a new perspective, focusing upon teacher retention in terms of teacher quality and effectiveness. It suggests that what is fundamentally required if schools are to continue to improve is a better understanding by policymakers of the factors which enable teachers, not simply to remain in teaching, but more importantly, to sustain their commitment, resilience and, therefore, effectiveness over the whole of their careers.

Notes

1. The percentage of pupils in a school eligible for free school meal (FSM) provides an indication of low income and social disadvantage. It was used to divide schools into four categories from least to most disadvantaged. FSM 1 describes schools with 0–8% of pupils eligible for free school meals. This percentage rises to 9–20% for FSM 2 schools, 21–35% for FSM 3 schools, and over 35% for FSM 4 schools.
2. Readers should note that this accounts for differences in the total number of teachers indicated in each of the figures and table in this chapter.

References

Acker, S. (1999). *The realities of teachers' work: Never a dull moment.* London: Cassell.
Ball, S. J. (2001). Teachers' soul and the terrors of performativity. *Research Students' Society*, Issue 38. London: University of London, Institute of Education.
Benard, B. (1991). Fostering resiliency in kids: *Protective factors in the family, school, and community.* Portland, OR: Western Center for Drug-Free Schools and Communities. (ERIC Document Reproduction Service No. ED 335 781.)
Bernstein, B. (1996). *Pedagogy, symbolic control and identity: Theory, research, critique.* London: Taylor and Francis.
Bryk, A. S., Lee, V. E., & Holland, P. B. (1993). *Catholic schools and the common good.* Cambridge, MA: Harvard University Press.
Castells, M. (1997). *The power of identity.* Oxford: Basil Blackwell.
Crosswell, L. (2006). *Understanding teacher commitment in times of change.* Submitted thesis for the degree of Doctor of Education, QUT, Australia.
Day, C. (2000). Stories of change and professional development: The costs of commitment. In C. Day, A. Fernandez, T. Hauge, & J. Moller (Eds.), *The life and work of teachers: International perspectives in changing times* (pp. 109–129). London: Falmer Press.
Day, C. (2004). *A passion for teaching.* London: Routledge Falmer.
Day, C. W., Elliott, B., & Kington, A. (2005). Reform, standards and teacher identity: Challenges of sustaining commitment. *Teaching and Teacher Education*, 21, 563–77, 0742051X.
Day, C., Sammons, P., Kington, A., Gu, Q., & Stobart, G. (2006). Methodological synergy in a national project: The VITAE story. *Evaluation and Research in Education*, 19(2), 102–125.
Ebmeier, J. & Nicklaus, H. (1999). The impact of peer and principal collaborative supervision on teachers' trust, commitment, desire for collaboration, and efficacy. *Journal of Curriculum and Supervision*, 14(4), 351–378.
Elliott, B. & Crosswell, L. (2001). Commitment to teaching: *Australian perspectives on the interplays of the professional and the personal in teachers' lives.* Paper presented at the International Symposium on Teacher Commitment at the European Conference on Educational Research, Lille, France.
Elkins, T. & Elliott, J. (2004). Competition and control: The impact of government regulation on teaching and learning in English schools. *Research Papers in Education*, 19(1), 15–30.
Evetts, J. (2005). The management of professionalism: A contemporary paradox. Paper presented to ESRC Seminar Series, *Changing Teacher Roles, Identities and Professionalism*, Kings College, London.
Firestone, W. A. (1996). Images of teaching and proposals for reform: A comparison of ideas from cognitive and organisational research. *Education Administration Quarterly*, 32(2), 209–235.
Gewirtz, S., Cribb, A., Mahony, P., & Hextall, I. (2006, June 26). Changing teacher roles, identities and professionalism: A review of key themes from the seminar papers. Paper for discussion

at Seminar 9 at the Changing Teacher Roles, *Identities and Professionalism seminar series*, Kings College, London.

Goodson, I. & Hargreaves, A. (Eds.) (1996). *Teachers' professional lives*. London: Falmer Press.

Goss, S. (2005). Counselling: *A quiet revolution*. London: Teacher Support Network.

Guardian (2003). *Workload hits teacher morale*. (Report on GTC/Guardian/Mori Teacher Survey) 7 January: 8.

Hargreaves, A. (1993). Individualism and individuality: Reinterpreting the teacher culture. In J. W. Little and M. W. McLaughlin (Eds.), *Teachers' work*: *Individuals, colleagues, and contexts* (pp. 51–76). New York: Teachers College Press.

Hargreaves, A. (2000). Four ages of professionalism and professional learning. *Teachers and Teaching: Theory and Practice*, 6(2), 151–82.

Hargreaves, A. (2001). The emotional geographies of teaching. *Teachers' College Record*, 103, 1056–1080.

Helsby, G. (1999). *Changing teachers' work*. Buckingham: Open University Press.

Henderson, N. & Milstein, M. M. (1996). *Resiliency in schools: Making it happen for students and educators*. Thousand Oaks, CA: Corwin Press.

Higgins, G. (1994). *Resilient adults: Overcoming a cruel past*. San Francisco, CA: Jossey-Bass.

Hodkinson, H. & Hodkinson, P. (2005). Improving schoolteachers' workplace learning. *Research Papers in Education*, 20(20), 109–131.

Huberman, M. (1993). *The lives of teachers*. London: Cassell.

Huberman, M. (1997). Coda: new paths for bold ventures. In S.A. Raizen and E.D. Britton (Eds.), *Bold ventures: Patterns among U.S. innovations in science and mathematics education*, Vol. 1. Boston, MA: Kluwer.

Ingersoll, R. M. (2003). *Who controls teachers' work?* Cambridge, MA: Harvard University Press.

James-Wilson, S. (2001). *The influence of ethnocultural identity on emotions and teaching*. Paper presented at the Annual Meeting of the American Educational Research Association, New Orleans, April 2000.

Kelchtermans, G. & Vandenberghe, R. (1994). Teachers' professional development: A biographic perspective. *Journal of Curriculum Studies*, 26(1), 45–62.

Kelchtermans, G. (1996). Teacher vulnerability: Understanding its moral and political roots. *Cambridge Journal of Education*, 26(1), 307–324.

Kelchtermans, G. (2005). Teachers' emotions in educational reforms: Self-understanding, vulnerable commitment and micropolitical literacy. *Teaching and Teacher Education*, 21(8), 995–1006.

Kushman, J. W. (1992). The organisational dynamics of teacher workplace commitment: A study of urban elementary and middle schools. *Educational Administration Quarterly*, 28(1), 5–42.

Kyriacou, C. (2000). *Stress busting for teachers*. Cheltenham: Stanley Thornes.

Louis, K. S. (1998). Effects of teacher quality worklife in secondary schools on commitment and sense of efficacy. *School Effectiveness and School Improvement*, 9(1), 1–27.

McLaughlin, M. & Talbert, J. E. (2006). *Building school-based teacher learning communities: Professional strategies to improve student achievement*. New York: Teachers College Press.

McNess, E., Broadfoot, P., & Osborn, M. (2003). Is the effective compromising the affective? *British Educational Research Journal*, 29(2), 243–57.

Nash, P. (2005, April 21). *Change and challenge. Speech to London Well-Being Conference*, British Library. Retrieved July 15, 2006 from http://www.teachersupport.info/upload/TeacherSupport/documents/Speechtowellbeingconference_210405.pdf

Nias, J. (1981). Commitment and motivation in primary school teachers. *Educational Review*, 33(3), 181–190.

OECD-PISA (2003). *PISA 2003 Assessment framework – mathematics, reading, science and problem solving knowledge and skills*. http://www.pisa.oecd.org.

Riehl, C. & Sipple, J. W. (1996). Making the most of time taken and talent: Secondary school organisational climates, teaching tasks environments, and teacher commitment. *American Educational Research Journal*, 33(4), 873–901.

Sachs, J. (2003). *The activist teaching profession*. Buckingham: Open University Press.

Tatto, M. T. (Ed.) (2007). *Reforming teaching globally*. Oxford: Symposium Books.

Troman, G. & Woods, P. (2001). *Primary teachers' stress*. London: Routledge.

Tschannen-Moran, M., Woolfolk Hoy, A., & Hoy, W. K. (1998). Teacher efficacy: Its meaning and measure. *Review of Educational Research*, 68, 202–48.

Tsui, K. T. & Cheng, Y. C. (1999). School organisational health and teacher commitment: A contingency study with multi-level analysis. *Educational Research and Evaluation*, 5(3), 249–265.

UNESCO (1998). *World Education Report: Teachers and teaching in a changing world*. Paris: UNESCO.

Werner, E. (1990). Protective factors and individual resilience. In S. J. Meisels and J. Shonkoff (Eds.), *Handbook of early childhood intervention* (pp. 97–116). New York: Cambridge University Press.

Woods, P., Jeffrey, B., & Troman, G. (1997). *Restructuring schools, reconstructing teachers*. Buckingham: Open University Press.

Chapter 4
On the Unacknowledged Significance of Teachers' Habitus and Dispositions

Jette Steensen

Introduction

In recent years, a growing number of studies have focused on teachers' career trajectories. At the same time there has been a special focus on attrition and retention, with worries about a sufficient supply of qualified teachers seemingly an almost worldwide phenomenon. In a comprehensive meta-analysis Borman and Dowling (2008) summarize 34 studies. The authors refer to Ingersoll (2001) in distancing themselves from previous work which they claim only quantifies the issue. Instead their goal is 'to understand why attrition occurs or, more formally, what factors moderate attrition outcomes' (p. 367). Their synthesis of research evidence points to five important constellations of variables affecting attrition and retention (i.e. teacher demographic characteristics, teacher qualifications, school organizational character-istics, school resources and school student body characteristics). They also indicate that teacher attrition rates and the reasons for attrition vary across the lifespan. This latter point is also taken up in the VITAE project (Day et al., 2006) which focuses on variations in teachers' work, lives and effectiveness during different phases of their careers. Both studies also point out the need for more complex theories and studies which might point to how combinations of factors influence teachers' career trajectories. However, although both studies are very comprehensive, neither of them touches upon the possibility that socio-economic and sociocultural factors might be mediating factors in explaining variations in trajectories. For Borman and Dowling, teacher demographic characteristics comprise gender, race, age, marital status and number of children, while Day et al. primarily focus on generational factors.

In the explorative study on which this chapter is based, I have made a prelimi-nary effort to show that socio-economic and sociocultural factors matter and might provide a missing link in research on teachers' lives and trajectories. Although this study focuses on teacher education students only, the results indicate that the basic orientations will influence career decisions and thus contribute in explaining dif-ferent teacher trajectories. However, further research will be needed to supplement and refine the instruments and put the results to scale.

In the first part of this chapter, a complex theoretical and meta-theoretical framework will be presented and theoretical points will be illustrated using empirical

M. Bayer et al. (eds.), *Teachers' Career Trajectories and Work Lives*,
Professional Learning and Development in Schools and Higher Education 3,
© Springer Science + Business Media B.V. 2009

data from the project. The second part of the chapter will summarize major findings and discuss implications for future research as well as some possible implications for practice.

Part One

Theoretical Framework: Life History, Habitus and Dispositions

Interest in life history and biography research has grown immensely since the beginning of the twentieth century from the first studies on the Polish peasants (Znaniecki & Znaniecki 1984) and the inspiration from the Chicago School over the French sociologist Daniel Bertaux's studies on bakers in France (Bertaux, 1981) to the growing number of studies on teachers' lives inspired by the works of Goodson (1992, 2003) among others. However, as the number of studies has grown, the methodological and theoretical frameworks have also diversified. One problem is that often life histories function as mere illustrations of other findings. Another issue pertains to the fact that the life history approach contains a tension between the interpretation of a purely subjective narrative and the contextual analysis, a tension which also reflects an invisible border between the humanities and the social sciences. As the project reported here lies firmly within the field of the social sciences, a theoretical and meta-theoretical framework has been developed in order to demonstrate underlying structural issues in addition to the more obvious subjective points of view which follow more naturally from the life history approach, and much effort has been made to discuss and elaborate a complex framework which could do this.

The main objective was to investigate the 'social conditions of teacher identity'. The research project analyses a number of life histories told by a sample of teacher education students in different institutional settings, one urban and one rural, in both Denmark and the USA. The study was carried out as an in-depth qualitative study with a view to investigating how sociocultural/economic background and life history might contribute in creating a specific 'identity' and orientation towards the teaching profession.

The project is based upon the theoretical and methodological framework of Pierre Bourdieu (Bourdieu & Passeron 1977; Bourdieu 1984, 1987a, b, 1988, 1990, 1999). Bourdieu's concepts of *habitus/dispositions* in relation to the concept of *field* constitute the backbone of the project. The two concepts of 'habitus' and 'dispositions' are developed at different stages of Bourdieu's work, but basically they allude to the same reality, and they will be used interchangeably in this text. Although still thought controversial by some researchers, dispositions/habitus have become increasingly popular in empirical studies. However, as discussed by Reay (2004), the concepts are too often used as a general explanation of social differences instead of being applied as working tools. Often it is less obvious how these dispositions/ habitus actually appear to the researcher. In other words, how can the habitus be sustained as a finding, what does it look like? This question is not easily answered since habitus/dispositions are *theoretical concepts* signifying that they cannot be directly observed. The habitus/dispositions can only be revealed through analysis of the content of the points of view as well as analysis of how these points of view are expressed. This analysis of the interviewee's life story must be supplemented by analysis of other types of data material (e.g. statistics, historical accounts, economic data and newspaper documentation) in order for the subjective points of view to be related to the contextual factors of social reality.

The objective of the project was to identify the underlying dispositions through analysis of the living conditions of the interviewees, including their own everyday descriptions of social reality. The assumption is that, in a preconscious way, living conditions mould the basic orientations of the individual. These dispositions do not exist as substantive entities for themselves, but only *relative to* other orientations. Therefore the analysis requires a methodology which is comparative and builds on a solid, well-documented framework. On the basis of this framework, the presence of different socio-economic and sociocultural backgrounds of interviewees has been ensured. This was done in order to apply a *relational analysis* of the points of view of the interviewees, i.e. male–female, urban–rural, different socio-economic backgrounds, etc. This has to do with the fact that in this study the researcher assumes that there is a certain social reality behind knowledge, feelings and practices. This social reality of a second order is the reality expressed through the concepts of habitus/dispositions. The habitus is difficult to grasp, it does not appear in a specific, definite form; it is to be understood as a certain orientation underlying various empirically observable utterances, feelings and actions. Habitus is embodied history and comes very close to culture, a concept which is generally acknowledged and widely understood and accepted, although at a closer look, just as complex. The habitus mediates between a specific position in social space, empirically ascertained through questions of the cultural and economic capital of the family of the interviewee (and of the interviewee himself or herself), and his or her points of view, in this case points of view concerning schools and future teaching career. In Bourdieu's theory, this connection is established as a relationship between a *position* in social space (i.e. society) and field (certain definite area of society, in this case education) and certain *positionings* (i.e. attitudes, statements and actions). The habitus is thus considered to be the mediator. The point here is that positions and positioning are directly observable empirical findings; the habitus, on the other hand, is not directly observable. However, we assume that it must be there, since we can empirically ascertain that certain positions are associated with certain positionings.

Teacher Education in Denmark and the USA

In this very limited space it will not be possible to give a thorough analysis of the complexities of the two educational systems and their historical backgrounds; however, for the sake of basic understanding, a few issues will be discussed in the following.

First, it is important to stress that usually the concept of 'teacher' in Denmark refers to the professional who teaches children aged 6 to 16 in primary and lower secondary school, whereas teachers within upper secondary and vocational education have other titles and are generally not included in the term. In the USA, the term 'teacher' comprises both primary and secondary teachers.

A very sensitive issue from a Danish point of view is whether teacher education is placed within the university system. Denmark still has a tradition of providing teacher education at separate independent 4-year colleges. Quite recently, the colleges have merged into larger institutions which, however, have not yet been able to achieve university status. At first glance the situation might appear quite different from the USA where teacher education appears to be university-based.

However, when the situation is investigated a little further, one realizes that the issue is much more complicated. Firstly the concept of 'college' is very important in the USA. To be or not to be at college is the decisive factor. Colleges might be public[1] or private, of 2 years or 4 years, be at a public grant university or a state university, and each type of institution has its own history. The two American universities included in this study represent two different public universities in the same state, only 1 hour's drive apart, but with quite distinctive differences. Fine-town University is a prestigious land grant university with a lot of research funds and only a very restricted intake of students into their teacher education programme. No-town University is a state university with very limited funding for research and no doctoral programme; instead they have a much more substantial intake of teacher students. Historically No-town developed as an institution from a 'normal school' (teacher training), then it became a teachers' college, which was then turned into a regional college until it achieved its present status as a state university.

In recent years, the traditional university-based teacher education programmes in the USA have had competition, as certification by private agencies makes short-cuts into teaching possible (Zeichner, 2008), even though the majority still follows the usual college route. Similarly, Denmark has seen the introduction of new shorter teacher training programmes, but these have not been privatized (yet).

Another distinctive difference between the two countries is that, due to the fact that teacher education in Denmark is placed at separate colleges, teacher education is considered and planned as a 4-year coherent professional programme striving to integrate subject theory, education and practice. In the USA, on the other hand, students start a 1.5-year general programme where they can choose a number of different courses before they apply to the 2.5-year teacher education programme at a School of Education. At some state universities with a large intake of teacher education students, the range of courses can be more limited and more focused on professional preparation from the beginning, and the programme might thus be more similar to the Danish programmes.

A Comparative Point of View

As stated above, the comparative/relational perspective is present throughout the analysis.

Often educational research tends to take the economic, historical and cultural context as given. This leads to a more or less consciously reflected rational choice thinking where a complex mix of reasons are boiled down to one dimension, and idealistic thinking prioritizes the well-intended educational objective. In reality a complex of factors are blended. Basically the comparative point of view is a methodological issue, it is a means of discovering influences distinctive of various contexts, so in principle comparisons between Swedish and Danish students and institutions (Steensen, 2005) might be as interesting as comparisons between England and France and in this case Denmark and the USA. Today, global educational policies and ideas often have American roots, whether they are spread across the globe through the borrowing and lending of national governments or through international agencies (Robertson, 2008); therefore, American educational policies and practices are of special interest in order to estimate the extent to which American trends might gain a foothold on the national scene. As many comparative researchers have pointed out (e.g. Archer, 1979), global trends, however, have to be translated into local contexts, making the actual results unpredictable.

Comparisons enable us to understand our own educational system, but they also enable us to see choice of education in a wider perspective, and from studies on the professions we know that exogenous factors also contribute in shaping the conditions of national professions (Abbott, 1988). This is why the socio-economic context has been the focus of the analysis in this project.

Empirical Data and Methodology

Data were collected at four institutions (colleges and universities), two in each country, each representing a prestige/research-oriented environment, Fine-town (USA) and City College (DK) and a more regional/non-research-oriented environment, No-town (USA) and Rural College (DK). In Denmark, students were selected on the basis of existing data from a previous large quantitative study (Steensen, 2005). They were selected according to their father's formal educational background as an important indicator of the sociocultural/economic background of the student. In Rural College, the fathers were unskilled, mainly employed in different functions within the fishing industry or within agriculture. In City College, all had college degrees, at least at master's level, i.e. engineers, physicians, veterinarians and high school teachers.[2] In the USA, I did not have any background knowledge about the students and had to rely on assistance from the university and college professors to find students for interviews. In the USA I interviewed eight students at each institution and I soon realized that the hypothesis was sustained, in that the similarities within each group were striking. In the analysis I have thus included six students from each institution representing the main group of students and then one or two students from each institution who represent some variations. Thus, at Fine-town, the majority of students had fathers with college degrees, mainly managers and engineers, whereas in No-town, no fathers had college degrees, but various forms of skilled and semi-skilled jobs. In comparison to Denmark, the students in No-town represent a more semi-rural/urban lifestyle and background where urban orientation is not far away. To avoid misunderstanding it is important to stress that the investigation was never intended to be representative in the general or statistical sense. I do not maintain that all students at each institution had the same background. In this study I was not interested in whether these students represent 5%, 10%, 20% or any other percentage of the total student body. The main objective was to find groups of students with similar social characteristics (positions) who could then be compared with one another as to dispositions and professional positionings. One might argue that mothers may be seen as equally important in influencing educational choice as fathers, which is also supported by the fact that in Fine-town five out of six mothers were in fact teachers. However, I had to choose one main indicator for the totality of the family position and status, and in social analysis, the father's position is still to be considered the major factor when estimating the social standing of the family as such. At any rate, while the father's position was used for the selection of cases, the analysis of course includes both parents.

Interviews were carried out as a combination of life history and thematic interviews. The main inspiration has been the interviews in the 'Weight of the World' (Bourdieu et al., 1999) in the sense that the effort was directed towards collecting the story and analysing it with a double perspective. On the one hand, student narratives were analysed from within their own perspective; on the other hand, the stories were analysed not only from an inside, but from an outside perspective as well. This is not some mysterious all-seeing eye or omniscient being, but a methodological choice which stems from the fact that when the stories are compared to each other and the narratives are interpreted according to the habitual circumstances of each student, systematic, though complex, regularities appear. The life history perspective was needed for two purposes: firstly, to establish the social background information in order to interpret the orientations and perspectives of each student; and secondly, also to provide contextual information which could be used to characterize the local environment. This subjective point of view was then supplemented by other types of data, e.g. statistical material, other research reports, and newspaper articles, in order to give a detailed contextual description. The thematic part of the interview was intended to provide information on the subjective perspectives (i.e. positionings) of individual students.

The dispositions cannot be detected as absolute entities; therefore, there needs to be a strict strategic choice behind the selection. Like any other point of view, the dispositions are constructed from a specific point in social space which is why prior indicators of social background factors are needed. The researcher must listen to what the interviewee says (or omits) as well as *how* it is said. Careful listening is also needed in order to be able to grasp the real subjective points of view and leave out official rhetoric which might be included for a lot of different reasons, e.g. that the interviewee tends to adapt to what she thinks the interviewer wants to hear etc. Thus close attention should be paid to both the outside and the inside perspective.

Basic Dispositions

In the section below I shall try to illustrate how the theoretical points of the concept of habitus have been applied to the interview material. As mentioned, I build on an understanding of social reality as a relational phenomenon. Therefore students have been selected from positions (social backgrounds) that clearly differ from one another in order to get an insight starting from a clear-cut material.

Fine-town

In general, students from Fine-town (a prestigious urban university) in the USA are characterized by *dispositions* which demonstrate familiarity with, and inside knowledge of, the world of education. Their parents have college degrees and thus economic as well as cultural capital. Interestingly this fact has led them to trust the educational system to such an extent that all but one has attended the public school system. They and their parents do not hesitate in contacting directors and teachers at their own discretion and they do not fear the school system, because they know how to handle it:

> I attended W-high school, it is inner-city and it was great there, there was a lot of theatre, music and dance which I have always been into. It was a very diverse inner-city school, and I was also in a great elementary school, where I got a Latino principal, a female black principal, and I was in an experimental bilingual first grade, so I was really exposed to Spanish. (Susan Fine-town, in Steensen, 2007: 221)

To grasp the real significance of the above statement, it should be compared to the statements of students from No-town who also deal with issues of inner-city schools and diversity, but from a position where the negative side is more imminently threatening, and in the interviews this is expressed in terms of safety.

> It was a very safe environment, my dad was a police officer, so he made sure that wherever we were, it was somewhere safe. (Karen No-town in Steensen, 2007: 215).

> A lot of it is safety issues, they are very safety conscious all over, and I have heard things about public schools I really do not want my daughter to be exposed to at this age, a lot of it is safety for me. (Jennie No-town in Steensen, 2007: 216).

Overall, all Fine-town students report that they have done well at school without really making a big issue out of it. A clear positioning which accompany these positions is that they trust teacher education to give them access to a world of opportunities.

> We would love to stay in Fine-town for a while, if we could; eventually we want to move abroad, hopefully. I would love to go to France or Quebec which are French speaking. If we can obtain a 5 year residence in France that would be fantastic. (Susan Fine-town in Steensen, 2007: 225)

> I think there are so many opportunities for teachers that I think they are not taking advantage of, you know there are summers off, and I think there is a lot of things I want to do,

there is an opportunity called 'teacher at sea' and you go to stay for 3 months with a marine
biologist at sea and you can communicate with your class via satellite and learn more about
science which is obviously something which interests me so. (Jennie Fine-town in
Steensen, 2007: 226)

On the *empirical* level, the above-mentioned two descriptions of job opportunities
might be understood as very different career perspectives. Some students express
a desire to move to another state (warmer and sunnier), one student wants to settle in Europe, another student instead explains how as a teacher she might have
the opportunity to participate in science expeditions and participate in research in
natural science which she feels will enhance the curiosity of children. However, the
underlying common tone in these interviews is optimism and a world of opportunities. Again this point of view should be contrasted, for example, with the concern
for 'safety' expressed by the students in No-town.

No-town

In *No-town* (semi-rural state university and former teachers' college) students
came mostly from unskilled or semi-skilled backgrounds. What might strike one
as strange at first glance is that the majority of students in this group have shunned
public schools and instead attended private, mostly small parochial schools, and
one even attended a more expensive Catholic private school, even though her parents were far from wealthy (her mother was a nurse's assistant and her father was
a policeman). However, she reports in detail and repeatedly how getting the right
schooling had been a top family priority and investment in her upbringing.

I went to an all-girls Catholic high school, and I think that was the greatest thing my parents
ever did for me. I did have options, but they definitely pushed for private school, because
we actually live in x-town, so they did not want me in the x-town school system, because
it is not as strong as some private schools, so private schools were definitely valued in my
family … private schools are better than the public schools if you want to pursue something
further beyond high school, they prepare you pretty well for that, so it is important. (Karen
No-town in Steensen, 2007: 218)

The values of her upbringing are then again reflected in her career orientation and
her attitudes to parents.

I know that families pay for their children to be at those private schools, and I know that
they pay a very good amount of money, so I know that they are going to be involved in
their children's lives academically, and I know that they are going to be at the schools more
than at some public school system, and the teacher I worked with said that sometimes she
has to hunt the parents down in order to have them involved, to have parent-teacher conferences with them. Sometimes parents will send their children to school at the beginning of
the year with a pencil that is half-used and that is all the kids get for the whole year, no
books, no folders and sometimes parents do not care what their kids are doing in schools,
they do not care about making sure their homework is done, and I know this will be emotionally a very difficult environment for me to work in, and so I know I will be more
confident in a private school setting. (Karen No-town in Steensen, 2007: 229–230)

Such a finding shows the complexity of social reality and how it might run counter
to everyday reasoning which tends to relate high status with private schooling and

low income with public schooling. This of course is true, but these cases show that it is a truth within the limits of a totality of factors. The relational methodology enables us to see the complex realities surrounding basic empirical responses, like the answer to a question such as 'Did you attend private or public schooling?'. In this social context, families see good schooling as the only way forward, and they are willing to invest hard work, money and a lot of effort in achieving their goal. They do not have the same basic familiarity with, trust in and ease with the public school system as appears in the narratives of Fine-town students. Their positioning as to their future career as well as their attitudes to the parents at the local school varies along the same lines. Where Fine-town students saw interesting opportunities, the narratives of No-town students are characterized by a much more focused attention on the importance of getting a decent job which will provide economic security in safe surroundings at the lowest possible cost. They do not put forward exciting dreams of travelling or glorious careers. Their plans for the future concentrate on 'going home' or at least getting a job in a 'safe' district, and they know the exact distinctions between the local schools.

> Many of the R school districts are not that good, B is not a good area, but if you get into the BT area that is good, that is a wealthier subdivision, even in J town. M is a better school than F because of the money in the area. MM has more money than W school area, so it just depend – if you need a job bad enough you will even go to those districts. (Jennie No-town in Steensen, 2007: 233)

Now sceptics might argue that these relational differences are accidental or merely the constructions of the researcher, a possibility which must always be taken into account. However, to substantiate the main points, the comparative (i.e. relational) approach is applied, and it is disclosed that when the Danish case is analysed, the same relational differences between urban and rural reappear, however, expressed according to a different national setting.

City College

In *City College* (Danish urban prestige college) we also meet students with upper-middle-class backgrounds; they come from family backgrounds of doctors, veterinarians and civil engineers. One of the important distinctions in Bourdieu's work is the distinction between 'economic' and 'cultural' capital. Where families in Fine-town had a balanced composition of cultural and economic capital (fathers in business and engineering and mothers in education), several students from City College seem to be leaning more towards the economic pole in that both the father and the mother work within business, accountancy, etc. This might explain their positionings which show that these students prioritize a career perspective which does not to the same extent focus on the opportunities within the public schooling system, but first and foremost will send them home into their 'habitual' upper-middle-class environment. They prefer to teach in private schools, get into management, advance into secondary school, etc. Compared to Fine-town, where the parents were quite sympathetic towards the public school system and ready to defend it, students at City College and their families see schools from a more external critical perspective in line with present-day political reform logic, although, like Fine-town, they handle the school system with ease. Their basic dispositions have consequences for their career ambitions in that they feel that their mission will be to improve school standards, preferably from a management point of view. Another striking feature is that male students in this group express that their main reason for choosing teaching was that they wanted their job 'to be fun', an indicator of ease. This statement should be related to the 'world of opportunities' of Fine-town students, and contrasted with the preoccupation with 'safety and going home' of No-town students as well as the modest optimism among students at Rural College whose main characteristics seem to be that they are in fact somewhat surprised that they finally made it, and they intend to remain in the local area.

Rural College

In Danish *Rural College* we meet students who come from unskilled backgrounds firmly rooted in the local rural traditions of agriculture and the fishing industry, or perhaps independent service activities. The majority are older second-career students who enter a teaching career through the back door and much to their own surprise. Their main strength, however, is a lifelong perspective of schooling seen from below, so to speak. They have experienced how it is not to be an obvious school success from the beginning, and although they are now about to enter a teaching career, they are still rather impressed that they have really made it. At the same time, they feel that finally they have got the recognition they deserve. New energy and a certain self-confidence appear because it turned out they were not that unqualified after all. Above all, most of them retain sensitivity to the fact that schools might be an oppressive experience for some students.

It is important to stress that there is absolutely no normative judgement in these observations and no evaluation as to who will become the best teachers; the effort has been to substantiate the point that social conditions (positions) matter in the formation of orientation of the initial teacher identity, but in very subtle ways.

The table below shows the major social characteristics and dispositions of the interviewed students at the four colleges. Please note that indicators of dispositions are statements constructed by the researcher on the basis of the totality of the stories where positions and positioning are analysed in relation to each other as well as to the positions and positionings of the other groups. The sentences and indicators of the dispositions are not labels of entities, but the names of the underlying connection between positions and positionings, a dynamic that must be assumed if we are to understand the coherence of the whole picture. Bourdieu's framework thus helps in revealing the complex patterns of similarities between students who share a certain social milieu.

	'Fine-town' (USA)	'No-town' (USA)
Socio-economic/ sociocultural characteristics	Parents with college degrees (fathers: businessmen, engineers, professionals)	Parents with some education (fathers: plumbers, policemen, farmers, etc.)
	High level of economic and cultural capital	Some economic and low cultural capital
	Working mothers (five out of six within education)	Non-working mothers
	Attended public schools	Attended parochial or private schools
Indicators of dispositions	*'I want to experience something new'*	*'I want to go home'*
	'The world is full of opportunities'	*'I work hard'*
	'I want to make a difference in life and do something good'	*'The world is dangerous'*
		'I will do my best to reach my goal'
	'Career orientation'	*'Home and family orientation'*
	'School familiarity'	*'School safety'*
	'City College' (DK)	**'Rural College' (DK)**
Socio-economic/ sociocultural characteristics	Parents with college degree	Parents with no formal education
	Engineers, doctors, professionals	Agriculture, fishing, local trade
	High level of economic and cultural capital	Low level of economic and cultural capital
	Some non-working mothers	Non-working mothers
	Public and private schools	Public schools
Indicators of dispositions	*'Revert to habitual status'*	*'Remain on the spot'*
	'Job must be fun'	*'I can do it '*
	'I have a calling to create school improvement'	*'They are not going to tell me my place'*
	'Career, private schools and further education'	*'Schools are not necessarily just'*
	'School familiarity'	*'Adaptation and some optimism in relation to their future new status'*
		'School distance'

Critical Realism as an Important Meta-theoretical Framework for the Analysis

Bourdieu can be understood within the framework of critical realism (Archer et al., 1998; Sayer, 2000; Maxwell, 2004) as an important epistemological and ontological position today, since habitus/dispositions (Bourdieu) can be understood as the 'causal mechanisms' influencing the attitudes and orientations of the actors.

These explanative 'causal'[3] mechanisms are not immediately accessible and can only be discovered through an analysis of the interview material as such, substantiated by observations during the interview and supplemented with other data material. Critical realism distinguishes analytically between three levels of reality:

1. The level of *the empirical* that consists of the collected data (in this case: interviews)
2. The level of *the actual* that consists of empirical material, which theoretically might have been collected, but which has been left out, since the research process always requires delimitations
3. The level of *the real* that cannot be observed directly, but must be analytically disclosed through its causal effects

Thus, the habitus and the reflexive modes are found at the *realm of the real* and might be revealed through *the way* things are being said as well as *what* the actors actually say at the level of the empirical. I assume that the actors can only to some extent have insight into their own *habitus* (Bourdieu).

In quantitative large-scale research, data are gathered from the level of the empirical only, and correlations are often mistaken for causality. The main methodological point in this study is that qualitative methods might have specific advantages when looking for causal mechanisms, an aspect often overlooked when quantitative and qualitative methods stand opposed to each other. Moreover, the application of the critical realist approach has a unique strategic strength at the present moment in time. With a trend that suggests that research ought to be restricted to producing evidence of what works, and expecting that only controlled experiments can produce reliable knowledge about the social world, it is paramount not only to claim diversity, but most of all to prove how small-scale qualitative contextualized research can detect what really 'works', i.e. *the causal mechanisms* beneath the immediately observable surface.

To give an example: two students at Fine-town express visions for the future that on the surface (empirical level) might sound very different.

> I thought about coming back for administration. You would be working on the policies and working with people who are running the schools and the teachers who are teaching and then you would be working with the people who make the higher level decisions and the decisions which are coming from above in a sense, I would love to work with administration. (Caroline Fine-town in Steensen, 2007: 224)

> I would probably want to move to Arizona actually, and I wanted to move out west and I am thinking of Colorado, California, Arizona, I have never lived out of state, well besides going abroad. I feel the need to move to something new and see something different and new places. (Linda Fine-town in Steensen, 2007: 225)

However, the point I try to illustrate here is that an interpretation of these ambitions from the empirical level alone might focus on the different ambitions, whereas in my search for *dispositions* I have to look beyond the empirical level and listen to how, in *similar ways*, they expressed their confidence of a world of opportunities opening up after graduation (for further examples compare the two statements above).

This underlying causal pattern can only be discovered through a relational approach, i.e. comparisons of life stories and statements made by students from different sociocultural and socio-economic conditions.

Part Two

Findings and Discussion

Differences Between Countries

The major objective in this chapter has been to show how underlying structural factors, identified as the habitus and dispositions underlying the diversity of positionings, are repeated in similar ways across national boundaries. Meanwhile, it is important also to acknowledge how economic as well as sociocultural and historic differences between the two countries influence the ways the challenges of a globalized world and neo-liberal policies are expressed in the interviews. The interview material reveals such trends in varied and often rather surprising ways, related to the students' daily lives.

One older American student from No-town describes the macroeconomic conditions and changes in her home town as she sees them in the following way:

> I see a trend in x-town, the demographics have changed, I have lived there all my life, 18 years, so you know, I used to … well we still do, we go round and look at the Christmas decorations in town, and since I was little we have done this, and they are all some really neat neighbourhoods you want to go through and check out the Christmas decorations, and as years have passed I have noticed that those really nice neighbourhoods that had all these neat decorations are now rental properties and they do not have the cool decorations and the condition of the houses is deteriorating, so it, we have changed, our town has changed, but our town is still growing, a lot of industries in inner town, you know they are starting wages at 7.50–9.50\$ an hour which, even if two people are working, it is difficult to raise a family on those kinds of wages. (Paula No-town in Steensen, 2007: 208)

Of course these changes are not only reflected in observations about Christmas decorations, but are also found in the conditions of the local schools. In another part of the interview this student continues:

> We have a free lunch programme and a free breakfast programme which does get utilized, you can tell by the conditions of the children's clothing, you know the dirtiness, that either someone is not there in the morning to get them dressed or they just do not have the facilities or the time or whatever to attend to the conditions of the clothing, I 'sub' [substitute teacher] in those schools and those kids are clingy, they want someone to pay attention to them … and I thought they are so needy and I have such a big heart and I would probably take them all home and give them all decent coats, and you know you cannot, and that does not solve the problem, it just makes it your problem. (Paula No-town in Steensen, 2007: 231)

In comparison, there is first and foremost a striking absence in the Danish interviews – an absence of the harsh social realities surrounding the situation in many American schools. The welfare system still seems to offer protection. Through the stories from Rural College, one gets a description of an environment which is struggling for survival, mainly because of a lack of job opportunities. However, all the students we meet seem to have adapted to the situation and live in a sort of equilibrium with the given surroundings. Their life is not based on huge consumption; they are accustomed to changing from unemployment benefit into temporary unskilled jobs and several types of reskilling projects. But this equilibrium is based on the continued presence of the welfare security net which ensures a basic income during unemployment as well as a minimum wage when in unskilled jobs. These students are satisfied with life where they are as long as they are assured a basic income. They are firmly rooted in the local community and opportunities (nature, music, etc.). For them, negative experiences with schools are individualized, basically related to their own experience. In City College the interviewed students come from privileged backgrounds and they have no worries. As mentioned above, half of them (male) even mention 'fun' as a main argument for choosing teaching. This of course does not mean that harsh social realities are non-existent, but due to the selection of students, those interviewed will probably not be the ones to take up the challenges in troubled schools, and overall these schools are seen more as rare exceptions.

Another indicator of the different national and economic context is related to the different conditions around their own studies. American teacher education students, both from Fine-town and No-town, share an early preoccupation with problems related to the financing of their studies as well as the provision of basic services (e.g. health insurance).

> [P]art of it was health insurance, I am still covered by my parents' health insurance. If I took time off, I would have lost the insurance, and I did not really want to look for a new insurance. (Christina No-town in Steensen, 2007: 215)

> I pay for it all by myself, in my high school I worked two jobs while going to school, one is a place called Shopco, it is like clothing and they also sell laundry, detergent and food, so it is an all purpose store, and then I worked at an ice cream dairy store called Dairy Queen, I would balance out the jobs and I would work at the store on Fridays through Sundays, probably 20 hours a week and then about 5–10 with the ice cream shop and then I would work full time during the summer. (Kristin No-town in Steensen, 2007: 202)

The financial worries result in few possibilities for experimentation in their choice of education: in a very literal sense, they cannot afford to make mistakes. In both countries there are a substantial number of second-career students; however, first-career teacher students in Denmark tend to be older than their American counterparts, primarily due to different conditions at the national level. Danish teacher education students both at City College and Rural College do not pay fees, receive general study grants, and basic services are in place. This fact provides them with more degrees of freedom in choice of education. They have often tried out different types of studies, often for several years, before they finally decide on teacher education. Many American teacher education students also reveal that originally they had other jobs in mind, but they settle for teacher education much faster, in that wrong decisions are very costly.

Similarities

In spite of the above-mentioned differences in national conditions, similarities across countries are even more striking. First and foremost, the relational distinctions between students in Fine-town/City College and No-town/Rural College are repeated across the countries.

The study thus sustains the hypothesis that students carry dispositions which can be attributed to their background and these affect the way they look at their future profession. However, it is important to stress that dispositions are the results of the incorporation of a complex mixture of contextual factors, they are created as intersections of local (rural/urban), national (the USA/Denmark), gender and socio-economic and sociocultural background. Ethnicity would be an obvious factor too; however, since all students are Caucasian, the study does not tell us anything about this. Many studies on teacher recruitment (Zumwalt & Craig, 2005) have shown that recruitment of teacher students is biased toward female (lower-) middle-class white students. This goes for both countries, although the male representation still seems to be higher in Denmark than in the USA.

The Significance of 'Moving Out' and 'Going Home'

One of the main findings of the study is that, irrespective of institutional context, most teacher students want to 'go home' to teach in familiar surroundings. However, this trend should be interpreted in a wider sense than mere geographical location. It must be understood also *habitually*, i.e. students are oriented to work within environments which correspond to their 'lifestyle' and values in the sense grasped by Bourdieu's concept of habitus. The study shows, for example, that students with high SES from Fine-town say that they are very interested in moving out to other states, even as far as Europe. At first glance this might seem a contradiction to the 'go home' statement; however, understood within the habitus framework, it seems reasonable to assume that their habitual orientation allows them a wider and more far-reaching perspective. It is part of their habitual orientation to have some experience of travelling and thus not to be tied to the same geographical location, as long as they can find companions who share the same outlook and world view. They look at the world from a top-down perspective rather than bottom-up and this makes the geographical range of familiarity much larger.

In the research project 'The Draw of Home: How Teachers' Preferences for Proximity Disadvantage Urban Schools', Boyd et al. (2003) have calculated the distance between the first job of newly educated teachers and the original environment and found that, during the period 1999 to 2002, 61% of new teachers in the state of New York taught at a school which was within a range of 15 miles from their own high school. They also make the conclusion that there might be other explanations than mere distance:

> These patterns may reflect more than just a preference for proximity. For example
> individuals may search for employment in regions where they are comfortable, independent
> of the distance from their home town. Teachers appear to prefer to teach in regions where
> they are comfortable, independent of the distance from their home town. Teachers appear
> to teach in regions similar to the one they grew up, if not the same region. Teachers grow-
> ing up in an urban area are much more likely to teach in an urban area, and those growing
> up in a suburban area are more likely to teach in a suburb. (Boyd et al., quoted in Hess
> et al., 2004: 162)

One interesting example which illustrates 'habitual going home' might be the case
of Charlotte, a Danish student from City College. She grew up in a provincial town
on the west coast of Jutland, approximately 350 km from the capital. Her father
was a physician at the local hospital and through her family she acquired a taste for
opera and classical theatre, but she felt isolated in the local school environment, so,
once she had graduated from high school, she left her family to settle in the capital.
She described how this move made her feel at home like never before, and she ven-
tured that she would never again move out of the city where her interests were no
longer an 'odd thing'. In other words, she has returned to familiar surroundings in
the 'habitual sense'. Although there are similarities between students of Fine-town
and students at City College, they differ in that the selected students at City College
do not have family members who would defend the public school system from an
inside point of view. The city contains a polarized mixture of urban multicultural
public schools, and private schools primarily serving middle-class parents. The
interview reveals that she sticks to this middle-class perspective. Although her own
experiences at a private school were not altogether happy, she sees public schools
as places to avoid since she considers many of them to be of 'inferior quality', and
teacher education has not succeeded in providing her with an alternative understanding of the challenges. On a more rational level, she also realizes the additional
workload involved, if she was to enter a mixed public school. Therefore she would
prefer to teach at a private school and has in fact already ensured a job in such a
school even before her graduation.

Thus, it is likely that many teacher students will contribute to the reproduction of local school cultures, and to the social stratification of the school system.
This might be labelled 'reproduction' or 'teacher tracking'. In the article 'Are
We Creating Separate and Unequal Tracks of Teachers?' Achinstein et al. (2004)
analyse the stories of two teachers who have very different qualifications and trajectories. Achinstein et al. also use the framework of Bourdieu and reach a conclusion close to the conclusions of this project. One student is a male with a Masters
degree, fully certified from a prestigious university. He grew up in a wealthy area
and attended a private Montessori school. The other is a female educated at the local
state university. This distinction is quite parallel to the distinctions between Fine-
town and No-town. The authors now follow up and find out that the male teacher
gets a position in a prestigious school in a wealthy district which allows him a
decent wage and substantial professional autonomy, whereas the female is hired by
a school in a problem area where teaching is 'scripted', which basically means that
there is not much freedom for professional judgement. One of the main points of

the article is, however, that these circumstances are also reflected in the professional identity of the two teachers, in that both of them seem to adhere to and defend the basic teaching principles of each school: i.e. institution and individual match.

> We found similar patterns of correspondence in our analysis of teachers' knowledge, access to learning and conceptions of themselves as professionals. Thus socialisation of novices may produce high and low tracks of teachers whose instructional beliefs and practices enact inequities in the socialization of high- and low track students. These tracks correspond with the capital of the district, thus ensuring that the 'rich' (high capital) get richer and the 'poor' (low capital) get poorer. This method of reproducing inequality is less obvious than student tracking, but all the more troubling. (Achinstein et al., 2004)

Habitual Idealism

Through the application of Bourdieu's, concepts various points of intersection between structure and agency are discovered, and these different intersections might contribute in explaining the development of preparedness for new challenges. Through these theoretical perspectives, the study, however, also indicates that there might be interesting exceptions to 'going home'. Interpreted through Bourdieu's concepts of habitus and field, there seems to be a certain homology between students from families with a high amount of sociocultural capital (college degrees and often one or both parents working in the educational system) and an idealistic engagement in multicultural issues. Multicultural schools might be considered a risk or a *threat* to students from a lower-middle-class background, or just causing too much *trouble* seen from the point of view of middle-class students close to the socio-economic pole. The multicultural perspective might, however, also turn out to be an *interesting experience* or a special enrichment in the upbringing of students closer to the sociocultural pole as shown in the following quotations:

> I was in an experimental bilingual first grade, so I was really exposed to Spanish and I attended W-high school, it is inner-city and it was great there. (Susan Fine-town in Steensen, 2007: 221)

Susan's parents both have college degrees, the father is a business manager and the mother has a degree in education and is now the principal of a 'progressive' private school. Jennie's parents have more or less the same background:

> [I]t was in high school I noticed that there were differences, … Latino kids would hang out on this one wall before school started and there was always a part of school that African American students hang out at, but while I was in middle school, there was no difference, we were all together, and there was not that kind of separation, and it was not until we came to high school that there came that separation which I thought was really interesting, well I grew up in middle school and had friends of all kinds of races, and it never occurred to me that it was not what the rest of the world was like. (Jennie Fine-town in Steensen, 2007: 196)

Thus a *habitual idealism* can be understood as a disposition, nurtured by a high amount of sociocultural capital. What remains to be seen is, however, whether this idealism will be sustainable faced with the harsh realities of everyday school practice. However, habitual idealism is not the only disposition which is open to change. From the life histories, another idealist disposition appears, idealism not with any particular connection to a certain habitus, but an idealism which seems to be developed more as an experience through life, in that, through the ups and downs of life, the subject is resettled in new social environments, often several times. These involuntary events seems to grow and nurture in the individual a cultural and social sensitivity and strength which might prove more sustainable, since many of them move from a less privileged to a more privileged position, and they have often experienced the school system from a less well-adjusted point of departure.[4] A few such students appear through both the Danish and the American material as exceptions to the general trend of 'going home'.

The American student Luiza is a case in point. She attends Fine-town University although she reports a quite different background. Her narrative is a story of loss and turbulence, since her parents are divorced, her mother disappears and her father more or less leaves her to herself. She refers to her parents as being working class, although she also mentions that they both started, but later dropped out of college. After her father left her, she spends her high school years in Germany with her uncle and returns to the USA for college. However, without a stable environment, she drops out and spends the next 10 years either working in service jobs or travelling around the USA and abroad, until she finally decides to enrol in teacher education at the age of 30, and she is now ready to make a difference in the lives of inner city kids with a lot of qualifications achieved through the various contexts she has taken part in before she enrolled as a teacher education student.

A small number of these students thus develop a commitment to the profession which is not restrained to reproduction, but open to change.[5]

Conclusion

The main conclusion is threefold, and all aspects are related. From a theoretical point of view, Bourdieu's concepts of habitus and dispositions provide new insights and understanding of teachers' careers, ambitions and ideas. Research on teachers and teacher education would benefit from including this perspective in the future, because a standardized ethos of professionalism alone cannot solve the issues of how to understand and acknowledge the impact of different cultural and social values. Culture and habitus are only rarely acknowledged as important factors, but life history interviews interpreted through the theoretical lenses of Bourdieu substantiate the claim that culture matters. Measures for recruitment, attrition and retention vary according to habitual preferences in different contexts, and teachers' comfort with local values is a neglected explanatory factor.

Finally I will try to argue how the preliminary results of this complexity research might be applied within present-day policies. In many OECD countries, the sociocultural backgrounds of the teacher education students have changed, in many cases as a consequence of the combined easier access to proper higher education, the low attractiveness because of increased outside control of working conditions, low salaries, the loss of status, feminization, etc. Thus teacher education today works with candidates who do not necessarily have the characteristics assumed by the standard image, and sometimes less of the characteristics advanced modernity suggests. Some standardized quantitative research seems to indicate a slight correspondence between teachers who have good test or examination results in their subject areas and good test results of their students (Muijs & Reynolds, 2002). However, such results totally oversee the underlying factor which might be that many of these teachers and students share the same social background characteristics, a tendency demonstrated in this project as well as by Achinstein et al. (2004). To spell it out, often students get good test results and have teachers who have good test results, because both teachers and students are attracted to the same schools. This fact is not disclosed by large-scale statistics and therefore educational evidence should pay more attention to supplementary qualitative research.

Regional, local and social diversity has increased. The preliminary suggestion pointed to in this project is that a unique standard education will no longer be sufficient, because very different categories of people may come to the profession, and they also face a more diverse student and parent population. The fact is that problems of recruitment and attrition are not equally distributed in all residential areas. Some teacher education students might fear the demands of parents in wealthy areas, and demands for high (subject area) quality often originate in middle-class requirements for (a certain type of) quality, but generally these schools are not really hard to staff. Rural areas as well as urban diverse schools might have more difficulty in attracting teachers, unless special measures are taken to remedy the situation. As the general rule seems to be that teacher education students prefer to teach in familiar surroundings, there are two paths that can be followed. One is to work intensively to recruit and prepare people from local, hard to staff areas, perhaps by offering additional courses and resources. The other is to diversify teacher education programmes in order to be able to take these different outlooks and career perspectives into account, and teacher education could benefit from working more intensely to make teachers' own 'habitual' outlook more conscious by acknowledging that, for example, 'habitual idealists' need to have guided practical exposure to the unfamiliar harsh practical realities in diverse urban areas. 'We cannot teach what we don't know' (Howard, 2006) is a statement which should be understood not only in terms of academic qualifications, but also as practical bodily experience in surviving under tough living conditions as well as in multicultural settings. However, different programmes will not be the solution alone; more attention should also be paid to the habitual experience of the students. Understanding and acting in different social realities should be treated as a resource, be taken into consideration and built upon rather than submitted to a standardized re-socialization.

Notes

1. The meaning of 'public' in the USA is today more a historical feature than a question of funding.
2. This does not imply that all students in each of the chosen institutions had the same background. Social reality is more varied than this. The main reason for the specific choice of these students was the intention to have the maximum possibility for contrast. There will of course be a lot of variations and overlapping in between these two extremes. However, it is important to point out that it has never been the intention to make the selection representative of the total number of students; this is where the understandings and reflections of critical realism on in-depth contextual analysis come in, the main intention being to look for causal explanations in different settings. All this put aside, the background of the students was not atypical: in each institution about 40% of the student population had the described background. This general hypothesis of a certain homology between type and prestige of institution and students' social background helped me in my work in the USA, where similar distinctions appeared although I did not have access to similar background information in advance.
3. I put causal within quotation marks here in order to avoid the misunderstanding that causal mechanism is seen as a mere direct and mechanical effect. The critical realist understanding of the concept is much more complex.
4. In my dissertation, 'Trajectories in a changing field' (Steensen, 2007), I have used an alternative framework developed by Margaret Archer (2003, 2007) to find an alternative way of analysing these cases in order to supplement the concept of habitus.
5. Habitual idealists are not the only ones who show idealistic potential, but are the most obvious in the present analysis. In my dissertation I also applied a supplementary framework developed by the British sociologist Margaret Archer, and in doing this I was able to add some additional explanations. In addition, it is worth pointing out that the interview material has been highly selective for reasons of achieving contrast.

References

Achinstein, B., Ogawa, R., & Speiglman, A. (2004). Are we creating separate and unequal tracks of teachers? *American Educational Research Journal*, 41(3), 557–603.

Archer, M. S. (1979). *Social origins of educational systems*. London: Sage.

Archer, M. S., Bhaskar, R., Collier, A., Lawson, T., & Norrie, A. (1998). *Critical realism essential readings*. London/New York: Routledge.

Archer, M. S. (2003). *Structure, agency and the internal conversation*. Cambridge: Cambridge University Press.

Archer, M. S. (2007). *Making our way through the world*. Cambridge: Cambridge University Press.

Bertaux, D. (Ed.) (1981). *Biography and society: the life story approach in the social sciences*. London: Sage.

Borman, G. D. & Dowling, N. M. (2008). Teacher attrition and retention: a meta-analytic and narrative review of the research. *Review of Educational Research*, 78(3), 367–409.

Bourdieu, P. & Passeron, J-Cl. (1977). *Reproduction in education, society and culture*. London: Sage.

Bourdieu, P. (1984). *Distinction, a social critique of the judgement of taste*. London: Routledge & Kegan Paul.

Bourdieu, P. (1987a). *The biographical illusion*. Working Papers and Proceedings of the Centre for Psychosocial Studies No. 14. Chicago: Centre for Psychosocial Studies.

Bourdieu, P. (1987b). What makes a social class. *Berkeley Journal of Sociology*, 32(1), 1–17.

Bourdieu, P. (1988). *Homo academicus*. Stanford: Stanford University Press.

Bourdieu, P. (1990). *The logic of practice*. Stanford: Stanford University Press.
Bourdieu, P. (1999). *The weight of the world*. Cambridge: Polity Press.
Boyd, D., Lankford, H., Loeb, S., Wyckoff, J. (2003). *The Draw of Home: How Teachers' Preferences for proximity Disadvantage Urban Schools*. NBER working paper 9953.
Day, C., Stobart, G., Sammons, P., Kington, A., Gu, Q., Smees, R., et al. (2006). *Variations in teachers' work, lives and their effects on pupils: VITAE Report* (DfeS Research Rep. No. 743). London: Department for Education and Skills.
Goodson, I. (Ed.) (1992). *Studying teachers' lives*. London: Routledge.
Goodson, I. (2003). *Professional knowledge, professional lives*. Philadelphia: Open University Press.
Hess, F. M., Rotherham, A. J., & Walsh, K. (2004). *A qualified teacher in every classroom? Appraising old answers and new ideas*. Cambridge: Harvard Education Press.
Howard, G. R. (2006). *We can't teach what we don't know*. New York: Teachers College Press.
Ingersoll, R. M. (2001). *Teacher turnover, teacher shortages, and the organization of schools*. Seattle: University of Washington, Center for the Study of Teaching and Policy.
Maxwell, J. A. (2004). Causal explanation, qualitative research, and scientific inquiry in education. *Educational Researcher*, 33(2), 3–11.
Muijs, D. & Reynolds, D. (2002). Students background and teacher effects on achievement and attainment in mathematics: A longitudinal study. *Educational Research and Evaluation*, 9(3), 289–314.
Reay, D. (2004). 'It's all becoming a habitus': Beyond the habitual use of habitus in educational research. *British Journal of Sociology of Education*, 25(4), 431–444.
Robertson, S. L. (2008). Remaking the world: Neoliberalism and the transformation of education and teachers' labour. In M. Compton & L. Weiner (Eds.), *The global assault on teaching, teachers and their unions*. New York: Palgrave Macmillan.
Sayer, A. (2000). *Method in social science, a realist approach*. London/New York: Routledge.
Steensen, J. (2007). *Veje og udveje i et felt under forandring (Trajectories in a changing field)*. Viborg: PUC.
Steensen, J. (2005). *Omstrukturering af læreruddannelse – En komparativ analyse Danmark – Sverige*. Uppsala Universitet: Pedagogiske Institutionen/Lärom.
Zeichner, K. (2008). Contradictions and tensions in the place of teachers in educational reform. In M. Compton & L. Weiner (Eds.), *The global assault on teaching, teachers and their unions*. New York: Palgrave Macmillan.
Znaniecki, W. I. T. & Znaniecki, F. (1984). The polish peasant in Europe and America. Urbana/Chicago: University of Illinois Press. (Edited and abridged by Eli Zaretsky).
Zumwalt, K. & Craig, E. (2005). Teachers' characteristics: Research on the demographic profile. In M. Cochran-Smith & K. M. Zeichner (Eds.), *Studying teacher education*. Mahwah: Erlbaum.

Chapter 5
Teachers' Professional Learning and the Workplace Curriculum

Martin Bayer and Ulf Brinkkjær

Introduction

Every year, a new set of Danish teachers graduate and begin work in a school, hereby embarking upon a career trajectory teaching various classes and subjects and meeting new colleagues, pupils, parents and the school management. This often represents a considerable challenge; indeed, so great are the challenges faced by new teachers that a number of them soon begin considering changing careers and leaving the profession. Among Danish teachers who graduated in 1997, almost one in four (23%) had left teaching by 2007 (FTF, 2007). Over time, those who remain develop career strategies, partly based on the various career opportunities and pathways which can be identified within the profession, partly based on their individual circumstances. In this chapter, we present the results of a case study which, by describing and analysing the teaching and collegial relations of two male teachers during their first 8 years in the profession, shows two very different career trajectories and career strategies. In other words, the two teachers trod two different pathways among the multitude of possible career trajectories open to teachers. The objective of this study was to shed light on teachers' professional learning and the relationship between their career strategies and career trajectories.

Teachers' career trajectories have been described and analysed by Sikes (1985), Fessler and Christensen (1992), Huberman (1993, 1997) and Day et al. (2007) among others. In studies of teachers' career trajectories, changes have usually been outlined in the form of a number of phases from entering the profession to retirement. Career trajectories are understood, as is the case here, as changes in relation to teachers' formal and informal positions within the school system, and in relation to their handling and perception of teaching, collegial relations and their role as teachers. Teachers' career trajectories and career strategies are, however, not universal, but rather situated within a particular context, influenced by a complex web of social, historical and institutional factors. The closer one studies the individual teacher's career trajectory, the more it appears almost unique. In this chapter, we attempt to strike a balance, primarily focusing upon the internal relationships between schools, teaching, colleagues and teachers' professional learning, career trajectories and career strategies.

M. Bayer et al. (eds.), *Teachers' Career Trajectories and Work Lives,*
Professional Learning and Development in Schools and Higher Education 3,
© Springer Science + Business Media B.V. 2009

To this end, the chapter makes use of the concept *workplace curriculum* (Bayer & Brinkkjær, 2005), understood as a post hoc curriculum which, more or less implicitly, prescribes certain elements in the content of teachers' professional learning. As such, professional learning is interpreted in this chapter as the establishment of a professional repertoire in the sense of a symbolic and practical way of managing the school's workplace curriculum. Our aim in describing and analysing professional learning as a gradual mastery of a workplace curriculum is to add a situated learning perspective to studies of teachers' career trajectories.

A workplace curriculum comprises a set of expectations to teachers' ways of practising the profession and learning how to do so. It partly concerns expectations relating to teachers' teaching, and partly relating to their collegial relations. These expectations are established on the basis of what we, inspired by Basil Bernstein (2000), refer to as a *segmental pedagogy* (Bayer & Brinkkjær, 2005), i.e. a number of, often highly contradictory, situated and tacit demands from pupils, colleagues, school management and parents to how teachers perceive and conduct their teaching and collegial relations. If teachers are able to manage the school's workplace curriculum, they gain access to the profession and can gradually begin to establish the necessary conditions for pursuing a career, that is to say moving between various formal or informal positions within the school, with their associated benefits and privileges.

The term workplace curriculum thereby refers in this chapter to a number of expectations which teachers meet on entering the profession, as stipulated by pupils, their parents, colleagues and school management, as we have been able to reconstruct them through our analysis of the data. This analysis shows that the workplace curriculum, in a Danish context, becomes particularly apparent on the basis of a segmental pedagogy. It should be underlined that the term workplace curriculum does *not* refer to a formal or explicit description of the expectations facing newly qualified teachers; there is no official workplace curriculum applicable to the Danish school system.

Methods

The case study was part of an extensive research council–funded project titled 'Teachers' and Pre-school Teachers' Professional Learning and Career Trajectories in Practice'. The project followed a group of teachers and a group of pre-school teachers, using questionnaires, from their graduation in 1998 over the following 2 years, then again in 2006, that is to say 8 years after entering the profession. The case study consisted of a series of classroom observations and interviews conducted with four teachers and four pre-school teachers over the same period. As mentioned, in this chapter we present selected results from this case study, following two male teachers from entering the profession in 1998 until 2006. The case study considers the following research questions:

1. Over the course of the first 8 years within the profession, can changes be registered in the ways in which teachers organize their teaching? How do the teachers themselves describe their organization of teaching and how do these descriptions change during the period?
2. How do teachers describe their collegial relations and their position within the school as a workplace, and how do these descriptions change during the period?

The theoretical and methodological inspiration for the case study was Bernstein's theory of pedagogic practice (Bernstein, 2000). As such, we focused on the teachers' teaching, as well as their interpretations of this, regarded as pedagogic codes characterized by either strong internal classification and framing with positional relations between teacher and pupils (visible pedagogic practice) or weak internal classification and framing with personal relations between teacher and pupils (invisible pedagogic practice). The various pedagogic codes draw upon various discourses which exist outside the school. Once again with inspiration from Bernstein, in order to describe and analyse how the teachers drew upon and re-contextualized different discourses we distinguished between vertical discourses, that is various more or less hierarchically structured knowledge systems, and horizontal discourses, that is flatly structured knowledge systems of an everyday nature. We will return to these concepts in our analysis of the two cases.

The employment of Bernstein's theory of pedagogic practice allowed us to describe and analyse some of the curricular conditions which comprised the foundation for the teachers' professional learning.

The Teachers

One of the teachers, Paul, was born in 1972 and began, but did not complete, an engineering degree prior to teacher training. In teacher training college, Paul's specialist subjects were English and Mathematics. It was here that he met his future wife, who likewise qualified as a teacher. On graduating, Paul found employment in a school quite far from their college and they therefore moved to the local area. The school (800 pupils, 75 teachers) is situated in a large provincial town and Paul was employed there throughout the period in which we followed him.

During the first year at the school (1998/99), Paul taught classes ranging from Grade 3 (9-year-olds) to Grade 8 (14-year-olds) in the following subjects: Natural

Fact box

The Danish school system can be considered an 'offer' to all between the ages of 6 and 16 in the sense that it is education itself and not school that is compulsory. The Danish system cannot be split into primary and lower secondary education, with pupils commonly remaining within the same school for the

(continued)

Fact box (continued)

entire period of compulsory education. Following the soon-to-be-compulsory nursery class and Grades 1–9, pupils can choose whether to continue by attending the non-compulsory Grade 10, enter an Upper Secondary Education programme, select a Vocational Education and Training programme, or leave the educational system and enter the labour market. In addition to the public schooling system, there also exists a fairly broad sector of private and independent schools which are attended by approximately 10% of a year group, although this figure can be as high as 25% in certain areas, particularly in the larger towns.

Danish teachers follow a 4-year programme at a teacher training college. Here, they follow a number of compulsory subjects and select specialist subjects. Each of the teachers we followed had two specialist subjects, although this number has since changed a number of times due to reforms of teacher training. Due to the unified nature of the Danish public schooling system, there is no split between primary and lower secondary in terms of teacher qualification requirements or training. All teachers are considered qualified to teach classes with pupils throughout the age range of 6–16.

Sciences/Technology, Visual Arts, Christianity Studies, Mathematics, Geography and Computer Science. The following year (1999/2000), Paul taught three different classes, namely Grade 1 (7-year-olds), Grade 9 (15-year-olds) and Grade 10 (16-year-olds) in Mathematics and/or Computer Science. During these 2 years, he also assumed the role of the school's IT-advisor. During the 2005/06 school year, Paul taught exclusively in a Grade 9 class in Mathematics and English (i.e. his two specialist subjects from teacher training college). In addition, he was the school's shop steward. Paul and his wife now had three children of their own.

The second teacher, Jacob, was born in 1971. Like Paul, he began but did not complete an education prior to enrolling in teacher training: in this case training as a shipping agent. Likewise, by the 2005/06 school year, Jacob was also married with three children, his wife a qualified nurse. Jacob's specialist subjects in teacher training college were English and Physical Education. On completing college, Jacob's wife had found work in another part of the country where he was able to find work at a small school (150 pupils, 11 teachers) catering for Grades 1–7. In 2005, however, he moved with his family to a small island in order to teach at a far smaller school (seven pupils, three teachers).

In his first year (1998/99), Jacob taught Grades 1, 2 and 5 classes in Danish, Natural Sciences/Technology, History and Physical Education. In addition, he acted as a support teacher for a few lessons a week in a Grade 1 class. The year after (1999/2000), Jacob had lessons with a Grade 2 class in Danish, Natural Sciences/Technology, Christianity Studies and Physical Education as well as Physical Education with Grades 1, 6 and 7 classes and swimming lessons for Grade 4. He also continued to act as a support teacher, now for classes in both Grades 2 and 4. At the new school, classes were generally not divided according to age with most subjects taught alongside at least one of Jacob's colleagues. He did, however, often conduct Physical Education lessons alone.

Teaching: The First 2 Years Within the Profession

There were some differences in the way the newly qualified teachers organized their lessons, irrespective of subject and age group. Paul's lessons were fairly uniform in their structure, despite the fact that, particularly in the first year, he taught a wide range of both subjects and age groups. The way he organized his lessons can be illustrated by the following example taken from a Grade 8 Mathematics class (24 pupils, age 14):

> Paul tells the class that they are going to have some homework and begins to hand out the assignments. He then returns to his place behind his desk and tells the pupils to get their calendars out. He begins by writing on the board which assignments they are to complete, and then the date for handing them in. 'Now we're going to talk a bit about the coordinate system' and he starts explaining longitude and latitude when a girl interrupts: 'But this isn't a Geography lesson!' Unperturbed, Paul continues drawing on the board and explaining. He then moves on to the homework the pupils had been set for the lesson. Pupils take turns going through the assignments on the board with Paul adding comments along the way and correcting them if they make a mistake. While Paul helps one of the girls, who is trying to solve a problem on the board, some of the other pupils have started work on the homework for the next lesson. When the girl has solved the problem, Paul tells the class that they are to complete the assignments up to and including number 21 for the next lesson. Those who haven't done so already immediately start work on the assignments. Some remain in the classroom while others take the work with them to the canteen. Paul wanders around assisting the pupils who ask for help. This continues until the end of the lesson. (Paul, year 1)

Paul's lessons often began with a brief teacher-controlled sequence addressed to the whole class followed by the pupils working individually. Sometimes, Paul concluded his lessons with a quick summary of the day's lesson.

With Jacob it was likewise possible to identify a clear pattern in the structure of his lessons, which again followed a similar pattern regardless of subject and age group. However, Jacob organized his lessons a little differently from Paul in that he tended to allow the pupils greater control over the lessons.

Naturally Paul and Jacob's lessons during this first year did not always go entirely according to plan. They had to learn that their organization of lessons and the sequences of content had to be adjusted according to how the pupils reacted. Pupil reactions, as they learnt, comprised one of teaching's more unpredictable, but nevertheless vital, elements. Sometimes the teachers found that what they did worked; on other occasions they had the clear sense that it didn't. As such, they had to learn that there is no 'right' way of teaching. Especially when teaching Grades 1–5, Jacob and Paul found it difficult at times to maintain control of the lesson's organization. If they tried to conduct a lesson characterized by strong internal classification and framing with positional relations between teacher and pupils, some of the pupils could challenge their decisions. Meanwhile, if they chose a structure characterized by weak internal classification and framing, some of the pupils didn't get any work done. As newly qualified teachers, Paul and Jacob had little experience of how pupils were likely to react to their teaching. This made it extremely difficult to incorporate this aspect in their lesson planning – which they describe as extremely thorough.

The problems were especially pronounced in certain classes they taught during the first year. They both had a particular class which they explicitly did not care for. In Paul's case, there was talk of a class which his colleagues also tried to avoid. Paul and Jacob differed, however, in their analysis of why they had problems with these classes. Jacob felt that his problems with a Grade 5 History class were due to 'beginner's errors':

> I have made a lot of stupid mistakes with that class. I guess I was probably too nice. And then I wanted to try out some teaching methods they weren't used to. It was too open, and that was stupid because I never should have started like that. It's a typical beginner's error. I've learnt that. (Jacob, year 1)

Jacob only had the class for 1 year. The problems had taught him that his preferred lesson design did not always work. The following year, another newly qualified teacher took the class in History, which, if nothing else, solved Jacob's problem. Paul's problems were with a Grade 4 class whom he taught both Natural Sciences/Technology and Christianity Studies. As mentioned, the class was considered a 'problem class' by the staff. He described the difficulties he experienced as a result of them having a class teacher who had 'clamped down on them':

> So, that's what he's done. But it also means that they have to let off steam at some point. And that's often during my lessons. I can't stand them, plain and simple. (Paul, year 1)

Again, Paul only taught the class during his first year at the school. He learnt, among other things, that, for a newly qualified teacher's lessons with a difficult class in periphery subjects, it is first and foremost a matter of surviving and not so much about right and wrong ways of organizing and preparing lessons.

Both Paul and Jacob were thereby exposed to classes which they explicitly did not care for. Meanwhile, it is interesting to note that Jacob puts the problems down to his own mistakes and naivety, while Paul largely places the blame elsewhere and on circumstances over which he had little or no control.

Changes in Teaching During the First 2 Years

The clearest and most dramatic changes during Paul's and Jacob's first 2 years of teaching were in their class and subject allocations, with both receiving very different timetables for their second year – the fundamental structure of their lessons did not change significantly. For Paul, this meant a considerable reduction in the number of subjects he taught, but his lessons still typically began with him providing a quick introduction to the day's activities after which he expected the pupils to get on with the assignments he set, whether individually or in groups. Finally, there might be some form of summary or evaluation of the lesson. Jacob's lessons were largely concentrated in one (Grade 2) class, where he still preferred an approach characterized by weak framing, placing a lot of importance on the pupils' opportunities to work independently.

Later in this chapter, we will present a number of changes regarding how the two teachers viewed teaching. We can begin by stating that their career strategies were primarily concerned with improving their possibilities for teaching in the ways they preferred and felt most comfortable. Therefore, it was largely a matter of getting rid of the classes and subjects where they found it difficult to conduct lessons following their favoured plan. This was due to three central factors.

Firstly, during the first 2 years it was essential for them to gain experience with a kind of 'survival' (Huberman, 1993), that is by managing and mastering their teaching, not by changing it. Part of surviving the first years involved building up and gaining experience with a repertoire of teaching methods which 'worked'. When they had done this, they stuck to it. They opted out of contexts which challenged their ways of doing things, including 'problem classes', and they did their best to reduce the number of different subjects and age groups they taught. Instead of adapting their way of teaching to suit a variety of different situations and contexts, both teachers sought to adapt the different situations and contexts they encountered to suit their way of teaching. Those changes which it is possible to identify can sooner be characterized as a refinement of their existing teaching practices than as actually breaking with or further expanding their established repertoires.

Secondly, we know from the interviews that the teachers themselves did not place an emphasis on changes to their teaching. Instead, they used a lot of resources in the *preparation* of lessons. Indeed, they described themselves as distinctly overprepared, especially when talking about their first 6 months in the job. They recounted gradually developing a far better sense of how much it is possible to get done in the course of a lesson and how this was considerably less than they expected, and therefore prepared for, during the first few months.

Thirdly, the apparent lack of major changes to their teaching draws attention to the relatively stable structure within which their practice was situated. Teaching is set and facilitated by a number of framing factors (Lundgren, 1981) which are outside teachers' sphere of influence, e.g. curriculum, timetable, class composition, physical confines and legal framework. On the one hand, these framing factors provide the school, the teaching and the pedagogy with relative autonomy; on the other hand, they also control, limit and regulate the outcomes of teaching. When newly qualified teachers' teaching tends to share many common characteristics, this cannot be reduced merely to a question of teachers' choice of strategy, but must also be seen as a result of both external and internal framing factors. The absence of systematic changes in teachers' teaching can, in this perspective, be regarded as an indication that precisely such framing factors give pedagogical practice a degree of stability and inertia. This inertia can perhaps contribute to teachers' career strategies not so much being about changing their teaching, but rather changing the circumstances in which they teach. It may also have contributed to the changes that could be registered mainly having to do with how Paul and Jacob viewed teaching.

Changes in How the Teachers Viewed Teaching During the First 2 Years

Both Paul's and Jacob's views of teaching changed over the course of their first 2 years in the job. On entering the profession and during the first year, they described how they preferred to conduct lessons involving a lot of individual or group work, maintaining what could be considered personal relations to the pupils. However, this approach could lead to friction with some of their more experienced colleagues:

> I mean, how strict should you be? That's something we can really disagree on. How much noise can the pupils make? Some people say they should be really quiet, while I say 'yeah, well…'. There might be certain times where I'm a bit stricter, not so much because of colleagues, but because I can't take any more myself. But I often do some activities out in the corridor. It can get a bit noisy, and then you get the others on your back. So you try and discuss it with them, but they're not interested in discussing it because, as they put it: 'Then we sit gazing at our navels!' (Paul, year 1)

Paul feels caught. On one side, his attitudes in relation to the pupils have been criticized by his colleagues; on the other side, his desire to discuss the matter with them was dismissed.

As mentioned previously, Jacob preferred an approach to teaching characterized by weak framing and personal relations to pupils. Along the way, however, he had to admit that this approach did not always work entirely the way he wanted. He states, for instance:

> [The pupils] aren't used to being taught in this way, I mean being involved in making decisions, having an opinion and working more freely. (Jacob, year 1)

He hereby also indicated that the more weakly framed approach, which he employed on the basis that the pupils learnt more when they were able to influence the lesson, was not always appreciated by pupils and therefore, in practice, it could be difficult to implement entirely according to plan.

The newly qualified teachers offered different pedagogical explanations for their way of organising lessons. Paul pointed out that he found it difficult to teach in other ways. He did not think traditional teacher-controlled class-oriented teaching was better as he considered it important that the pupils were actively involved in lessons and:

> there are certain teachers who can talk and talk, and then they have some smart rhymes or ways of remembering things. That's fair enough, I'm a bit envious of them, because I can't do that, so I make use of the means I have. (Paul, year 1)

Jacob considered the pupils' well-being a prerequisite for their academic learning processes:

> If the kids are feeling good, then I think they learn more. He continued by explaining how he saw his role as a kind of initiator who … helps the pupils, makes sure they get something done. I believe that pupils get more out of a lesson like that, where they have to make their own rules for the things they're working with. (Jacob, year 1)

They ascribe the differences they registered between themselves and their colleagues to the fact that many of their colleagues were trained a long time ago. As Jacob puts it:

> Of course, they are influenced by which teacher training college they attended and when they went there. I mean, the ones who trained 40 years ago learnt different things and have different opinions from us. (Jacob, year 1)

This statement is interesting as it shows the way in which an important role is given to the teacher training programme in explaining the formation of pedagogical views on teaching. Not just in relation to themselves, which would not be surprising bearing in mind the close proximity of their student days, but also in relation to colleagues who have spent a considerable number of years within the profession. It may seem a little odd that they expected teachers with so many years of experience to still be holding on to the views on teaching they were presented with in college, especially in light of Jacob at the same time stating that he did not learn anything from subjects like Didactics in college.

The two teachers disagreed on the importance of their time in college for their own professional performance. Paul felt that his education had equipped him with a toolbox for teaching his subjects and for understanding, for example, pupils with different ethnic backgrounds. At the same time, he strongly believed there are a great number of skills and competences which the newly qualified teacher first can acquire 'on the job'. These skills and competences could not be taught in an auditorium, or even in conjunction with the programme's practical classroom training.

As already suggested, Jacob was far more sceptical in assessing the importance of teacher training. He expressed some disappointment in relation to the teacher training programme which he felt did not provide the opportunity to acquire the necessary skills and competences required by a newly qualified teacher in order to deal with the challenges they met in their work. Jacob thereby disagreed with Paul regarding the contribution of the training programme to the performance of the profession and indirectly indicated his expectations that his time at college could and should have better equipped him to deal with everyday life as a schoolteacher. The differences in their assessments of the importance of teacher training, and the extent to which they felt well-equipped for the challenges they faced, likely also influenced their differing views on teaching.

As has been apparent, the two teachers had different views on teaching and thereby also on the role of the school: For Paul, it was important that the pupils' activities and his teaching were centred on academic goals, as such drawing upon a vertical discourse; meanwhile Jacob regarded pupils' well-being as a prerequisite for, and perhaps even of equal importance to, achieving academic goals. He thereby drew upon a horizontal discourse of domesticity (Bayer & Brinkkjær, 2005). It is possible that these differences are also due to the fact that they taught different age groups and different subjects, although in the interviews they both expressed their views as more general opinions. It therefore seems reasonable to interpret this as an expression of different preferences.

This interpretation is also indirectly supported by Paul expressing in one of the earliest interviews that he could recognize himself in the oldest pupils, which could be described as adopting a pupil perspective. After a year of teaching, however, he saw himself as a 'Mathematics teacher'. The role as 'reserve dad', often conferred by the very youngest pupils, is one he now highlighted as undesirable:

> I have kids of my own at home ... I'd preferably like to have the older classes, but also Grade 1, because I haven't tried that. But I don't much care for the role as reserve dad. Where they hang off you and want to tell you their life story. That's not really my thing. Rather Grade 9 who can be a bit lippy, but can also get something done. (Paul, year 2)

Paul simultaneously indicated a preference for older classes and an interest in teaching Grade 1. This statement suggests that the apparent ambiguity does not signal any doubts in relation to actual teaching in the younger classes, but rather an unwillingness to meet the pupils' expectations that he, at the same time, ought to act as some kind of personal confidant. He thereby favoured a more 'professional' relationship with his pupils than the smaller children seemingly expected of him. Paul's preferences can therefore be described as for less personal and more positional relations to his pupils and, as such, a desire to draw mainly upon a vertical discourse.

Jacob clearly had other preferences. After a year within the profession, he described himself as 'a friend, playmate and teacher'. He thematized his relationship with an older female colleague as a 'mother–son relationship' during an interview. These statements, which draw extensively on a discourse of domesticity, indicated that Jacob had a basic preference for relations where the personal aspects were key, thereby drawing on a horizontal discourse to a much greater extent than Paul.

As we have shown, Paul and Jacob had different views on their role as teachers, and also on their career trajectories. While Paul largely left a pupil perspective and an understanding of himself as the pupils' 'friend' behind after his first year of teaching, Jacob held on to this position and pupil-centred view of teaching. It may be significant that Paul was voted 'Teacher of the Year' by the school's pupils in his first year. This would seem to have been almost a kind of 'critical incident' (Measor, 1985) for him. He was far from pleased to receive the award and considered it a sign that he was likely doing something wrong, for example acting too much like a friend with the pupils. Additionally, he may have been concerned that the award could be regarded as a sign of weakness by colleagues. He therefore organized his lessons according to a far stronger framing the following year. Jacob, on the other hand, saw the fact that his pupils liked him as an indication that he was doing something right.

In any case, Paul's view of teaching changed. Whereas, the first year, he pointed to large holes in and clear limits to his repertoire, after the second year he said:

> The good teacher is the one who, apart from knowing things, is capable of conducting a lesson. It may seem obvious, but it's a matter of setting targets for the individual pupil, for the whole class, for the lesson, for the month. ... The difficult part is making professional choices. Anyone can go out and teach, but if it's left to chance then it's bad teaching, no matter if it works. (Paul, year 2)

This shows how Paul's reflections had become more differentiated than was the case previously. While the central criterion when he began teaching was finding something that 'worked', he now explicitly stated that this was not enough. He hereby indirectly indicated that he had now found teaching strategies that, in his opinion, worked.

After 2 years of teaching, Paul increasingly expressed a preference for what could be considered lessons characterized by strong internal classification and framing, as well as positional relations to pupils. He had already attempted to conduct lessons in this fashion during his first year at the school when teaching the 'problem class', but these attempts had been largely unsuccessful:

> The first six months, I really tried to stamp my authority. But then the parents complained. They thought I was treating their children unfairly. It's not more than 14 days since complaints have been lodged about me with their class teacher. (Paul, year 1)

Both teachers changed their views on teaching, even though these changes, as mentioned, were not clearly reflected in their actual teaching. Paul and Jacob now also considered themselves better at making decisions which suggests they had also now accepted making decisions as part of being a proper teacher.

Teaching: After 8 Years Within the Profession

When we contacted them again in 2005, Jacob and Paul had spent 8 years as teachers. As mentioned previously, Paul was still employed at the same school and now only had lessons with one Grade 9 class where he taught his specialist subjects from college. A considerable amount of his mandatory working hours were assigned to his duties as shop steward and duties tied to positions on a number of councils and committees. After 6 years, Jacob had found a new job teaching at a school on a small island.

Paul's way of organizing his lessons still followed the same template that he had established during the first 2 years. The following example from a Mathematics lesson (Grade 9, 13 pupils) can help illustrate:

> 'Now you need to get ready for something that's a bit difficult' says Paul and draws a triangle up on the board. He then asks the class how you calculate the perimeter of a triangle. Some of the pupils raise their hands and answer when called upon. 'Ok, so you know everything that a Grade 4 class needs to know about triangles! This next bit's a little trickier. You can write it down if you want.' None of the pupils take notes, Paul runs through different ways of calculating the lengths of sides of triangles. He asks the class how to work out the area. A pupil gives the correct answer. They are now instructed to get out their books and a pencil. 'Turn to page 40 in your books. Yes, well you have to use your books at some point.' He tells them which assignments he wants them to work on. 'Carry on with the questions on page 41. I want them finished by next time, maybe page 42 as well, so you'd better get a move on.' They get to work while Paul helps a girl who raises her hand. He moves on to one of the boys who had also put his hand up. Three pupils aren't doing anything, the rest are working. Paul intervenes in an argument between two of the boys over a red pen and then addresses the class: '…some of you are having trouble with Pythagoras'. He then runs through different ways of using the formula. There is a fair amount of talking among the pupils, both related to the lesson and private conversations. Paul announces that they have pages 41 and 42 as homework. (Paul, year 8)

As such, Paul retained the template of starting the lesson with class instruction, then individual work and perhaps a summary at the end. He now knew there was a 'right' way of teaching – for him at least. As the above example shows, this lesson form was both secure and natural for him. The fundamental basis of Paul's way of organizing lessons did not change during the first 8 years.

Paul had made a considerable effort at the end of his first year to get rid of the Grade 4 class he at the time described as the school's 'problem class'. With this in mind, it is worth noting that he had now become one of the teachers who willingly took on the classes no one else wanted. These were usually difficult Grade 7 or 8 classes which other teachers had more or less given up on.

Jacob taught most of his lessons with the school's eight pupils alongside one or other of his two colleagues. The other teachers decided how these lessons were organized. Jacob therefore often stood on the sideline while a colleague followed a similar template to the one used by Paul. Only in Physical Education lessons was Jacob alone with the pupils. These lessons were generally strongly governed by Jacob and often involved highly physical activities where the pupils had to, for example, box, run after each other, etc. In the interview, Jacob explained that the reason for the physically demanding nature of these lessons was that most of the pupils were overweight.

The conditions under which Jacob worked made it difficult to identify possible changes in his way of organizing lessons compared to previously. The lessons were, as mentioned, largely controlled by the other teachers. To Jacob's considerable dissatisfaction, he now functioned more or less as a support teacher in the majority of lessons.

Views on Teaching: After 8 Years Within the Profession

The teachers' views on teaching had changed during their first 8 years in the job. Paul felt that his way of organizing lessons improved his opportunities of relating to the pupils' varying academic levels. As such, he had now added another explanation for his way of doing things. Furthermore, as opposed to at the beginning of his career, he now felt entirely capable of conducing class-based teaching for a whole (45 minute) lesson, but at the same time pointed out, referring to what he'd learnt at teacher training college, that this wasn't the right way to learn things. He had, however, become more critical in his views on teacher training. He now expressed the opinion that the instructors did not know enough about the tasks and the problems teachers faced in schools. 'All teachers have the same problems' (Paul, year 8). He was aware of a change in his view on pupils in that he was now more concerned with differentiating with regard to pupils' learning processes, and less with any perceived gaps in his own teaching abilities:

> In the beginning I was worried about making a mistake in an equation in Grade 8; whether the pupils could read my writing; whether I'd made proper use of the time available; and what I should do with the pupil who was ahead of the class. I don't worry so much about that anymore, because now I have something to offer each of them. I have the courage to say: '[Y]ou don't have to get as far as the others, you just have to enjoy sitting there

grappling with the first three questions, and never mind if him over there is doing something completely different.' ... Before, it was much more about the ability to know a lot, to be able to remember, keep control of a whole class with twenty pupils, and where there's two who are chatting to each other while you're writing a formula up on the board. Now I'm a bit vaguer, trying to create a framework where the kids can develop, and that's something different. So I've probably gone from a slightly old-fashioned view to a bit more of a touchy-feely pedagogy. (Paul, year 8)

Paul has moved from primarily focusing on his own performance, mistakes and (lacking) competences to a much greater focus on the pupils' academic development. Maintaining classroom control, for example, is no longer mentioned as an issue; now it's more a matter of how to manage pupils' different abilities.

Jacob's perspective was still a kind of critical pupil-centred perspective. This was likely linked to his periphery position at the school and in lessons. He disagreed with the way lessons were conducted and was shocked by the treatment of the pupils. He referred to it as like going 30 years back in time:

My authority is at rock bottom in relation to the pupils. Luckily, I like them and they like me, otherwise it would be hell. (Jacob, year 8)

Despite maintaining a pupil-centred view of teaching, he had little in the way of possibilities for implementing it, and was in a lot of ways more like a kind of friend with the pupils, discretely encouraging them to rebel against the other teachers:

Sometimes it's fun to do things we're not supposed to; sometimes you [the pupils] have to knock down some walls. (Jacob to pupils, year 8)

Eight Years of Teaching: A Summary

In Denmark, the first couple of years as a teacher are commonly described in terms of moving to the other side of the teacher's desk. This journey can also, over the course of 8 years within the profession, be described as gradually learning to manage the school's workplace curriculum in that Paul and Jacob had to learn the following:

- Lessons can be organized in different ways on the basis of different pedagogic codes. In spite of these, however, the outcome and results cannot be reliably predicted as teaching involves too many unpredictable factors. Other than trial and error, there is no obvious method, e.g. thorough preparation, which can help predict whether a lesson will work or not. When, through years of experience, you have discovered what works for you, then hang onto it. The unpredictability of teaching thereby becomes predictable and can be used constructively. It will now only rarely and under special circumstances cause major disturbances.
- Organizing lessons is primarily a matter of maintaining control in that it will often be necessary to enter into negotiations with pupils. As a newly qualified teacher, you have to learn to take control of lessons. You, therefore, have to replace a personal relationship to the pupils with a more positional relationship. Having, over the years, established a positional relationship, you can slowly

begin to relinquish control again, i.e. re-establish a more personal relationship to the pupils.

- You often start off being preoccupied with your own teaching activities and any problems you experience in conducting lessons. Over time, this perspective can be expanded to also include pupils' learning processes. Lessons should be organized in such a way that they provide the teacher with the opportunity to take the pupils' differing academic abilities and backgrounds into account. Pupils are different, what they learn is different and what they achieve is different. Teaching can do little to change these things.
- Teaching is a private matter which can be explained by (or confused with) pedagogical autonomy. Therefore, teachers can, and indeed should, teach in their own way as long as it does not cause problems for their colleagues. There are no expectations from colleagues that teachers change their teaching in a particular direction. Teachers' professional development is therefore individual and self-directed.

Teachers' Views on Colleagues: The First 2 Years Within the Profession

Schools and teachers' work involve more than teaching. An ever-growing part of Danish teachers' working lives is spent holding meetings, taking part in team planning, completing documentation, and other activities with no direct contact to pupils. The school should therefore also be studied as a place of work with both a formal and an informal hierarchy and a workplace culture. Just like the vast majority of newly qualified teachers, the knowledge of teaching which Paul and Jacob could draw upon largely stemmed from their schooldays, observing their own teachers at work – what Lortie refers to as the 'apprenticeship of observation' (Lortie, 1975). On joining the profession, there were relatively few opportunities to see how colleagues taught, and likewise few opportunities to show their 'abilities' in front of colleagues. As such, teaching rarely played a part in determining the school's hierarchy, resulting in an increase in the importance afforded to seniority.

Already during their first year of teaching, Paul and Jacob told that they had come into contact with a wide range of ways of managing the teaching job among their colleagues. These differences were particularly apparent during the so-called team collaboration meetings which have become a growing part of everyday life in Danish schools since their introduction in 1993. Teaching teams are comprised of the teachers attached to particular year groups and/or particular subjects. Among the areas they work with are curriculum planning, field trips, projects, and disciplinary matters. The newly qualified teachers both approached this team collaboration with a positive attitude and a good deal of interest, presumably because it offered them the chance to learn from more experienced colleagues, gain recognition, and negotiate their positions in the informal hierarchy. Team collaboration also provided Paul and Jacob with the opportunity to observe how certain colleagues, with the others' tacit acceptance, were able to more or less entirely avoid contributing or participating. Jacob articulates this experience:

> There are some teachers who've been here a long time and with a proven track record – you're not going to say much to teachers like that, are you? (Jacob, year 1)

Paul also talks about his experiences of team collaboration:

> The 'underperformers' turn up to the meetings they have to, hold two team meetings a year, because then they've held one every half year. They have a repertoire they rely on. That's accepted too. Then there's the teachers who just keep going on and on and spend a lot of time discussing. (Paul, year 1)

Thereby, both teachers discovered at a relatively early stage that a key element of the workplace culture was a widespread acceptance that teachers taught in different ways. This acceptance, which was clear both when talking to colleagues and during various forms of collaboration such as team collaboration, was related to colleagues' understanding of, for example, methodological freedom and, as a result, the relative autonomy which the teachers considered as intrinsic to pedagogical work. Such freedom at the same time gave leeway for an almost legitimate difference in teachers' levels of commitment, which have previously been classified as follows (cf. Due & Madsen, 1990):

- The standard-bearers who always line up at the forefront of change and go beyond the call of duty
- A group right behind them who also involve themselves in school life beyond the confines of their own classrooms
- The underperformers who seldom contribute to school activities

Apart from gaining this insight into the wide range in how different teachers tackle the job, Paul and Jacob also found that, perhaps for this very reason, certain colleagues were highly critical towards their suggestions, e.g. for more interdisciplinary collaboration. These colleagues would either flat out refuse to spend time on that kind of thing, or suggest that their suggestions would never work.

> If you stand out as one of the standard-bearers, then they give you the thumbs down. That's kind of my impression. They feel provoked and they think you're a little crazy. But that doesn't mean you can't do some exciting things. Just don't go around saying, for example, 'let's have some more differential teaching'. (Paul, year 1)

The new teachers thus discovered that their association with colleagues, among other things in conjunction with team collaboration, demanded of them that they, for example, were capable of correctly decoding the workplace culture and acting mainly in accordance with it. In other words, they needed to find their place. In Paul's statement above, it is not only a matter of there existing different positions as a teacher, but that not all these positions are open to new recruits. In order to be taken seriously as a recently qualified teacher, one should not act like a standard-bearer. If one instead chooses to go a little more quietly about one's business, it is possible to achieve quite a lot. As such, Paul and Jacob gradually learnt to position themselves within the group just behind the standard-bearers.

Paul, however, had a sort of double position: on the one hand, as a new employee he was on the periphery; on the other hand, as the school's IT-advisor he possessed knowledge which many of his colleagues did not and frequently required. Paul himself was well aware of the special status of the role as IT-advisor:

> I think it's very important that things are kept reasonably simple for them, because one of the worst things for a teacher is feeling like an idiot. They can handle all kinds of things, but they can't deal with that. (Paul, year 1)

Paul has clearly carefully considered his relationships with colleagues in his role as IT-advisor. In practice, however, it led him to a position parallel to the one he described in relation to team collaboration, namely looking to get things done without making a big deal of it with regard to colleagues.

That their colleagues were almost unanimous in praising diversity and freedom, regardless of how much they actually differed in practice in their performance of the job, was evidence of a clear discourse that such differences existed and were entirely legitimate. 'Everyone's committed in their own way', as Jacob put it. Paul felt that there were some highly skilled teachers at the school, teachers he considered experts, but he considered it problematic that they were extremely guarded, generally keeping their expertise to themselves:

> They don't talk too loudly. It's a real problem because they're doing some of the most exciting things. (Paul, year 2)

Quietly going about one's business could be a fruitful career strategy, as Paul and Jacob discovered at the end of their first year when it was time to compile the timetable for the following year. Jacob was very interested in teaching some English lessons, English being one of his specialist subjects from college. He therefore wrote his name up on the list in the staffroom. A few days later, however, it became clear to him that this perhaps was not the accepted way of registering one's wishes for the new timetable. The teachers who had made English their domain at the school had written their names against the same lessons as Jacob, after which he felt obliged to remove his name again. This taught Jacob that things like distribution of lessons were often decided in the corridors or the staffroom and that a good relationship with heads, deputies, etc. was important in such matters. Another example of a clear informal hierarchy, where new teachers are shown their place, was Jacob as a new employee repeatedly having enquiries met by the statement that 'we'll do it the usual way' without being given any further explanation.

This power and control over privileges within the school generally, they found, had a direct correlation to how long a teacher had been at the school, i.e. seniority. Paul and Jacob had to learn how to manage and fight this, which they did in different ways. During the first 2 years, Jacob maintained a highly critical view of this form of hierarchy:

> There is absolutely no difference between the teacher who does nothing and the teacher who would do anything for his place of work. The pay's the same; you have the same rights, the same duties. (Jacob, year 2)

Jacob was able, to some degree, to influence the lessons he was assigned after his first year at the school, but kept a critical view. This was in tune with his pupil-centred perspective on teaching, even though it weakened a little along the way. In this sense, Jacob was a teacher who only gradually edged towards a more central position in the school's informal hierarchy and its reward system. He persisted in taking a critical stance to a number of colleagues' teaching, to the workplace culture at the school, and thereby to the school's code. Jacob approached the profession with a child-centred perspective and an idealistic notion that reward could, or at least should, reflect effort and expertise.

Paul, on the other hand, found himself in a somewhat different position, chiefly due to his role as IT-advisor; something he was able to exploit in order to follow a somewhat different career trajectory. This was made possible largely due to the central position he was given by the role.

> I don't think we should act like complete idiots and work for free. We've done that enough already. I've worked for free a lot during the first year and a half. I won't do that any more. I don't mind doing more team collaboration, but they'll have to pay me for it. (Paul, year 2)

Here, he stressed that the commitment he had shown for nearly 2 years at the school had become more focused than it had been. Over the same period, his view of the role as teacher had also changed:

> I think you have to be prepared for conflicts; not just with your employer, you also have to be tough when it comes to pupils, parents, colleagues, the head and the administration. (Paul, year 2)

In this way, Paul approached the profession with a self-identification as a 'Maths teacher' and an employee. He developed another career strategy and thereby followed a different career strategy where he as predominantly a Mathematics teacher – a prestigious subject – could paint himself as a subject teacher, and where he, helped considerably by his role as an IT-advisor, was able to assume a central position within the workplace culture over the course of the first 2 years. This central position is, for example, apparent in Paul's rhetoric regarding 'we teachers'. At the same time, he now prioritized his commitment by being more careful in how he chose to allocate his energy and was able to direct criticism towards his employers and others outside the workplace culture.

Both teachers expressed frustration that they, as newly qualified teachers, automatically occupied a position at the bottom of the hierarchy, where one is not rewarded for one's efforts. Meanwhile, they had very different ways of tackling this situation. Jacob focused on teaching and on earning some extra money by taking on extra lessons, while Paul instead spent time and resources on, for example, committee work at the school. He thereby ended up working more than he was paid for, but the rewards became apparent as he slowly rose in both the formal and informal hierarchy at the school. Paul can be said to have employed a more long-term career strategy, where he gradually learnt to target his efforts in the form of which committees bestowed the greatest prestige among colleagues and school management – a form of professional learning of the workplace curriculum. Jacob's involvement in committee work remained more haphazard. He felt obliged to display commitment by getting involved, but did not gain an understanding of how best to target such efforts.

Teachers' Views on Colleagues: After 8 Years Within the Profession

The teachers were, as mentioned, positioned very differently within the workplace organization. Paul was now a centrally positioned teacher, one of the standard-bearers, who, due to his involvement in a number of key councils and committees and his post as shop steward, had a close relationship with the school management. Jacob, meanwhile, had more or less found himself back at the foot of the ladder at his new school. He was highly critical of colleagues' teaching methods, but his own suggestions were brushed aside with the comment that 'that isn't how we do things on a small island'. He now found himself, if anything, in a more peripheral position than at the beginning of his career and therefore decided to seek a return to his previous place of work.

The two teachers' career trajectories were thereby very different, with Paul successfully following a progressive trajectory at the same school, while Jacob less successfully tried to climb the career ladder by changing schools, but ended up remaining in more or less the same position. Jacob had also applied for, but not got, a position at an European Union (EU) school abroad. Both teachers planned on applying for a management position at some point. However, Paul had postponed these plans as he was concerned it would mean he would have considerably less time to spend with his family; Jacob, who had also considered leaving the profession entirely, told that he had started to give up hope:

> I just seem to end up doing the wrong thing all the time, everyone gets annoyed with me. I don't have much to offer right now, because I've only been a teacher for eight years and have three small children and a wife who works. (Jacob, year 8)

After 8 years of teaching, Jacob had therefore entered a period characterized by what Huberman (1993) describes as 'self-doubt'. Adding to this is the close bond he had felt with his pupils and the distance he felt in relation to school management in particular. While his pupil-centred approach was apparent from his earliest teaching days, an episode during his third year within the profession likely reinforced his relationship with pupils and school management respectively. The seeming importance of this episode was underlined by the fact that he, unsolicited, brought it up 5 years later during an interview. Here Jacob told how the mother of one of his pupils accused him of looking at the female pupils when they showered after Physical Education lessons. These accusations were rubbished by the parents of the other pupils in the class and the matter was therefore brought to a swift conclusion. While Jacob was extremely appreciative of the support he received from the parents, he did not feel he had got sufficient backing from the headmaster:

> That was the first blow to my relationship with school management. (Jacob, year 8)

Already during his first year of teaching, problems with some of the parents in a Grade 5 class had led Jacob to consider his future in the profession. Seven years later, he still had doubts as to whether he would continue teaching. The move to the new school seemed only to have reinforced this 'self-doubt'.

Paul, who was widely regarded as one of the senior members of staff, had, to a large extent, changed his views on his colleagues. From his position as one of the standard-bearers, he now saw a good teacher as

> one who knows his subject and how to teach it, knows his stuff, but is also able to put pupils in a situation where they have the opportunity to stretch themselves, to move to a different level. (Paul, year 8)

As such, he had now become uncertain whether the teachers he had previously classified as experts really were:

> I have my doubts *as to how accomplished they really are.* (Paul, year 8).

He felt that there was a group of teachers, some of whom were newly qualified and some with up to 30-years experience, who were virtually talentless when it came to teaching, who took personal offence at any criticism of their teaching, were incapable of understanding constructive criticism and could not select 'the means according to the situation' (Paul, year 8). in these situations, he nearly always aligned himself with a pupil's perspective:

> [T]here are some teachers who can't see the potential in other people's children, and that's something I can't take. I have a strong opinion on that since I've had children of my own. Then some teachers, old or new, come along and say this child here is stupid, and then I get angry. There are no stupid children in that way, but there are loads of children who need a helping hand. I think I've become more conscious of the fact that children are people too. I think some of my colleagues can't understand that, and I can't stand that. (Paul, year 8)

The teachers' relationships with the teaching profession and their colleagues changed over the course of 8 years. Paul and Jacob, from their original peripheral positions, both started by differentiating between 'them and me' when discussing colleagues. After 2 years, Paul spoke of 'we teachers', while Jacob still largely spoke in terms of 'them and me', reflecting the changes in their respective positions. After 8 years within the profession, Paul now increasingly talked about 'the teachers' as though he no longer belonged to that group; something which, bearing in mind his close ties to the school management, was not entirely untrue.

The teachers could also be said to have changed regarding the criteria by which they assessed their colleagues. The first years were characterized by a concern at the levels of commitment displayed by colleagues and themselves. Colleagues could therefore be categorized as either standard-bearers, the following group or underperformers. After 8 years, Paul now distinguished more between the talentless and the talented on the basis of how his colleagues related to their pupils. He no longer framed the question of talent in terms of seniority. For example, he stressed that teachers with a low level of commitment could well be good and competent teachers of their subject:

> [T]he teachers with low commitment levels are the ones who've been at the school for years and who have started to consider retirement, for example female teachers over fifty who can't see many career opportunities ahead. They do their job, and do it well, but they can't be bothered getting involved in other areas of school life. (Paul, year 8)

Paul's classification, or hierarchy, thereby now seemed to be formed as a sort of two-level model, where the first level is divided according to an assessment of the teacher's abilities in the classroom, i.e. whether a teacher could teach or not. If they couldn't, they were 'hopeless'. The second level is ordered in relation to a number of factors which have nothing to do with the teacher's knowledge of his or her subject, but rather his or her commitment to the job outside of teaching, including commitment to more general pedagogical matters. This was apparent in Paul's discussion of whether or not a teacher acts appropriately in conflict situations with teachers and/or their parents. For Paul, an appropriate reaction involves the teacher not using stronger means than necessary.

Changing Views on Colleagues: A Summary

When it comes to participating in the school's organization and the workplace culture, once again, the teachers had to gradually learn to manage the school's workplace curriculum. They had to learn that:

- Newly qualified teachers should be committed, and loyal to their peripheral position. They should therefore take their place in the group behind the group of standard-bearers who remain highly committed after several years within the profession.
- Highly committed teachers are not necessarily competent teachers, while teachers with low levels of commitment can be perfectly competent.
- Both the newly qualified and those with a great deal of experience can be either talented or talentless as teachers; seniority does not determine talent.
- Newly qualified teachers must submit to privileges mainly corresponding to seniority as opposed to expertise, talent or commitment.

Conclusion: Two Different Career Trajectories

There undoubtedly exist different career trajectories within the teaching profession. These take the form of more or less unique career paths, which should not necessarily be understood in terms of a movement through a series of different positions, but also as a change in teachers' working conditions; in their ways of teaching; and in their views on teaching, pupils, parents, colleagues, school management, and on themselves as teachers. After 8 years within the profession, Paul and Jacob were following very different career trajectories: one vertical and continuous; the other horizontal and fractured.

A Vertical Career Trajectory

If a teacher career is understood in terms of a hierarchical system of positions, then Paul could be considered as being a step higher on the ladder than Jacob right from day one on account of his role as IT-advisor, a role which meant both fewer timetabled lessons and the opportunity to relate to colleagues from a position as an expert. Paul's working conditions in terms of the number of lessons, subjects and different classes he taught changed significantly during the 8 years with a progressive reduction in number.

Changes concerning his teaching were far less noticeable, although he undoubtedly adopted a more differentiated view of the relationship between teaching and pupils' varying academic abilities, backgrounds and outcomes. There were no significant changes in Paul's organization of lessons, but he continued to learn more about the effects of his teaching on pupils' academic learning processes, which constituted his primary field of interest, i.e. teaching's vertical discourse.

One could say that Paul had learnt the rules of the game and, by and large, followed these rules, no longer considering the workplace culture at the school esoteric. He had become a part of this culture and was also positioned close to the school management in the form of the head teacher. He was a member of the Parent–Teacher Association, was shop steward, and belonged to various councils and committees. The only time he had given serious consideration to leaving the profession was during the first year when he experienced some teething trouble with a 'problem class'. He had considered applying for positions at other schools, but without doing so. He thereby followed a more or less established vertical career trajectory within the school.

A Horizontal Career Trajectory

In comparison, Jacob could be described as having followed a more horizontal career trajectory, changing schools, but without climbing the career ladder. In his first job, he began on the lowest rung and his working conditions changed very slowly; perhaps so slowly that it caused him to apply for other jobs at other schools. He first applied for a position at an international EU school abroad, but did not get the job. He then applied for and got a job at an unusual school on a small island, where he also applied for the position as head teacher, but was turned down. At his first school, Jacob was involved in what might be described as a critical incident, and this may have been another reason why he sought pastures anew.

The Two Main Challenges

There were two challenges which it was essential that the teachers learnt to tackle. Firstly, they had to learn the effect of their teaching on pupils. They went about this in different ways and with different results. Following a career trajectory within the same school meant that Paul, becoming one of the 'older' teachers, had opportunities to change his views on pupils along the way: first predominantly personal relations, then more positional, and finally more personal again. It was possible to trace a similar pattern in his views on their parents: at first he kept his distance and regarded them as a problem; later he learnt how to deal with them and no longer viewed his relationship with parents as problematic. He developed a closer relationship to the school management, which he at one point had been highly critical of, but later became almost an unofficial part of. As has been apparent, Paul's focus was not on experimenting with his teaching to any great degree, but rather on improving the conditions for his work and his position within the school. His career trajectory was characterized by identification with the school system and drew upon a vertical academic discourse.

Jacob, on the other hand, was primarily concerned with establishing personal relations with his pupils. He attempted to improve his position by moving to a new school, but maintained a career strategy characterized by identification with his pupils and a degree of pastoral care, thereby drawing upon a horizontal discourse of domesticity. It is, of course, also interesting in this regard that no major changes were registered in the teachers' ways of organizing lessons as they gained in experience.

Secondly, they had to learn to deal with the unwritten rules within the school as a workplace, in particular concerning their relationships with colleagues and school management, and their positions within the school organization. The first year as a newly qualified teacher is clearly quite distinct. This is due to certain structural properties which make it extremely difficult to place new teachers in classes where they will be teaching their specialist subjects. Schools vary considerably in how they assign classes to new employees. Paul, for example, was assigned Physics lessons because he had spent a year studying engineering. He was given what he himself referred to as the 'garbage' – that is the subjects and classes which hadn't been covered when all his colleagues had got their timetables. Jacob had particular problems with History lessons in Grade 5. The lack of influence in determining their timetables made the first year a unique and somewhat testing experience for the newly qualified teachers. To ensure things are different after this first year, new teachers have to learn how to decode and master the rules of the game as they are manifested at the particular school. If they complete what might be regarded as a rite of passage which virtually all Danish teachers have faced, new possibilities become available. Both teachers took advantage of this, but employing different strategies: either prioritizing cutting down on the number of different classes (Paul) or the number of different subjects (Jacob). At first, Paul fought against the system, but later in his career, he increasingly became a part of this very system and fought for it. Jacob, meanwhile, continued to fight against it, but to some degree seemed to want to become more of a part of it, although he did not succeed. After 8 years within the profession, he had become a self-doubter.

Perspectives

Using the terms professional learning, career trajectories and workplace curriculum, we have described and analysed a number of important characteristics of teachers' teaching and their participation in other aspects of school life over the course of 8 years within the profession.

It strikes us that the school's workplace curriculum does not, to any great extent, give any indication that teachers are expected to get better at teaching over time. Teaching itself can rather be seen as a form of condition for gaining access to the profession and to various career trajectories. Teaching has to be managed, and this can be done in a wide variety of ways. If this does not happen, it can undermine a teacher's career, but, on the other hand, mastery of teaching does not necessarily result in any great benefit to a teacher's career. Teaching cannot in this regard be considered a career in a positional sense, but as a kind of entrance requirement or threshold.

There exist vertical and horizontal career trajectories within the profession. Access to the vertical trajectory is not provided by a system of rewards directly relating to teaching, but rather to active involvement in the school's other activities, such as participation in committee work. The horizontal trajectory centred on teaching is far more unpredictable. If this path is followed, as e.g. Fessler & Christensen (1992) and Tickle (1994, 2000) have noted, one must be prepared to start again, as acquired teaching competences alone do not provide access to privileges.

References

Bayer, M. & Brinkkjær, U. (2005). *Professional learning in practice: Newly qualified teachers' and educators' encounter with practice.* Copenhagen: Danish University of Education Press.

Bernstein, B. (2000). *Pedagogy symbolic control and identity.* London: Rowman & Littlefield.

Day, C., Sammons, P., Stobart, G., Kington, A., & Gu, Q. (2007). *Teachers matter: Connecting work, lives and effectiveness.* Maidenhead: Open University Press.

Due, J. & Madsen, J. S. (1990). *Man Kan kun Gå på To Ben.* Copenhagen: DLF.

Fessler, R. & Christensen, J. (1992). *The teacher career cycle: Understanding and guiding the professional development of teachers.* Needham Heights, MA: Allyn & Bacon.

Funktionærernes og Tjenestemændenes Fællesforbund (FTF) (2007). *FTF'ernes mobilitet på arbejdsmarkedet.*

Huberman, M. (1993). *The lives of teachers.* London: Cassell.

Huberman, M., Thomson, C. L., & Weiland, S. (1997). Perspectives on the teaching career. In B. J. Biddle, T. L. Good, & I. F. Goodson (Eds.), *International handbook of teachers and teaching* (pp. 11–77). Dordrecht: Kluwer.

Lortie, D. (1975). *Schoolteacher: A sociological study.* Chicago: University of Chicago Press.

Lundgren, U. P. (1981). *Model analysis of pedagogical process,* second edition. Lund, Sweden: CWK/Gleerup.

Measor, L. (1985). Critical incidents in the classroom: Identities, choices and careers. In S. Ball & I. Goodson (Eds.), *Teachers' lives and careers* (pp. 61–77). Lewes: Falmer.

Sikes, P. (1985). The life cycle of the teacher. In S. Ball & I. Goodson (Eds.), *Teachers' lives and careers* (pp. 27–60). Lewes: Falmer.

Tickle, L. (1994). *The induction of new teachers.* London: Cassell.

Tickle, L. (2000). *Teacher induction: The way ahead.* Maidenhead: Open University Press.

Chapter 6
Careers Under Stress: Teacher Adaptations at a Time of Intensive Reform*

Geoff Troman and Peter Woods

Introduction: Teacher Careers

The time is ripe for a reconsideration of teacher careers. Evetts (1987) argues that some studies of teacher careers assume a continuous and progressive trajectory. This model, it is argued, is founded on the concept of an 'objective' occupational career which is an ordered sequence of development extending over a period of years and involving steadily more responsible roles within an occupation. In teaching, there are fewer and fewer opportunities for promotion as one ascends the scale, and the model is a kind of 'flattened pyramid' (Woods et al., 1997). Ethnographers, by contrast, have explored teachers' 'subjective' experiences of career (Sikes et al., 1985; Ball & Goodson, 1985; Cherniss, 1995). Here the 'emphasis is on the individual's construction of meaning and the career as a continuous process in which the individual changes in accordance with his or her own choices, aims and intentions' (Woods, 1983, p. 153). Individuals 'negotiate and re-negotiate in their own minds as their careers proceed and they continually set and reset the goals themselves in that process' (ibid.). Work carried out in this tradition has shown the centrality of the teachers' selves in this process and how their values and commitments shape their careers (Woods, 1981; Nias, 1980, 1995).

Feminist inspired work has challenged what it sees as the male-centred concept of 'objective career' by showing how the careers of the women teachers studied are 'discontinuous', 'broken', or 'interrupted' owing to child-rearing and other family commitments (Evetts, 1987). Acker (1992), for instance, shows in her analysis of women teachers that female careers in teaching are influenced by 'daily experiences in a workplace context'. Whereas males are often seen as 'rational career planners, busily plotting career maps and climbing career ladders', in contrast, women's 'career plans are provisional and changeable', influenced by 'family stage and the work needs of teachers' spouses, as well as unexpected life events' (ibid., pp. 148–149).

Career theorists have recognized that sometimes the steps and paths in careers are not definite and some careers end badly (Strauss, 1971). Maclean (1992) and

---

*Chapter originally published as an article in the *Journal of Educational Change* Vol. 1, No. 3 (September 2000)

M. Bayer et al. (eds.), *Teachers' Career Trajectories and Work Lives,*
Professional Learning and Development in Schools and Higher Education 3,
© Springer Science + Business Media B.V. 2009

Maclean and McKenzie (1991) seem to presuppose an exit from the occupation at retirement age, though briefly touch on the issues of 'dissatisfied leavers' and 'wastage' to the profession. Huberman (1993) discovered a professional trajectory in the professional life cycle which sometimes terminated in 'reassessment' leading to 'bitter disengagement' from teaching. Some reasons for leaving the career before retirement age were 'fatigue', 'routine', 'frustration', and 'nervous tension'. With this exception, however, career researchers/theorists have not given much attention to teachers' experience of early exit or the adaptations of those who change course in their teacher careers. An opportunity to investigate this phenomenon has been afforded by recent developments in teaching which have caused increasing levels of stress and brought the whole profession into crisis.

Teacher Stress

Gardner and Oswald (1999) argue that while teachers are not the 'unhappiest workers' in the UK, they are 'low by public sector standards compared, especially, to nurses'. These large-scale survey data indicate that the 'dissatisfiers' (Nias, 1989) of primary teaching may be beginning to outweigh the 'satisfiers'. In terms of retention, the numbers receiving breakdown pensions and those leaving teaching before retirement age have risen dramatically through the 1990s (Brown & Ralph, 1998; Woods et al., 1997). Stress-related illness has been cited as the reason for this trend (Brown & Ralph, 1998). While occupational stress is a problem amongst the caring professionals generally, it is of particular concern in the teaching profession. There is now a considerable body of work which links teacher stress with the wholesale restructuring of national education systems which began in the 1980s. Travers and Cooper (1996), for instance, argue that it is no coincidence that rising stress levels in the profession coincided with the introduction of the Education Reform Act 1988. Since this time, the nature and demands of teaching have changed resulting in the intensification of teachers' work (Apple, 1986; Densmore, 1987; Hargreaves, 1994; Woods, 1995a; Campbell & Neill, 1994; Troman, 1997). Apple (1986) argues that, in late-twentieth-century capitalist societies, work intensifies as capital experiences an accumulation crisis and pressure for efficiency mounts in public and private sectors. Intensification leads to reduced time for relaxation and reskilling, causes chronic and persistent work overload, reduces quality of service, and separates the conceptualization from the execution of tasks, making teachers dependent on outside expertise and reducing them to technicians (also see Hargreaves, 1994, pp. 118–119). Similar trends have been noted in Europe (Vandenberghe & Huberman, 1999), North America (Leithwood et al., 1999; Smylie, 1999), and Australia (Dinham, 1992; Dinham & Scott, 1996).

Consequently, there are growing numbers of redundancies and redeployments (Woods et al., 1997), and increasing problems in teacher recruitment. The increased casualization of teaching (Lawn, 1995) with temporary and short-term contracts further increases insecurity. Menter et al. (1999) argue that the vacancy rates have created a culture of heavy reliance on supply teachers. This is particularly acute in London where many 'Commonwealth' (Australia, New Zealand, and Canada) supplied teachers, not trained in the National Curriculum, are employed (Menter et al., 1999). Relf and Hobbs (1999) argue that there is a downward spiral of low recruitment leading to low standards leading to further low recruitment (Sutherland, 1997; Young, 1997). Many job vacancies remain unfilled (Howson, 1998, 1999), particularly for headteacher and senior manager posts in London schools (Menter et al., 1999). Such jobs have become 'blocked off from teachers who formerly would have applied for them. The pressures of the head teacher role have become too great and the salary levels not high enough to compensate for them (Woods et al., 1997). The career structure base has become even wider in consequence.

In an attempt to boost recruitment, the government has launched the national advertising campaign '*No-one Forgets a Good Teacher*' (Booth in Macleod, 1998) and has published a *Green Paper* (Department for Education and Employment, 1998) aimed at 'modernizing' teaching, introducing what it views as a more attractive (performance-related) pay structure in order to attract recruits to teaching. However, Dainton (1999, p. 45) argues that:

> Fifty per cent of the teaching workforce is over 45 years old. Yet proposals in the Green Paper have little to offer this important group of teachers who help form the backbone of the profession. What are the prospects for an ageing, demoralised and disaffected workforce, already working under considerable stress and carrying a heavy workload, which saw the last Government's arrangements as blocking off the only career prospects which had kept many going?

These developments have had radical implications for teacher careers. Drawing on a 3-year study of teacher stress, we investigate the consequences of stress for teacher careers, and teachers' own strategies and adaptations in adjusting their careers. First, we outline the methods of the study.

Methods

Most research on teacher stress has adopted large-scale survey methods (e.g. Travers & Cooper, 1996). While these studies reveal likely causes of stress and patterns of stress-related illness in large populations, the individual and detailed testimony of teachers is often missing. Thus, we know little of the teachers' perceptions of sources of stress, how it feels to experience it and what strategies are used to cope with it. By way of contrast, this research is qualitative. The principal method was semi-structured and open-ended, in-depth, life history interviewing. A sample of teachers was assembled with the assistance of a Local Authority Occupational Health Unit which was engaged in counselling employees who had been self-referred, or referred by their doctors. All had been diagnosed as suffering from anxiety, depression, or stress-related illness. The Unit also had knowledge of those teachers who had returned to school or who had retired early or otherwise left teaching for stress-related reasons. Attendance at the Unit for counselling, receiving medical treatment for stress-related illness and having a prolonged period off work provided an operational definition of stress for our research. All such teachers were circulated with our letter inviting them to take part in the research. The eventual sample consisted of 20 teachers – 13 women and 7 men. These were working, or had worked, in schools representing a range of urban and rural locations. The gender proportions and ages represented those found in the teaching profession generally in that they were predominantly women and a large majority was 40years of age or above (Wragg et al., 1998). A range of positions was represented, though the majority were teachers (mostly coordinators of subject areas) in mid- to late-career. There were three headteachers (two male, one female) and two newly qualified teachers (female). Some of the teachers were on sickness absence, some had returned to work, and some had left teaching.

The teachers were interviewed in their own homes. Each interview was normally of 1.5–2h duration with the length being determined by the interviewee. There were a minimum of two and a maximum of five interviews with respondents over a 2-year period. This adds a longitudinal dimension to the research, something which is often missing in research on stress in teaching (Kelchtermans, 1995), and which allows us to see what impact stress-related illness was having on the teachers' careers. Analysis of transcripts, conducted in parallel with ongoing comparisons with related research literature, fed into future data collection facilitating 'progressive focusing' (Glaser & Strauss, 1967).

It might be argued that such a sample, containing a majority who were suffering from stress-related illness, could be atypical of teachers generally. However, these teachers are dealing with the same educational changes affecting their work as all other teachers in the education system. Additionally, there are considerable numbers of teachers who report stress (Travers & Cooper, 1996) and those who are thinking of leaving (Dinham & Scott, 1996) or who have resigned (Dinham, 1992). The teachers in this sample, therefore, might be regarded as 'critical cases' in that they highlight issues common to all to some extent rather than peculiar to themselves (Hammersley & Atkinson, 1995).

Change Views of Careers

How did the teachers perceive what was happening to them in career terms? Their comments led us to the view that periods of teacher stress can be considered as 'epiphanies' (Denzin, in Richardson, 1994) or 'fateful moments' in the career:

> [W]hen individuals are called on to take decisions that are particularly consequential for their ambitions, or more generally for their future lives. Fateful moments are highly consequential for a person's identity. (Giddens, 1991, p. 112)

They are likely to occur during 'periods of strain' and like 'critical incidents' (Sikes et al., 1985, p. 57), are 'key events in an individual's life, around which pivotal decisions revolve. They provoke the individual into selecting particular kinds of actions which lead in particular directions', and in which 'new aspects of the self are brought into being' (Becker, 1966, p. xiv). During episodes of stress, individuals may experience 'fateful moments' or 'critical incidents' in which processes of 'rumination' (Lazarus, 1990), 'reassessment' (Huberman, 1993) and 'redefinition' (Sikes et al., 1985) of self and career take place. A succession of such moments during a period of stress has the potential for bringing about conditions where the individual takes a different career direction or terminates the career. In this process, the individual 'chooses' a way and 'makes a self' (ibid., p. 57).

Convery (1999) argues that such 'critical incidents' are commonly deployed by researchers to illustrate teachers' professional and personal development. In these cases, the transformative nature of the incidents is used to suggest 'progressive moral improvement'. However, in the teachers' experience, the stress-related illness episodes were, like their subsequent thoughts of leaving teaching or having to modify their roles, wholly unanticipated and usually not at all transformative in a positive sense. The result was more like Goffman's (1968) 'spoiled careers', in that they were 'untimely terminated, or have otherwise taken a turn out of line with the occupants' intentions' (Woods, 1983, p. 163; see also Riseborough, 1981). A common phrase used by the teachers in the stress research was, 'I was the last person I thought it (stress) would happen to'. The occupational changes they experienced as a consequence of their adaptations were in many cases out of their control. Some felt 'forced out' of teaching while others were 'trapped within' it (Woods et al., 1997).

Those teachers who had extended absence reported that they had thoughts of leaving teaching during their time off work with stress-related illness, yet the negative financial consequences of doing so loomed large. As in Becker's (1977) conception of career, these teachers had 'side-bets' and were, at this stage, committed **by** their work as much as **to** it. Those who had partners said that they had extensive discussions during their illness deciding whether they could afford not to return to work in teaching. This process, while a form of 'strategic life planning' (Giddens, 1991), was heavily constrained by such factors as age, gender, experience, the state of the labour market, and the marketization of schooling. Judith (43 years) was effectively facing career curtailment:

> I was very scared, let down I think. I didn't feel the headteacher had supported me – well any of us, I mean not just me, because everybody was feeling scared about it, had been since Christmas really. I was anxious because I obviously had the mortgage; I had to pay the mortgage. And I was really worried that I couldn't get another job because I was expensive. Although I'd only been teaching for six years, I think that would probably have taken me up to the top of the grade anyway, but because I was an adult – a mature student – I'd been given enhanced points when I started so I was right at the top of the scale, so I was expensive. So every job I applied for they were all saying, 'Newly qualified teachers welcome to apply'. So I thought, 'Well, that's code for "we don't want anybody who's expensive basically"'. Also, I wanted to look for a permanent contract and they were all of them temporary – one term, two terms, that kind of thing. I knew that I would have some redundancy payment, I mean that was in the letter, it was all laid down. So I was determined not to take just a one term contract. Because I knew I could cope with one or two terms, that wouldn't have been too difficult. But I didn't really want to have a break if I could avoid it.'

Michael (52 years) considered that he had been 'bullied' in the workplace and felt that his career was in the hands of the management who had been bullying him. On his return to school after extended sick leave he found management's behaviour towards him increased his stress and further confused his thinking about his career, and decisions concerning it seemed out of his control:

> I was still fatigued and finding it a struggle – the stress was continuing. They were keeping me on tenterhooks all the time. Nothing resolved, no issue clarified, no review of my job description, no clear-cut pointers about my future. 'Would I still be a co-ordinator?' 'If not, where did that leave me?' I was a relatively highly paid older member of staff ripe for being made redundant. They hadn't said, 'We've got to have two redundancies, can we have volunteers?' but there was this implication.

The experience of stress had changed the way all the teachers viewed their careers. While some (men and women) had held notions of the 'objective' career with its predictable stages (onwards and upwards) now, following stressful episodes, they were more focused on merely coping. Many of the teachers (particularly in mid-career) wondered if they could keep going until they were 60 years of age. For Jackie (50 years) this involved the loss of ambition:

> But I do think my career reached its limit. I'm not going to go anywhere now. I think that's it. I've got no ambition left in me any more. I was actually going for deputy headships and jobs like that but I'm not any longer. I was getting interviews but I just don't care any more. I'm not interested in career other than doing what I'm doing now. I'm interested in teaching. I like teaching the way I am at the moment. And I'm not particularly interested in management any more. I think I've had so much of the stuffing knocked out of me, I just haven't got enough energy left. I just don't want to be bothered. So although it might have made me more capable of resisting bullying or pressure, it dampened down any ambition; it's just dampened it down completely.

Teacher Adaptations

Given these changing views, how did our teachers adapt? Some were determined to stay in teaching in some form and would not consider the early retirement or break-down pensions they were offered, saying they would not 'let the system beat' them. Most of the teachers argued that the work they were expected to do was not the job they had trained for or entered teaching to do. For all of the teachers, no matter what age or career stage, stress meant a shift in their values from purely expressive to more instrumental commitment, a pattern that others have observed in primary teachers since the Education Reform Act of 1988 (Broadfoot & Osborn, 1988; Pollard et al., 1994; Jeffrey & Woods, 1996). In these circumstances, what for some teachers had once been a vocation now became just a job. Apart from this, however, they chose three different kinds of adaptation: *retreatism*, *downshifting*, and *self-actualization*.

Retreatism

Woods (1995b, p. 9) argues that retreatism involves, 'submitting to the imposed changes in professional ideology leading to stress and anxiety. This can be alleviated in a number of ways including leaving the job'. Pollard et al. (1994) found 'considerable evidence' of retreatism in response to the introduction of the National Curriculum and attendant intensification of work. This adaptation was particularly pronounced among the older teachers and at the time they were interviewed, the authors report, they were 'about to take early retirement or were strongly considering it' (p. 101). Until recently, internal retreatism, involving withdrawal to the classroom and working in isolation, was one form of 'escape' for teachers that might have been possible. However, this is no longer a viable adaptation given the levels of monitoring and surveillance and the ethos in schools today of constant improvement in a culture of managerial teamwork.[1]

The teachers in the stress research who adapted in this way had gained or were seeking a breakdown pension considerably before the 'official' retirement age. They had no plans to return to teaching. Indeed, as part of the settlement for this form of early retirement, it is against the regulations to return to teaching in any form as the individual has been deemed to be physically and psychologically unfit for teaching work. All the teachers in this category felt 'forced out' of teaching.

Marion (50 years), for example, was very committed to child-centred teaching in an inner-city context, and experienced stress with her over-conscientious approach to nurturing individual children (Campbell & Neill, 1994). Others have noted the association of guilt with burnout (Hargreaves, 1994). She grieved for a lost self (Nias, 1991) when she had to leave teaching with a breakdown pension because of her depressive illness. She had a very strong conception of 'normality' and 'abnormality' in work and felt that her career had finished 'abnormally'. Interestingly, for Marion, 'normal' life refers to the working life at school and 'abnormal' refers to a life where one can 'visit galleries', 'go out for lunch' (things she has done since being retired). Retirement was, therefore, seen as an 'abnormal' state. Also, she had a conception of a 'normal' career with a 'normal' end to it, presumably with an appropriate rite of passage (party and presentation at school, letter from the director of education, a clock). Marion's end of career was 'abnormal' and undesirable, termination taking the form of a disabling illness caused by stress and burnout. Her friends said 'you can't leave like this', and she said 'I didn't want it to end this way, there is still a great sadness'. To her, her career was unfinished and incomplete.

Ben (38 years), who was very young to be considering retirement, could not envisage continuing in the job 'that has made me so ill'. He said that returning to a reduced role would be unthinkable for this reason, and he would feel that he had 'cheated' the school by not fulfilling the role for which he had been appointed:

I don't think I'm going to be able to cope with teaching any more, with the way the system is and the pressures of the job. No. I think I've had enough of that. I mean the job is a very stressful one and having experienced what I've experienced since April there's no way I want to put myself in a situation where I can be made ill again. It's taken much longer than I anticipated to start getting well. The doctor said to me yesterday, 'It could take two or three years before you really feel a hundred per cent'. And I think he's right. I couldn't cope with it now. If I could find a job that was sufficiently lucrative without the pressure, I would get out of education. And I'm not bothered. I'll just see what happens. I mean, I look in the jobs section in the newspaper, more to give me an idea of what I might like to do. If I can manage, I'll work part-time to begin with. I think what I want to do is just get a pretty mundane job to begin with and just settle back into work and then take it from there. I have no desire to start a new career as such. I don't want a career. I don't want to go into something where there are prospects of management and moving up. I've been there and I've done it. I could just cope with working in a shop, something like that with very little responsibility. I'm no longer planning; just taking one day at a time.

Julie (35 years) redefined her role outside teaching. She left following her school's failure of an external inspection and now works part-time in an office doing clerical work. At the time she left her school:

Everyone said, 'Oh don't go – what a loss to the profession'. So I got given a nice plant at Christmas and that was it, I left – end of career as far as everyone was concerned.

She was really worried about getting another job doing anything because of the stigma. She said, 'I didn't want people to think I was a lousy teacher. I wondered if people would employ me if they knew I hadn't coped with teaching and was working in a school that had failed'.

She finds her new work frustrating but no longer has the stresses and strains of teaching:

I am a bit frustrated now because the job is the other end of the scale. I have gone from an alarming amount of responsibility to virtually none at all. I just do what I'm told and I'm doing a job you just leave behind at five o'clock.

Although engaging in very different work, Julie initially retained aspects of her teacher identity. She gave advice to workmates and friends about the education of their children and regarding some tasks in the office colleagues said, 'Oh, Julie's a teacher, she'll do that'.

Mary (52 years) had returned to school after a two-term absence which she considered had been caused by the simultaneous intensification of her work and the violent and acrimonious breakdown of her relationship with her partner. In the first week of her return, the headteacher placed her on competency procedures because of complaints from parents concerning her lengthy absence and her alleged ineffectiveness as a class teacher. After a term in which she had to conform to the competency procedures but was frequently absent, she again left for extended sick leave. She now feels that it will be impossible for her to satisfy the school that she is competent and has decided to leave teaching rather than go back to face further humiliation and stress. Having left under these circumstances, she feels that she will have to leave teaching altogether since transfer to another school would be difficult or impossible to achieve owing to her having to tell a potential employer about the competency procedures and receiving a negative reference from her current headteacher. Consequently, Mary felt 'forced out' of teaching.

For these teachers, their teaching careers are clearly at an end. Two of them, Marion and Ben, are suffering from a depressive illness and felt they could not return. Ben has become disillusioned with the concept and experience of 'career', no matter what the occupation. Return for Mary and Julie would involve overcoming major stigmas surrounding 'incompetency' and school 'failure' respectively, something they seemed unlikely to do.

Downshifting

Downshifting involved reducing workload, responsibilities, and status. Some felt able to return to teaching after a break. Others departed radically from notions of 'objective' or 'normal' traditional career. Several teachers adjusted their 'working conditions and their degree of personal investment' to the job (Huberman, 1993, p. 153). In effect, all were curtailing their careers. The ways they sought to modify their work took the form of *planned demotion*, *role-reduction*, or *role-redefinition*.

Planned Demotion

This form of adaptation involves the teacher voluntarily occupying a role that is lower in status than the one they are seeking to leave. This kind of adaptation involving, for instance, a headteacher who moved vertically downwards in career, to become a deputy headteacher, used to be an extremely rare phenomenon prior to the recent reforms (Woods, 1983).

Merryl (35 years) had been a headteacher in a small school. She felt she was over-promoted and realized she could not fulfil the requirements of the role. She took a job as a deputy head in a larger school following her illness and found that this work was less stressful and that it also comprised improved staff relationships:

> There are a lot more people to share things with. I think one of my big things is that I'm not the final buffer. There's somebody else there as well. The actual curriculum responsibilities are shared out because we've got fourteen staff. So instead of three of you doing nine subjects, there are fourteen of you doing nine subjects. And just generally the interaction that you get as well.

However, there was stigma (Goffman, 1963) attached to her career change which threatened her identity:

> In the interview, I was asked why I was going from a headship to a deputy headship. I just said honestly – well, of course I couldn't say I couldn't cope with headship. I said, 'I'd done my stint at my last school but I wasn't sure whether I was ready for another headship. So I wanted to step back a little bit and experience life in a larger school'. And it was truthful. I did want to move into a different situation just to try and analyse whether it was me or the job. ... I felt a bit of an anomaly when I met heads and deputies in partnership schools at the beginning of term. They would say, 'Oh, you were a head weren't you? Oh, why did you become a deputy?' They kept asking **why**. I felt a bit like a talking point really.

The stigma, the previous experience of stress and lack of self-confidence in the headteacher role made it unlikely that Merryl would seek to (re)develop her career by seeking headteacher posts.

Role-Reduction

Teachers adapting through role-reduction relinquished posts of responsibility and the payments that went with them. Unlike planned demotion, this form of adaptation was a smaller step down and was sometimes suggested or imposed by management as a condition of return to work. This mode of adaptation resulted in the teachers having to do less administrative work, like paperwork and attending meetings. The resulting reduction in role pressures, while making life 'more bearable' in and out of school, signalled a dilution in the role occupant's career. Role-reduction involves progressive 'disengagement' (Huberman, 1993).

William (45 years) returned to school after a depressive illness and reduced his several coordination roles and, while not experiencing stigma from the other teachers in the school (all female), found difficulties with relationships with some colleagues after he relinquished his status and formal, paid responsibilities for science, design, and technology, as well as games and audio-visual aids):

> A few weeks ago, the person who'd taken my science post was talking about reorganising the science resources and in fact it was how it used to be, how I used to have it, and I was told it had to change because we had this new room in school. And she said, 'I think we ought to do this, that and the other', and I just said something about, 'well we used to do that, and I was told at the time that it had to change because that wasn't meeting the National Curriculum blah, blah'. And somebody else said, 'But you must, William, let other people to their own, or make their own mistakes or have a go themselves sort of thing'. And I was saying, 'Well I wasn't meaning it in an unpleasant way. I was just trying to save you time by doing something that perhaps wouldn't work'. But, as I say, basically I haven't volunteered for anything this term. I've just really kept my head down most of the time. I've just gone into school a bit later than I used to. I just do my job and mark the books more or less quite a lot of breaks and lunchtimes. I don't go in the staff room quite as much, I try to keep out of the way I suppose. I have to keep on top of all the marking. And then I don't run any clubs at all after school which is the first time ever.

Feeling 'trapped' with many years to go until retirement, William's commitment is now one of 'career continuance' (Nias, 1980). He considers he is too old to retrain in an alternative occupation and too young to leave with a reasonable pension (he does not qualify for early retirement). William is attempting to 'sit it out' until retirement but is finding that this strategy will probably be unsuccessful in the long term owing to the demands being made on all the teachers at his school for constant improvement.

Role-Redefinition

Some of the teachers left full-time employment for part-time contracts or to work as supply teachers. While this was seemingly done voluntarily, the teachers actually felt they had little choice. They could not continue in the role that had made them ill. By redefining the role and reducing commitment, these teachers no longer had the responsibility for displays, being a subject coordinator, writing reports, writing curriculum programmes for the year, attending parents' evenings, attending curriculum meetings, and many of the other tasks they found stressful.

Olivia (58 years) left the school where she had felt 'bullied' by management and was appointed in another small school but this was a part-time fixed-term job rather than her previous full-time, permanent contract.

Rita (45 years) left her school where she was undergoing competency procedures in order to do supply teaching:

> I agonised because being the only breadwinner I have to earn enough money to pay the
> mortgage. But the job was making me ill. I thought I should work to live not the other way
> round. So I have a lot of friends who've gone into supply. I thought I would give up full-
> time teaching and go into supply.

Lorraine (30 years) had been pressured to be a music coordinator. Initially, she
refused the role, though the school insisted. She said, 'they were so pleased to get
me because I could play the piano and music coordinators are as rare as rocking
horse droppings'. After a year in this post she found the work too demanding and
had an extended sickness absence. She returned to her school and took a post as a
'floating' teacher. In this role, she covered for the other teachers to give them non-
contact time or substituted when a member of staff was absent, thus relinquishing
the many duties of a class teacher.

As noted earlier, career breaks and returning to teaching as supply or temporary
teachers have been part of the female teacher employment pattern for many years
(Evetts, 1987; Acker, 1992). However, now, for some teachers, the reason for the
break is illness rather than child-rearing and the choice of supply or temporary
work is not as a stepping stone to restart a career but an end in itself. Teaching may
be becoming (re)feminized not only in being an occupation with a large female
majority workforce, but in the sense that men are being offered or obliged to accept
types of work and work conditions which women have always experienced in State
schooling. This study supports Acker's finding that women teachers' careers are
influenced by 'unexpected life events' and stressful work is a major factor in this
respect. Additionally, it is not only women who are living through a crisis in careers.
Men, too, are experiencing forced career breaks (and all that this entails in terms of
getting back into teaching) or early termination of career. Changing schools or making a 'gentle' return to teaching after a prolonged period of stress-related illness is
unlikely to be facilitated by the kinds of supportive, informal and influential networks
of colleagues, headteachers, and local inspectors that Evetts (1987) described in the
current climate of intensification and accountability (Jeffrey & Woods, 1998).

Self-Actualizing

A number of teachers laid emphasis on adapting to stress by making the most of
change and looking for opportunities for development or realization of the self,
seeking new identities. The main means were through re-routeing or relocating.

Re-routeing

Whereas retreatism involves 'little choice in the face of superior hostile forces' re-
routeing is a 'positive act of removal or redirection' (Woods, 1995b, p. 9). Re-routeing

involves 'finding new opportunities for lifelong ambitions. It is a 'strategy to save and promote the self'. Even though transferring to new careers from teaching is difficult and some suffer occupational 'locking in' (Travers & Cooper, 1996) some of the teachers felt that they could no longer remain in teaching and, therefore, must re-route. This allowed them to preserve the values that they had previously invested in teaching.

Thomas (46 years), who had been prominent in creative and artistic education and at the forefront of progressive primary education throughout his career, was taking early retirement. After spending the past 2 years successfully getting his school off Special Measures (instituted by inspectors because they had judged the school to be 'failing'), he resigned as headteacher after

> giving considerable thought as to whether I wanted to be part of this any more. The experiences I have gone through in the past years have been so negative and have cost me so much personally that the answer is 'no'. I could no longer stomach the climate of blame that the harsh and unyielding system of school inspections had created. Not only is it stifling individuality and destroying teachers' self-confidence, it is driving many headteachers out and making headships increasingly difficult to fill.

With, potentially, a further 20 years to go in headship, his pupils' parents and his friends find it difficult to understand his decision:

> It was partly professional pride and also knowing the picture given by the inspection report was flawed. I was also determined not to be a victim. I look at parents and see the process that is going on. They're thinking, 'Is he cracking up; Is he just not up to it; Is it a mid-life crisis?' Friends cannot understand why I would want to leave a relatively well-paid job.

He refused to continue in headship and is beginning a new career as a writer of children's books and plays about schoolteachers. In this role he can express his strong commitment to education in a wider sense but faces the uncertainty involved in adopting the new role with poor financial prospects.

Barbara (48 years), who was strongly committed to early years teaching in an inner-city school, lost her father and her job (redundancy forced by school closure) in the same week. She explained that she had 'lost the two things she loved most' and her period of grieving for her father and her lost identity as a teacher (Nias, 1991) is currently continuing. She had experienced a breaking of the 'essential link' between a person's sense of identity and the work she performed (Berger, 1964). Recently she has been appointed as an educational liaison worker to work with mothers on an inner-city housing estate to develop stronger relationships between school and home. In this way she can begin to redevelop the human relationships she found so important in her work as an infant teacher. However, the work is part-time and on a 1-year contract basis. Consequently she is suffering insecurity as well as major reduction in salary.

Although they found the curtailment of the teaching career painful, these teachers did have the 'luxury' of some measure of financial security (small pension or redundancy payment) to cushion their entry into and development of an alternative career which would allow them to reinvest their values.

Relocating

Some of the teachers found self-fulfilment by relocating to a different school and doing work more in line with their values (see Nias, 1989). Anna (25 years) had difficulties in her previous school teaching Key Stage 2 children and trying to fit into a hostile teacher culture. She found it easy to change schools (she had taught at three in her short career) because as a young teacher she was relatively inexpensive to employ. Her move enabled her to join a school staff to whom she thought she could relate more easily and teach nursery children with whom she felt more comfortable.

Vanessa (45 years) experienced stress in her work in a 'failing school' but did not have extended sick leave. She perceived the sources of her stress to be the intensification of her work and not being recognized as a good teacher by the management in the school. Despite the stigma of the 'failing school' label she was appointed as Humanities coordinator, which was a promotion, at another school. She described her new school and job as follows:

> I think the catchment area is a lot tougher and I am stressed but now I can tell the difference between unhealthy stress and healthy stress. What I was suffering from was not a healthy form of stress. I think stress is part of life, it is definitely part of a teacher's life. In my present job I have bad times when I get in a panic and everything goes to hell in a basket but I'm doing fine. I'm really enjoying it.

Susan (33 years) had not taken time off work even though she was stressed. This was because she did not want a 'stain' to be on her record and affect future appointments and planned on 'leaving in a dignified fashion'. She felt capable of continuing full-time by relocating, an option not open to retreating and downshifting teachers. She found self-fulfilment by leaving a school with a culture of 'bureaucracy' and 'overwork' for more human relationships and part-time work which enabled her to spend more time with her daughter at home. Her commitment was now more towards herself and family than to school (Healy, 1999):

> I think I said it in my letter of application. I was regrettably having to leave my job because I needed to spend time with my young daughter. Which was perfectly true. And it's never ever been questioned. And in fact I had a conversation with him (headteacher) along those lines the other night. Not specifically talking about me. But how teaching doesn't tend to allow you to spend much time with your family. And I was saying that's exactly why I had to make this kind of decision. Because it was either be a teacher or be a parent. There didn't seem to be much in between. But fortunately I found this part-time job which is working out well. I mean the financial side is dreadful because you're working a small proportion of what you were but it's a long way away and you're only doing two hours a day. All this kind of thing. But it's done me the world of good in getting back to somewhere where they actually seem to be quite human ... (for example) ... in the way that they talk and they laugh. They seem to enjoy themselves. Without a shadow of a doubt I would say that the school that I've just come out of is populated by very grey, very knackered looking people. And I just don't understand why it just seems like there's a culture of overwork and a culture of over-bureaucracy."

She anticipated gradually building up to full-time work again as her daughter became older. In this way she could continue developing her career.

While it was the women who sought self-fulfilment in children and the family and reduced their commitment to work by changing it in the way Susan describes, some of the men coped with stressful work and gained self-fulfilment by increasing their commitment to activities outside school or home. Examples of this included voluntary youth work; voluntary administrative work in county cricket; playing tennis; and frequent involvement at a religious social club.

George (45 years) found self-fulfilment by leaving his full-time job in teaching, which he had found stressful, in order to raise his children while his wife who was employed on a series of short-term contracts as a lecturer became the principal breadwinner. Once the children reached school age he returned to teaching on supply in order to 'use my capacity to earn as a supply teacher; that's the bits that make up the gaps. But I wouldn't take even a temporary full-time job. It's too much'. This lifestyle allows him to develop his interest in renovating vintage cars and attending car rallies. Although he 'takes work as it comes', he is prepared to return to teaching full-time if his wife's career falters.

This does not mean that we are witnessing the rise of a self-actualizing generation of teachers which has been described by some writers (Cherniss, 1995; Bartlett, 1998). Teachers faced with reinventing themselves and their careers are limited by more than just their aspirations. As Cherniss (1995, p. 166) explains; 'People can make their lives better or worse but what they think, how they feel and what they do are strongly shaped by the social contexts in which they live.'

Conclusion

In the light of the evidence presented in this paper, the notion of 'career' needs reconceptualizing. Certainly, 'objective career' theory and research, even though it briefly touches on early leavers from, and 'wastage', to the profession, does not engage with the types of adaptations and their consequences described in this study. Many of the teachers in the sample also appeared to lack the degree of agency and control which is stressed in theories of 'subjective careers', suggesting that these theories may also need development.

Teaching, for many, is no longer a job for life. The notion of a career being hierarchical (in terms of moving vertically upwards) and continuous to the age of 60 or 65 years of age is breaking down. Many careers are now fragmented by the forced interruptions of redundancy, early retirement, or breakdown retirement. Increasingly, careers are becoming discontinuous, or are experienced as being on a plateau, or involve vertical movement downwards through strategies of downshifting (Sennett, 1998). In conditions of turbulence and anxiety, teachers face these insecurities largely unprepared and alone. Macnicol (1999, p. 30) argues that 'being continually exposed to such risks eats away at one's sense of character; the destruction of personal narratives by which people make sense of their past engenders confusion and alienation'.

Perhaps change is necessary to remove some of the ineffective and inefficient teachers from the system in order to accelerate improvement in educational provision. The replacement of older teachers with younger, cheaper, more instrumentally committed, compliant, and malleable ones well versed in the National Curriculum may be the answer. Indeed, Her Majesty's Chief Inspector of Schools with his idea of dismissing 15,000 incompetent teachers (Woodhead, 1995, p. 15) may be seeking not only to remove the type of teachers he considers a hindrance to educational progress but also to use the threat of sacking in order to gain greater control of those teachers who remain in the system. It may be, of course, that it is this public 'discourse of derision' (Ball, 1994), and images of the stressful and discontinuous career, that make teaching an increasingly unattractive proposition to potential recruits.

Whatever the intention, the result is a huge personal cost to some teachers and to the education system in general. The system suffers in terms of the loss of experienced teachers and the money that was invested in their skills and knowledge in terms of training and staff development. This cultural and economic loss is increased considerably if sick pay, redundancy payments, pensions, and in some cases compensation payments are added. The annual cost of stress to the Education Service has been estimated at £230 million (Brown & Ralph, 1998). Further, there is evidence that the profession may be losing some of its best teachers. Woods (1990, p. 185), for instance, argues that for some teachers:

> [R]edefinition or adaptation, for some reason or another, is difficult, painful, or impossible. Among these are those teachers who are highly committed, vocationally oriented and 'caring', for there is no escape route open to them. They will not weaken their commitment. There is nothing left to give way but themselves. The best teachers, arguably, are the most vulnerable.

The data on which this article is based gives insights into the personal and social consequences of change. Rapid and wide-ranging changes in the nature of teachers' work are producing conditions of uncertainty in which traditions and social structures are crumbling (Giddens, 1991; Jeffrey, 1998) and the tension and interplay between the global and local are experienced. Giddens (1991, p. 5) argues that:

> One of the distinctive features of (high) modernity is an increasing interconnection between the two extremes of extensionality and intentionality. Globalising influences on the one hand and personal dispositions on the other. ... The more tradition loses its hold, and the more daily life is reconstituted in terms of the dialectical interplay of the local and the global, the more individuals are forced to negotiate lifestyle choices among a diversity of options. ... Reflexively organized life-planning ... becomes a central feature of the structuring of self-identity.

In the conditions of late modernity, planning becomes more difficult as traditional social and cultural landmarks disappear and nothing stands still. However, individuals in these circumstances cannot choose not to choose, for in the absence of traditional status passages and attendant rites of passage they have to continually reinvent themselves (Woods, 1999). For many of the phases in the unpredictable new career, there are no scripts which people can follow (Ford, 1992). Careers must be negotiated and renegotiated repeatedly. Lifestyle choices involving the reinvention of identity are reoccurring aspects of late modernity and the demise of the regularized society. Making these choices in the circumstances described in this article is, of course, a highly constrained, convoluted and stressful process in itself. As Woods (1983, p. 160) points out: '[C]areer structures cannot be re-formulated in one's head over-night'.

The head of the governmental organization responsible for teacher supply has recently announced that 'people should be encouraged to spend just a few years teaching during more flexible and varied careers' (Barnard, 1999, p. 1). He clearly recognizes the physically, psychologically, and emotionally demanding nature of teaching in contemporary schooling and seems to have in mind co-opting teaching personnel, on a temporary basis, from other occupations, when he says that:

> We have to make it possible for people to come in and give some very enthusiastic, ener-getic years. There's a bit of teacher in all of us ... we can do quite well to get people fired up to teach for ten years of their career rather than the whole thing." (ibid.)

One wonders what kind of teacher will be recruited to the 'officially' discontinuous career. Will they be the kind of stress-proofed technicians that Jeffrey and Woods (1996) describe, driven by instrumental commitment at the outset? And what will happen to those vocationally oriented teachers who thought they had chosen a career for life once they are burned out after a decade? Currently, there is no provi-sion for teachers to change career 'escalators' (Strauss, 1971), either by retraining for work in a different phase of education (though this is possible in Scotland) or in a new occupation. Further, the measures the policymakers have devised so far do little to change the conditions of teachers' work to make them less stressful and supportive of career development and workplace commitment (Rosenholtz, 1989) – rather the reverse. For example, the zero-tolerance policy of school 'improvement' by 'naming, blaming, and shaming' schools that are judged to be 'failing', has been a major source of teacher stress and impetus for early exit for all kinds of teachers, 'failing' or not (Troman & Woods, 2001). The break-up of the teacher career as it has been known seems set to continue.

Note

1. I am grateful to Martyn Hammersley for suggesting this point. In our own study, external retreatism was therefore the route that some teachers took instead.

References

Acker, S. (1992). Creating careers: Women teachers at work. *Curriculum Enquiry*, 22(2), 141–163.
Apple, N. (1986). *Teachers and texts*. London: Routledge and Kegan Paul.

Ball, S. J. (1994). *Education reform: A critical and post-structural approach*. Buckingham: Open University Press.

Ball, S. J. & Goodson, I. F. (Eds.) (1985). *Teachers' lives and careers*. Lewes: Falmer Press.

Barnard, N. (1999). New TTA chief calls for 'radical' change. In *The Times Educational Supplement* (p. 1). London: The Time Educational Supplement.

Bartlett, D. (1998). *Stress: Perspectives and processes*. Buckingham: Open University Press.

Becker, H. (1966). *Introduction to Shaw, C.R.: The Jack-Roller*. Chicago, IL: University of Chicago Press.

Becker, H. (1977). Personal change in adult life. In B.R. Cosin et al. (Eds.), *School and society*, second edition. London: Routledge and Kegan Paul.

Berger, P. L. (1964). The human shape of work. In G. Esland, G. Salaman, & G. Speakman (Eds.) (1975) *People and Work*. Edinburgh: Holmes McDougal/The Open University Press.

Broadfoot, P. & Osborn, M. (1988). What professional responsibility means to teacher: National contexts and classroom constants. *British Journal of Sociology of Education*, 9(3), 265–288.

Brown, M. & Ralph, S. (1998). Change-linked stress in British teachers. Paper presented to the *British Educational Research Association Conference*. Queen's University, Belfast.

Campbell, R. J. & St. J. Neill, S. R. (1994). *Primary teachers at work*. London: Routledge.

Cherniss, C. (1995). *Beyond burnout: Helping teachers, nurses, therapists and lawyers recover from stress and disillusionment*. New York: Routledge.

Convery, A. (1999). Listening to teachers' stories: Are we sitting comfortably? *Qualitative Studies in Education*, 12(2), 131–146.

Dainton, S. (1999). Think again, Mr Blunkett. *Forum*, 41(2), 43–45.

Densmore, K. (1987). Professionalism, proletarianization and teachers' work. In T. Popkewitz (Ed.), *Critical studies in teacher education*. Lewes: Falmer Press.

Department for Education and Employment (1998). *Teachers meeting the challenge of change*. London: DfEE.

Dinham, S. K. (1992). *Human perspectives on the resignation of teachers from the New South Wales public school system: Towards a model of teacher persistence*. Unpublished Ph.D. thesis. University of New England, Armidale.

Dinham, S. K. & Scott, C. (1996). *The teacher 2000 project: A study of teacher satisfaction*. Nepean: Motivation and Health, Faculty of Education, University of Western Sydney.

Evetts, J. (1987). Becoming career ambitious: The career strategies of married women who became primary headteachers in the 1960s and 1970s. *Educational Review*, 39(1), 15–29.

Ford, M. E. (1992). *Motivating humans, goals, emotions and personal agency beliefs*. London: Sage.

Gardner, J. A. & Oswald, A. J. (1999). *The determinants of job-satisfaction in Britain*. A summary of the research at http://www.warwick.ac.uk/news/pr/business/82

Giddens, A. (1991). *Modernity and self – identity*. Cambridge: Polity Press.

Glaser, B. G. & Strauss, A. L. (1967). *The discovery of grounded theory*. Chicago, IL: Aldine.

Goffman, E. (1963). *Stigma: Notes on the management of spoiled identity*. London: Penguin.

Goffman, E. (1968). *Asylums*. Harmondsworth: Penguin.

Hammersley, M. & Atkinson, P. (1995). *Ethnography: Principles in practice*, second edition. London: Routledge.

Hargreaves, A. (1994). *Changing teachers, changing times: Teachers' work and culture in the postmodern age*. London: Cassell.

Healy, G. (1999). Structuring commitments in interrupted careers: Career breaks, commitment and the life cycle in teaching. *Gender Work and Organization*, 6(4), 185–201.

Howson, J. (1998). 'Situations vacant', school management section. *The Times Educational Supplement* (January 23rd) 24.

Howson, J. (1999). Male primary teachers still elusive. Briefing research focus. *The Times Educational Supplement* (April 2nd) 19.

Huberman, M. (1993). *The lives of teachers*. London: Cassell.

Jeffrey, B. (1998). The intensification of primary teachers' work through new forms of accountability. Paper presented to the *European Educational Research Association Conference*. University of Ljubljana, Slovenia, September.

Jeffrey, B. & Woods, P. (1996). Feeling deprofessionalized: The social construction of emotions during an Ofsted inspection. *Cambridge Journal of Education*, 26(3), 325–343.

Jeffrey, B. & Woods, P. (1998). *Testing teachers: The effect of school inspections on primary teachers*. London: Falmer Press.

Kelchtermans, G. (1995). Teacher stress and burnout: Summary of the *Conference of J. Jacobs Foundation* at Marbach Castle. 2–4 November.

Lawn, M. (1995). Restructuring teaching in the USA and England: Moving towards the differentiated, flexible teacher. *Journal of Education Policy*, 10(4), 347–360.

Lazarus, R. S. (1990). Stress, coping and illness. In H. A. Friedman (Ed.), *Personality and disease*. New York: Wiley.

Leithwood, K. A., Menzies, T., Jantzi, D., & Leithwood, J. (1999). Teacher burnout: A critical challenge for leaders of restructuring schools. In R. Vandenberghe & Hubermanz A.M. (Eds.), *Understanding and preventing teacher burnout*. Cambridge: Cambridge University Press.

Maclean, R. (1992). *Teachers' career and promotional patterns*. London: Falmer.

Maclean, R. & McKenzie, P. (Eds.) (1991). *Australian teachers' careers*. Hawthorn, Victoria: ACER.

Macleod, D. (1998). Happy days are here again? *Guardian Education* (September 29) 4.

Macnicol, J. (1999). A review of Sennet, R. The corrosion of character: The personal consequences of work in the new capitalism. In *The Times Higher Education Supplement* (April 30) 30.

Menter, I. & Thomson, D. with Ross, A., Hutchings, M., & Bedford, D. (1999). Leaving and joining London's teaching force. Paper presented at the *British Educational Research Association Conference*. University of Sussex, Brighton, September.

Nias, J. (1980). *Commitment and motivation in primary teachers*. Cambridge: Cambridge Institute of Education, unpublished paper.

Nias, J. (1989). *Primary teachers talking: A study of teaching as work*. London: Routledge.

Nias, J. (1991). Changing times, changing identities: Grieving for a lost self. In R.G. Burgess (Ed.), *Educational research and evaluation*. London: Falmer Press.

Nias, J. (1995). Teachers' moral purposes; Sources of vulnerability and strength. Paper presented at Conference on *Teacher Burnout*, Marbach, Germany.

Pollard, A., Broadfoot, P., Croll, P., Osborn, M., & Abbot, D. (1994). *Changing English primary schools: The impact of the education reform act at key stage one*. London: Cassell.

Relf, S. & Hobbs, D. (1999). The recruitment and selection of new teachers of mathematics: The needs of secondary schools versus the teacher training agenda. *Research Papers in Education*, 14(2), 165–180.

Richardson, L. (1994). Nine poems, marriage and the family. *Journal of Contemporary Ethnography*, 23(1), 3–13.

Riseborough, G. F. (1981). Teacher careers and comprehensive schooling: An empirical study. *Sociology*, 15(3), 352–381.

Rosenholtz, S. (1989). Workplace conditions that affect quality and commitment: Implications for teacher induction programs. *The Elementary School Journal*, 89(4), 421–439.

Sennett, R. (1998). *The corrosion of character: The personal consequences of work in the new capitalism*. New York: Norton.

Sikes, P., Measor, L., & Woods, P. (1985). *Teacher careers: Crises and continuities*. Lewes: Falmer Press.

Smylie, M. (1999). Teacher stress in a time of reform. In R. Vandenberghe & A.M. Huberman (Eds.), *Understanding and preventing teacher burnout*. Cambridge: Cambridge University Press.

Strauss, A. L. (1971). *Professions, work and careers*. San Francisco, CA: The Sociology Press.

Sutherland, S. (1997). *Teacher education and training: A study, an appendix to* The Dearing Report. London: HMSO.

Travers, C. J. & Cooper, C. L. (1996). *Teachers under pressure: Stress in the teaching profession*. London: Routledge.

Troman, G. (1997). *The effects of restructuring on primary teachers' work: A sociological analysis*. Unpublished Ph.D. thesis, The Open University, Buckingham.

Troman, G. & Woods, P. (2001). *The social construction of teacher stress*. London: Routledge.

Vandenberghe, R. & Huberman, A. M. (1999). *Understanding and preventing teacher burnout*. Cambridge: Cambridge University Press.

Woods, P. (1981). Strategies, commitment and identity: Making and breaking the teacher role. In L. Barton & S. Walker (Eds.), *Schools, teachers and teaching*. Lewes: Falmer Press.

Woods, P. (1983). *Sociology and the school: An interactionist viewpoint*. London: Routledge and Kegan Paul.

Woods, P. (1990). *Teacher skills and strategies*. Buckingham: Open University Press.

Woods, P. (1995a). The intensification of the teacher's self. Presented at the *Conference on Teacher Burnout*. Marbach, November.

Woods, P. (1995b). *Creative teachers in primary schools*. Buckingham: Open University Press.

Woods, P. (1999). Teaching and learning in the new millennium. Keynote address given at *Malaysian Educational Research Association Conference (MERA)*. Malacca, 1–3 December.

Woods, P., Jeffrey, B., Troman, G., & Boyle, M. (1997). *Restructuring schools; reconstructing teachers: Responding to change in the primary school*. Buckingham: Open University Press.

Woodhead, C. (1995). *A question of standards: Finding the balance*. London: Politea.

Wragg. E. C., Wragg, C. M., Haynes, G. S., & Chamberlain, R. P. (1998). *Teaching competence project, occasional paper 1*. University of Exeter School of Education.

Young, S. (1997). Recruitment crisis looms. *The Time Educational Supplement*, 2nd May.

Postscript to 'Careers Under Stress: Teacher Adaptations at a Time of Intensive Reform'

Geoff Troman and Peter Woods

The research which provides the basis for this *Postscript* (*Primary Teacher Identity, Commitment and Career in Performative School Cultures* – PTICC – ESRC – RES-000-23-0748) builds on our previous projects (e.g. Woods et al., 1997) into primary teachers' responses to educational reforms. We charted the adaptations of 'creative teachers' to the National Curriculum and other policy changes during the 1990s (Woods & Jeffrey, 1996), showing teachers both responding to policy prescriptions and playing a creative role in its implementation. Since 1995 three allied projects have focused on teachers developing creative learning (Woods, 1995), school restructuring (Troman, 1997), and the impact of Office for Standards in Education inspections (Jeffrey & Woods, 1998) with a reported growth of constraint, intensification of work, and increasing managerialism; and the social aspects of stress and teachers' careers and identity reconstructions (Troman & Woods, 2001). This current research extends this work by mapping changes in primary teachers' identity, commitment, and perspectives and subjective experiences of occupational career in the context of performative primary school cultures. Cultures of performativity in English primary schools refer to systems and relationships of target-setting, OFSTED inspections, school league tables constructed from pupil test scores, performance management, performance-related pay, threshold assessment, and advanced skills teachers – systems which demand that teachers 'perform' and in which individuals are made accountable. These policy measures, introduced to improve levels of achievement and increased international economic competitiveness, have, potentially, profound implications for the meaning and experience of primary teachers' work; their identities; their commitment to teaching; and how they view their careers.

Research Methods

Fieldwork on the project commenced in May 2005. Following negotiations with headteachers of the schools we conducted initial interviews and recorded life-history details with 5 headteachers (3 female and 2 male) and 37 teachers

M. Bayer et al. (eds.), *Teachers' Career Trajectories and Work Lives,*
Professional Learning and Development in Schools and Higher Education 3,
© Springer Science + Business Media B.V. 2009

(32 female and 5 male) of a range of ages and career stages. These represented the gender proportions in primary schools nationally in that approximately 85% of our sample was female. Analysis of the interview and documentation was ongoing. Our methodological approach was ethnographic. Data collection involving informal conversations and participant observation over 1 school year enabled us to follow identity trajectories, expose some contradictions and developments, as well as gaining deeper analysis. We mapped changes in teachers' experiences and changes in national, local, and school policy and changing schoolwork cultures. An 'intermittent' approach (Jeffrey & Troman, 2005) to data collection was adopted. This mode is one where the length of time spent doing the research is longer, for example, from 3 months to 2 years, but with a very flexible approach to the frequency of site visits. The frequency depends on the researcher selecting particular foci as the research develops and selecting the relevant events. The dominant criterion is depth of study, entailing progressive focusing for a sustained period. Apart from the initial period of broad familiarization, specific rich contexts are selected for examination and interpretation. There is less 'hanging around' as the research develops than there might be in a compressed approach where a continuous length of time in the field is stipulated. This type of research specifies the area for investigation, such as a curriculum, hierarchies, gender relations, micro-politics, student–teacher relations, but the researcher would be continually selective about the place and the people with whom they spent time. This approach enabled us to visit the sample schools at both routine and significant times, high and low points, during the school year to observe and record events where performativity was overt (e.g. threshold payment assessments, pupil testing) and other, potentially, creative occasions (activity weeks, outings, celebrations). The research was based in six primary schools across five English Local Education Authorities: one in the South West, two in the South Midlands, and three contrasting London boroughs. We also achieved some significant contrasts in terms of size and socio-economic status (SES): for instance, large inner-city, large suburban, small rural. These were important influencing factors on teacher identity and teacher and school culture. Hence, data were collected within these school contexts (Rosenholtz, 1989). Our starting conceptions of 'identity', 'commitment', 'career', and 'culture', were derived from Symbolic Interactionist theory developed in our previous researches. Data analysis (theme analysis) was conducted jointly by the two researchers and this was assisted by the use of Atlas Ti. This was necessary to facilitate a comparative dimension since Raggl had conducted the fieldwork in the London schools and Troman had carried out the fieldwork in the Midlands and South West. The preliminary analyses and resulting analytical memos and working papers were then discussed at meetings involving the whole team. This process was facilitated by the overlapping of project personnel with *Creativity and Performativity in Teaching and Learning* – CAPITAL (ESRC – RES-000-23-1281) (See Troman et al., 2007). Literature review was ongoing, facilitated by our involvement in the *Teaching and Learning Research Project* – TLRP – *Changing Teacher Roles, Identities and Professionalism* C-TRIP Seminar Series (See ESRC, 2007).

Turning to Teaching: New Developments in Professional and Teacher Careers

The reforms in educational, economic, and social policies in the 1990s have been accompanied by increases in low teacher morale, stress levels, and high rates of burnout (Troman & Woods, 2001). Consequently, the education system in England in the recent past has experienced problems in recruiting and retaining sufficient teachers (Smithers & Robinson, 2004). The policy response has been to try to increase recruitment and retention through 'modernization' of the workforce, to offer financial incentives for the recruits and the creation of new routes into teaching to attract career changers. These changes are taking place in the context of wholesale reconfiguration of work (Edwards & Wajcman, 2005) and family life in late modernity and widespread Equal Opportunities and Practices such as the Equal Pay Act and Sex Discrimination Act (see Women and Work Commission, 2006) aimed at increasing female participation in the workforce.

As the largest public sector institution in the United Kingdom, education is a key site for studying the context of 'choice' and changes in the identities of professional workers in contemporary society. In this *Postscript* I focus on 18 career changers within our project who entered teaching from different private sector occupations. Of these 15 are women and 3 men. These figures represent the predominantly female composition (85%) of the primary teaching workforce (DFES, 2004). A workforce, which, it is argued, is becoming increasingly 'feminized', at least in terms of numbers (Carrington, 2002; Skelton, 2002). We analysed the choices of these career changers and were interested in the bases on which these choices were made and the impact of gender and other influencing factors on career decisions.

Primary Teacher Careers

Analysis of career changer narratives indicated that career plans were provisional, influenced by personal and family stage, structural factors, and unexpected life events (Acker, 1992). For most women, the 'critical career event' was childbirth. Other turning points involved redundancy and changes in partner's careers. There are more turning points when people reviewed their former career and realized they didn't enjoy it enough or 'wanted more' taking major financial cuts to achieve this. Narratives of our female respondents show 'career women' as mothers had to abandon that career in favour of teaching which fitted better with childcare responsibilities. Also there are those career changers from less secure employment who turned to teaching after displacement.

With the exception of the London schools, pay was seen as satisfactory for dual-earner households. Promotion and increased salary seemed significant to a minority. Teachers, generally, did not express strong interest in promotion and the additional payment that would bring. One said: '[T]he pay is not enough to offset the head's role'. However, those interested in developing a career were engaged in fast-track promotion to management and National Professional Qualification for Headteacher schemes.

An unexpected finding was the number of teachers (18) who had entered teaching after following another occupation. Most of the career changers came into teaching via new routes. Of these, 15 were women and 3 men. We analysed the choices of these career changers in terms of 'turning points' in the participants' lives to assess the extent to which these choices were 'self-initiated', 'forced', or 'structural' (Strauss, 1962; Hodkinson & Sparkes, 1997) and found all three represented in our sample. The high number of career changers in our sample (42%) indicates that it is now, perhaps, more common to change careers than it used to be (Edwards & Wajcman, 2005).

The data led us to develop the following categories of 'turners': The *Parent Turners*, *Self-Initiated Turners* and *Displaced Turners*, corresponding to the forced, self-initiated, and structural indicated above. In each category there appears to be a general level of satisfaction with the change, albeit for different reasons.

Parent Turners

Teaching traditionally attracted female workers with its reputation as a 'woman's job' (Steedman, 1986), fitting in with family life unlike private sector occupations from where career changers came. More suited to parental responsibilities there were also gains in moving to a culture in which care and humane relations were considerations. Teaching in performative cultures was not without its tensions between managing a professional role and the family. But, in contrast, in other occupations juggling the two roles was harder. Hannah, a former journalist, found the period following child-birth 'very hard because of the hours in journalism' which involved '6 o'clock shifts in the morning' and having to work on weekends. She explained that 'it was a night-mare to arrange childcare'. And that working part-time would have meant that 'you would have lost so much respect'. So 'you've got to be able to do the hours basically' There were also problems for those who had taken pay cuts reflecting the Women and Work Commission Report (2006) which states that despite policy changes the 'opportunity gap for women remains' and women 'are crowded into a narrow range of lower paying occupations, mainly those available part time' (p. 19).

Self-Initiated Turners

Career changers who left well-paid 'career' jobs turned to teaching because they did not enjoy their previous professions, got bored, or 'wanted to learn again'. Theresa worked in finance, for 10 years and 'got to quite a high level', when she was 'put up for a big promotion' to become a senior requiring 'taking on more responsibility'. During this process she re-evaluated her career and 'felt I'm not interested ... enough in business and finance'. One main 'problem was it was such long hours' and because of 'tight time scales' she had to 'work more than full-time, there is no way to do it part-time'. Theresa stated: 'I was more ambitious when I was younger' but at 30 she realized 'there are too many sacrifices' and 'I should do something which I enjoy'. In a flexible market place teaching is benefiting from a group who bring experience from other professions.

Displaced Turners

Some career changers experienced a structural turning when facing redundancy. Jan as a flight attendant 'got made redundant after September 11th' (9/11/2001) together with 500 colleagues. Jan's narrative illustrates how much personal decisions can be influenced by structural global events. Looking back at her former career she said 'I'd had enough of travelling' pointing out that being a flight attendant can be restrictive by age, because 'airlines are phasing older employees out'. Jan is an example of turners who enjoyed being a teacher: 'I really found my niche'. She 'decided to give teaching a try' in order to work more creatively.

'New' Teacher Careers

This influx of turners is bringing new commitments, values, and expertise to primary schools. However, on the evidence presented here, primary teaching may no longer be considered as a job for life. Schools, like other organizations in post-industrial society, are no longer bureaucratic institutions offering bureaucratic careers in which individuals invest their 'selves' for a working lifetime. Initial and career-change decisions were characterized by a great deal of uncertainty around choices (Duncan, 2003) and preferences (Hakim, 2000) of career in post-industrial society (Hage & Powers, 1992). In terms of portfolio careers, then, we must ask what kinds of commitment(s) were the teachers investing in their previous occupations and what happened to it.

Work also may no longer be the major area of human activity around which personal and occupational identities are formed. In this respect then, the primary schools of our research can be said to have undergone a major change in the identities, commitments and careers of those working in them since our research reported in *Careers Under Stress* was conducted.

References

Acker, S. (1992). Creating careers: Women teachers at work. *Curriculum Enquiry*, 22(2), 141–163.
Carrington, B. (2002). A quintessentially feminine domain? *Educational Studies*, 28(3), 287–303.
Department for Education and Skills (2004). *Statistics of Education: Schools in England*. London: DfES. Accessed at http://www.dcsf.gov.uk/rsgateway/DB/VOL/v000495/schools_04_final.pdf/

Edwards, P. & Wajcman, J. (2005) *The politics of working life.* Oxford: Oxford University Press.

ESRC Teaching and Learning Research Project (2007). 'Changing Teacher Roles, Identities and Professionalism, (C-Trip) Seminar Series, Annotated bibliography and annex on the historical development of scholarship on teachers' work and teacher professionalism before 2000. accessed at: http://www.tlrp.org/themes/seminar/gewirtz/contact.html (with Gewirtz, S., Mahony, P., Hextall, I. and Cribb, A.)

Hage, J. & Powers, C. (1992). *Post-industrial lives: Roles and relationships in the 21st century.* Newbury Park: Sage.

Hakim, C. (2000). *Work-lifestyle choices in the 21st century.* Oxford: Oxford University Press.

Hodkinson, P. & Sparkes, A. (1997). Careership: A sociological theory of career decision making. *British Journal of Sociology of Education,* 18(1), 29–44.

Jeffrey, B. & Troman, G. (2004). Time for ethnography. *British Educational Research Journal,* 30(4), 535–548.

Jeffrey, B. & Woods, P. (1998). *Testing teachers: The effect of school inspections on primary teachers.* London: Falmer Press.

Rosenholtz, S. (1989) *Teachers' workplace.* New York: Longman.

Skelton, C. (2002). The 'feminisation' of schooling or 're-masculinising' primary education. *International Studies in Sociology of Education,* 12(1), 77–96.

Smithers, A. & Robinson, P. (2004). *Teacher turnover, wastage and destinations,* Research Report No. 553, University of Liverpool.

Steedman, C. (1986). *Landscape for a good woman.* London: Virago.

Strauss, A. (1962). Transformations of identity. In A.M. Rose (Ed.), *Human behaviour and social processes: An interactionist approach.* London: Routledge and Kegan Paul.

Troman, G. (1997). *The effects of restructuring on primary teachers' work: A sociological analysis,* unpublished Ph.D. thesis. The Open University, Buckingham.

Troman, G. & Woods, P. (2001). *Primary teachers' stress.* London: RoutledgeFalmer.

Troman, G., Jeffrey, B., & Raggl, A. (2007). Creativity and performativity policies in primary school cultures. *Journal of Education Policy,* 22(5), 549–572, September.

Women and Work Commission (2006). *Shaping a fairer future.* London.

Woods, P. (1995). *Creative teachers in primary schools.* Buckingham: Open University Press.

Woods, P. & Jeffrey, R. J. (1996). *Teachable moments: The art of teaching in primary schools.* Buckingham: Open University Press.

Chapter 7
The Careers of Urban Teachers: A Synthesis of Findings from UCLA's Longitudinal Study of Urban Educators

Karen Hunter Quartz

Educating young people in Los Angeles – and other massive, diverse cities throughout the world – requires the commitment and hard work of many, particularly teachers. Students in urban centers face a set of historically rooted challenges, including living in poverty and densely populated neighborhoods, attending large overcrowded schools often miles from their home, learning a language different than their parents, and many more. With notable exceptions, urban schools have been unable to attract, support, and retain a highly qualified workforce to address these challenges. Urban schools lose an average of one fifth of their teaching staff every year (Ingersoll, 2003a). In a typical Los Angeles urban high school, this might translate into 50 teachers coming and going each fall and spring. And in many of these schools the uncredentialled teachers outnumber those professionally prepared to do a good job. Imagine the flux, the induction challenge, and the disruption and collegial challenge to those teachers committed to a campus for the long haul.

In 1995, this dire situation led my colleagues at the University of California, Los Angeles (UCLA) to create an experimental teacher education program to recruit, prepare, and retain teachers in Los Angeles' most challenging schools. This program was part of a new center, named "Center X," to capture both the intersection of research and practice as well as its roots as an activist community. First conceived in response to upheaval and self-examination stemming from race-related uprisings in Los Angeles (Oakes, 1995), Center X is now a community of more than 200 educators working across 12 programs: two graduate credential programs and ten professional development initiatives. Together, these educators work to transform public schooling to create a more just, equitable, and humane society. This work involves supporting the learning of educators, from novices to accomplished practitioners; partnering with schools, districts, and communities; and integrating research and practice (Quartz, Priselac & Franke, in press).

From 2000 to 2007, I participated in a research group[1] to study the careers of more than a thousand urban teachers prepared by Center X's experimental teacher education program. Using both quantitative and qualitative methods,

M. Bayer et al. (eds.), *Teachers' Career Trajectories and Work Lives,*
Professional Learning and Development in Schools and Higher Education 3,
© Springer Science + Business Media B.V. 2009

my colleagues and I conducted a range of studies to answer the following questions:

1. What is the effect of specialized teacher preparation on retention?
2. What is the effect of career advancement on attrition among highly qualified urban educators?
3. What individual and school characteristics are associated with retention in high-poverty schools?

In this chapter, I synthesize the main findings of our longitudinal study and discuss promising policy responses for curbing the attrition of well-prepared urban teachers.

Part One: UCLA's Longitudinal Study of Urban Educators, 2000–2007

Research Context

Each fall, Center X's Teacher Education Program welcomes 170 new novice teachers – each eager to join the profession of education. The program, an intensive, 2-year preservice program leading to state certification and a Master's degree in Education, works to specifically prepare its participants for careers in urban, high-poverty schools (Oakes, 1996; Oakes & Lipton, 2003). Part of a growing national movement towards multicultural teacher education, Center X creates opportunities for teacher learning that "challenge the ideological underpinnings of traditional programs, place knowledge about culture and racism front and center in the teacher education curriculum, include teaching for social justice as a major outcome, and value the cultural knowledge of local communities" (Cochran-Smith, 2003).

Prior to certification, Center X students are required to take coursework in the selection and adaptation of materials and learning theory and are required to spend at least 120h observing experienced teachers in their classrooms before engaging in their own practice teaching. In addition, they spend 15 weeks of supervised classroom teaching and receive feedback on that teaching. An analysis of national data revealed that approximately 9% of first-year teachers in the United States enter the profession with a similar level of preparation (Lyons, 2007). We interpret the results of our study as generalizable to this population of well-prepared teachers, with one exception. Although most Center X graduates are female (79%), which is similar to national trends, the group's ethnic and racial diversity contrasts sharply with national norms (though it reflects California's increasing diversity): 31% are White, 27% are Latino/Latina, 6% are African-American, and 31% are Asian. This is significant given the growing "demographic divide" in the United States between increasingly diverse student populations and a still overwhelmingly White, middle-class teaching force.

Most of the program's teaching candidates are graduates of selective undergraduate institutions, and many grew up in the same type of urban communities they seek to serve as educators. In the United States, fewer than 6% of all education graduates express a desire for inner-city placements (The National Partnership for Excellence and Accountability in Teaching, 2000), yet for Center X graduates, teaching in such schools defines their professional identity. The majority of Center X candidates report that they are motivated by activist ideals. For example, nearly three quarters of incoming students stated that their belief that "teaching helps change the world and further social justice" was extremely important to their decision to pursue a teaching credential.

Study Overview

Each spring, for 6 years, we sent surveys to Center X graduates in order to track their career retention and movement. These surveys also provided information regarding the factors that keep teachers teaching and push and pull them away from the classroom – allowing for a deeper understanding of the motivators behind teachers' professional decisions. Additionally, surveys were also administered to participants just prior to entering and exiting UCLA's program, in order to better track the perceptions and intentions of teachers just starting their preparation and their employment as teachers. These survey data were matched to national data in an attempt to determine the effect of the program. In addition, a supplementary survey was created to understand the effect of social networks on career advancement and retention. Qualitative interview data were also collected to further understand the many factors that shape teachers' careers over time. Further detail is available in the project's technical report and papers (Quartz & TEP, 2003; Quartz et al., 2005, 2008, 2009; Anderson & Olsen, 2006; Olsen & Anderson, 2007; Lyons, 2007; Thomas, 2005, 2007; Masyn et al., submitted). In what follows, I present the findings from these studies according to themes that correspond to our three main research questions.

Findings Theme 1: Preparing to Stay

Researching the effect of specialized teacher preparation on retention involves a number of challenges. First, constructing an appropriate matched sample is difficult. The dearth of common measures across teacher education programs coupled with the challenge of capturing differences in culture and pedagogical principles means that comparisons across programs must rely on a relatively narrow and straightforward set of measures. In addition, it is difficult to control for the characteristics and motivations of individual students beyond gender, race/ethnicity, age, etc. Finally, as we detail in our related studies, career development and retention is a complex social phenomenon explained by factors that extend far beyond an individual's formal preparation to become a teacher.

Considering these limitations, we designed a comparative study of Center X graduates and similar teachers nationwide in their first through fifth year of the profession. This study was led by Lyons (2007) who created binary and multinomial logistic regression models of a national sample of beginning teachers, the data for which were extracted from the 1999–2000 National Center for Education Statistics' Schools and Staffing Survey (SASS) and its companion Teacher Follow-up Survey (TFS). The SASS/TFS databases comprise the largest set of data available on public school teachers in the United States; the 1999–2000 database contains responses from a probability sample of 42,086 public school teachers, representing the nearly 3 million across the nation (weighted $N = 2,984,782$). Data on the quality of respondents' teacher preparation experiences are captured by SASS according to a set of questions regarding the inclusion of coursework in the selection and adaptation of materials, coursework in learning theory or psychology, classroom observations, feedback on teaching, and 10 or more weeks of practice teaching. The TFS data capture retention in 1-year intervals. Using these variables as well as the credential type a teacher earned, Lyons studied the effect of Center X's specialized program on retention.

Before I turn to Lyons' findings, it is crucial to define what we mean by retention. Our studies include five different categories of retention and its correlate attrition. First, teachers are retained by educational role, i.e. they decide to remain classroom teachers (*teacher stayers*) or leave to take on a variety of other roles, within the education profession (*role changers*) or out of education entirely (*leavers*). We call this role retention and its study provides insight into the larger educational workforce. Second, teachers are retained by school or workplace; they decide to stay at particular schools (*same school stayers*) or move to another school (*movers*). We call this workplace retention and its study provides insight into the creation of stable professional learning communities at school sites.

In Lyons' study, important differences emerged across these five retention categories. The results from regression analyses of the national data allowed her to predict the rates of Center X graduates' retention in and out of the classroom and the field of education. Differences in the predicted and actual retention rates of Center X graduates served as the bases for judging the impact of the program. Lyons was able to control for school characteristics related to student poverty using a three-category variable based on the percentage of students who qualify for free or reduced price lunch. This variable allowed her to distinguish between schools that were highly impacted by poverty (i.e. greater than 80% poor students), moderately impacted (40–79%), and slightly impacted (less than 40%). This is significant because Center X places its students exclusively in high-poverty schools. Therefore, controlling for school poverty in this way allowed Lyons to test the hypothesis that Center X graduates would be more likely than others to stay in these challenging schools.

Predictions are based on three separate regression analyses for teacher and other role retention and workplace retention. For more detail, see Lyons (2007).

Table 7.1 Predicted and actual fifth-year cumulative retention rates for Center X graduates

	Predicted (%)	Actual (%)	Actual: Predicted
Role retention			
Stay in teaching	67.8	59.8	0.88
Change roles in education	30.2	28.4	0.94
Workplace retention			
Stay in same school	11.2	29.3	2.62

As Table 7.1 summarizes, Center X seems to have had a positive impact on workplace retention, but not role retention. Given their characteristics, workplaces, and intensive preparation, Lyons' model, based on the national SASS/TFS data, predicted that 67.8% of Center X graduates would be retained as full-time classroom teachers after 5 years when in fact only 59.8% were. Alongside this result, Lyons found that Center X graduates were slightly less likely over time to change roles within the field of education than similar teachers nationwide. However, looking at the annual – not cumulative – role-changing rate, Lyons found that from their fifth to sixth career year, Center X graduates were four times more likely to change roles than similarly prepared teachers. One interpretation of these findings is that Center X graduates enter the program with career advancement in mind and/or are encouraged by the program and others to take on leadership positions beyond the classroom. More discussion on this issue follows in the next section.

The results for workplace retention are more promising for Center X. If they decide to stay in teaching, Center X graduates are much more likely than similar teachers nationwide to stay put in the same school over time. This finding has important implications for the organizational stability and potential reform of urban schools. As Ingersoll persuasively argues, also based on analyses of the SASS/TFS data, what schools should be concerned with is turnover – any outflow of teachers from a school – not simply attrition from the profession. Ingersoll focuses his analyses on the school-level measure of turnover because the movement of teachers from school to school, although not representing a net loss from the "system," creates important transaction costs and fuels organizational instability. In 1999, for instance, Ingersoll calculated that nearly 290,000 left the occupation altogether (Ingersoll, 2003b) and approximately 250,000 more teachers moved or migrated from one school to another – more often away from "hard to staff" high-poverty schools (Ingersoll, 2003a). Overall, this represents a turnover rate of roughly 15% for all schools and 20% for high-poverty schools.

Although our research did not include school-level measures of turnover, we would expect based on our data that over time the heightened workplace retention of Center X graduates would contribute to decreased turnover in several urban schools across Los Angeles. As suggested above, many factors contribute to teachers' career decisions. Lyons' comparative analysis of Center X graduates with similar teachers nationwide suggests that specialized urban teacher preparation may contribute to workplace retention, particularly in high-poverty schools.

Findings Theme 2: Sanctioned Attrition

Focusing in on the issue of role retention allowed us to study the proportion of teacher attrition that is due to career advancement. This is a form of sanctioned attrition that is rarely included in the study of teacher retention. Most retention research focuses on the factors that contribute to teacher dissatisfaction and hence attrition. According to this essentially negative conception, dissatisfaction pushes teachers away from the classroom. In contrast, by distinguishing between leaving teaching, changing schools, and changing roles, our study adds another dimension to what may motivate teachers' career moves. Lack of resources or poor administration may drive a teacher from an urban school to a suburban school, but some other factor entirely may prove influential in a teacher's decision to become a district official. As discussed below, our data suggest that many teachers make a positive decision to change roles, perhaps based on the increased "influence" that other positions in the field of education promise. Rather than being pushed, these teachers are pulled out of the classroom. Our study population of diverse, high-achieving individuals working in challenging urban settings provided a unique opportunity to learn more about this form of sanctioned attrition.

Figure 7.1 describes the proportion of attrition among Center X graduates that is due to changing roles within the field of education. After 8 years, this proportion is 70%; that is, seven out of ten teachers who leave the classroom after 8 years do so to pursue another professional role. Looking across career years, what is

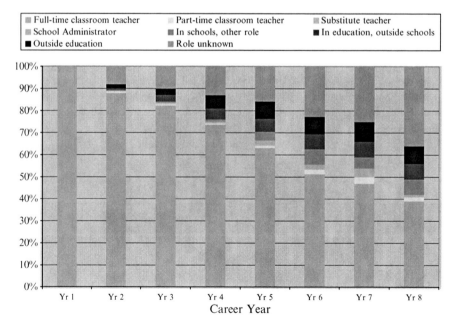

Fig. 7.1 Role retention of Center X graduates by career year

the distribution of roles for those who make such a career move? As illustrated, a substantial proportion of role changing within this population is career movement outside the kindergarten to 12th Grade (K–12) educational system, the publicly funded set of schools and districts in the United States that serve 5- to 18-year-old students. Also significant is the proportion of role changers who reported "working in K–12 school/district in another role." Not surprisingly, our data indicate a range of roles within these latter two categories. We are able to detail some of these roles based on handwritten explanations and survey items that probed the nature of professional activities and leadership roles taken on by respondents.

Not all respondents chose to further specify their roles by handwriting additional information on the survey; however, of those who did, "working in K–12 school/district in another role" included, for example, work as an instructional (literacy or math) coach, a bilingual coordinator, a dual-language immersion program coordinator, or a director of an after-school program at a family resource center. Examples of "working in education outside K–12 school/district" included work as a college professor, a college academic advisor, a museum educator, a curriculum developer, an educational software developer, or a marketing director for an educational media company.

Survey data about professional activities showed that both categories of role changers (i.e. in and out of K–12 schools) were positively correlated with conducting "observational visits to other schools" and "presenting at workshops, conferences or training sessions." Role changers "inside K–12 schools in another role" reported taking on a variety of leadership roles: 59% assumed the duties of trainers or staff developers; 52% reported coaching; and 41% reported coordinating testing, technology, beginning teacher support, or other programs. Engaging in these types of professional activities seemed to set the stage for a role change within the profession.

In addition to enumerating and describing the variety of non-teaching roles into which the teachers in this study moved, we are able to document the patterns of movement, or the "pathways" that teachers take out of the classroom and into other educational roles, and then sometimes back to the classroom again. In an attempt to understand the dynamics of these career pathways, we mapped movement across, or through, roles over time. In an analysis of 432 Center X graduates for whom we had complete role data on at least 3 but as many as 8 *consecutive* career years each year, there were 57 unique observed pathways – underscoring the fluidity and movement within careers in education. Of those graduate in this sample, 95% had been teaching for 3 consecutive years at the year 3 mark. Of the graduates for whom we had 7 consecutive years of data, 68% had been teaching for all 7 years at the year 7 mark. In total, "stayers" like these who remained in classroom teaching over their entire observed pathway (between 3 and 8 career years beginning in the first year of teaching) represented 76% of the sample, whereas those who changed roles or left one or more times represented 24% of the sample. Of those who changed roles or left one or more times, 59% changed roles/left once and 41% changed roles/left two or more times.

Studying graduates' career pathways over time complicates the issue of retention because it calls into question retention rates reported in cross-sectional studies. Consider the career pathway of a person who teaches for 1 year, leaves in year 2, returns to teach in another school in year 3, moves to the district office in years 5 and 6, and returns to the classroom in year 7. Depending on the time frame of the cross-sectional research, this person could be considered a stayer, leaver, mover, or role changer.

Going beyond a description of role-retention rates to understand the individual-level characteristics that correlate with this form of sanctioned attrition, we constructed a discrete time survival model to capture the influence of race/ethnicity, gender, credential type, and age on the timing of the *first* departure from full-time classroom teaching. Consistent with prior research that White teachers leave teaching at higher rates than teachers of color, the Latino teachers in our population had a significantly lower attrition rate from education than White teachers. However, when we examined differences within the competing risk model between those who leave and those who change roles, we found that race/ethnicity had very little effect on role changing. This finding may reflect the wide array of opportunities open to our young, well-prepared, and diverse subject population, many of whom work in a predominantly Latino school district. Being pulled out of teaching by leadership and advancement opportunities may be especially likely among this particular graduate population given their placement in schools that tend, like most high-poverty urban schools, to have a relative scarcity of well-prepared and veteran educators. In such circumstances, there is perhaps an increased likelihood of being "cherry-picked" into the advancement pipeline.

Unlike race, gender and credential type did have an effect on role changing. After year 3, men were more likely to change roles than women, suggesting that even among our well-prepared sample of teachers, traditional gender bias around career advancement may be an issue. Assuming that most role changing is movement up the career ladder, men seem to be more likely than women to be promoted. Teaching has a long history as a female-dominated profession in which men have been overrepresented in higher status positions. Our research informs this trend. We also found that teachers with single-subject (secondary) credentials were more likely to leave teaching for a role change in education than their colleagues who hold multiple-subject (elementary) credentials, suggesting that elementary and secondary schools cultivate different norms and opportunities for career advancement.

With respect to age, we found that younger teachers were much more likely to change roles than to leave education entirely – pointing to a broader theme about age and generation. Today's teachers may be entering the profession with long-term career goals that differ from those of previous generations of career educators. As Johnson & The Project on the Next Generation of American Teachers (2004) and her colleagues have written about the next generation of teachers, "Those who consider teaching today have an array of alternative career options, many offering greater social status, providing more comfortable work environments, and offering far higher pay than teaching" (p. 19). A myriad of factors explain this apparent generational turn in the educational workforce. In three related follow-up studies, we looked deeper at this phenomenon of role changing within our study population.

In their qualitative study of 15 Center X graduates, Olsen and Anderson (2007) probed teachers' reasons for anticipated role changes. Jiao, one of the fifth-year teachers they followed, was planning to leave for graduate school and reported always having viewed teaching as a "stepping stone" – in his case, to a district position working with curriculum and instruction. Although Jiao reported that he would have taken this path regardless, there are several aspects of teaching with which he expressed frustration. He described the profession as "stagnant," especially concerning salary and status: "In the business world, you can always become an 'associate-' this and then you can become 'vice-' this and then 'director.' In teaching, you're just a teacher." Olsen and Anderson outlined other reported reasons for role changing, including the desire to make a bigger impact in urban education, family pressure to achieve higher status, and more typical career dissatisfaction variables such as the lack of administrative support and the emotional and physical toll of day-to-day teaching. The authors also noted the potential role of professional development and leadership opportunities in influencing the construction of career pathways that differentiate and expand teachers' work and influence while keeping them closely connected to the schools where they are arguably most needed (Anderson & Olsen, 2006).

In a second study, Thomas (2005) explored the career-related discussion networks (i.e. who talked to whom about their career choices) of a sub-sample of this study population. Thomas found that social capital – as manifested in the age, occupational, and status-level diversity of a teacher's professional contacts – was positively associated with role changing. Teachers who changed roles were those who maintained and mobilized a diverse group of professional contacts who tended to occupy non-teaching positions in the educational system, whereas teachers who continued full-time classroom teaching tended to be closely linked to their in-school colleagues and to value collegiality highly.

In a third qualitative study (Quartz et al., 2009), we analyzed the careers of seven Center X graduates – all of whom had changed roles at least once. We framed their careers in the context of the history, structures, and culture of schooling, making sense of their efforts to exercise professional autonomy, build supportive social networks, and make a difference in the lives of urban students and communities. In a monograph for teachers, we examined how these seven educators engaged in a common struggle: how to stay connected to the core work of teaching – student learning – in a profession that rewards them for taking on roles and responsibilities beyond the classroom.

Although largely hidden from policy view, role changing, as documented above, is a form of sanctioned attrition that should be added to the landscape of teacher retention research. Policymakers currently struggle with how best to sanction or encourage attrition among "bad" teachers, yet there is virtually no attention paid to all the ways that the educational system sanctions attrition of the nation's most well-prepared teachers.

Findings Theme 3: Professional Learning Communities

Johnson and Birkeland (2003), in their qualitative study of teacher retention, found that many teachers move around voluntarily in search of "schools that make good teaching possible" (p. 21). This is often a search for supportive principals and colleagues, reasonable teaching assignments and workloads, and sufficient resources. Given the scarcity of these conditions in high-poverty schools, teacher migration patterns typically flow from less affluent to more affluent school contexts. As described above, Center X graduates are less likely to make such a move than similarly prepared educators. What explains their staying power was the topic of the research group's final analysis.

Within our population of diverse, specially prepared teachers, we found two individual attributes associated with workplace retention: gender and race. Results from a longitudinal multinomial logistic regression model suggest that among active teachers in a given year, men are less likely than women in our population to move from school to school or leave teaching for the following year. Traditional gender differences such as childbearing may explain this finding of higher workplace and teacher attrition between years among women, although we suspect there are other factors that contribute as well. This complicates our understanding of the influence of gender in retention as our findings from Theme 2 also demonstrated men being more likely than women, upon their first departure from teaching, to change roles within education. We also found that Latino teachers were less likely than White teachers to move from school to school or leave teaching, as noted above. This finding echoes prior research on the heightened retention of teachers of color, yet it has particular significance in Los Angeles, a city that is predominantly Latino. Many Center X graduates grew up in Los Angeles schools and remain teaching in these same schools as a form of service to their communities; as one teacher explained: "My calling to become a teacher stems from my challenging experiences as a student in the Los Angeles public school system. I attended one of the worst academic performing schools in the state. I am determined to provide quality education and work to keep children from falling through the cracks as I almost did."

In addition to the individual characteristics of "same school stayers," we also found that student disadvantage contributed to workplace retention. Our findings stand in stark contrast to a number of studies that have found teachers systematically move away from schools with low levels of achievement and high concentrations of poor children of color (Carroll et al., 2000; Hanushek et al., 2004; Lankford et al., 2002). For our population of Center X graduates, just the opposite was true. If a Center X graduate were either going to stay or change schools but remain teaching, he or she is less likely to move to a different workplace to continue teaching if he or she is currently teaching in a high-priority school. Using a latent class cluster analysis, we define a "high priority" school in terms of student disadvantage in the educational system – students who are most in need of good teachers. The measurement model for the latent class variable, a three-category priority school status variable (high, medium, and low priority), was based on four school-level measures: (1) average percentage of students in the school receiving free or reduced price lunch (family socio-economic status or SES); (2) average percentage of students whose parents have some education beyond high school (parent education); (3) average percentage of students with English Language Learner status (English proficiency); and (4) average school base Academic Performance Index score (academic achievement). In the construction of this variable, our intent was to distinguish between schools that are a priority for teacher retention with respect to student disadvantage without directly confounding, in our measurement model, other correlated school-level workplace characteristics that may also, independently, influence teacher and workplace retention.

Our finding that Center X graduates are less likely to move away from high-priority schools contributes to research that disentangles school working conditions from student characteristics as factors pushing teachers out of certain schools or away from teaching altogether. For example, although attributes of students appear to influence attrition in many studies, when Loeb et al. (2005) added district salary levels and teachers' ratings of working conditions – including large class sizes, facilities and space problems, multi-track schools, and lack of textbooks – to student variables in their model, they found that student characteristics become insignificant predictors of teacher turnover. Similarly, Horng (2004) found that when teachers were asked to make trade-offs among school and student characteristics, the former were often considered more important than the latter. To explore this idea further, we developed a model that included school priority status as well as measures of workplace quality.

The workplace measures we included were based on publicly available California state data on schools. The following school-related variables were considered: (1) school type (elementary versus secondary); (2) multitrack year-round school; (3) percentage of teachers at school with full teaching credentials; and (4) percentage of teachers at school with emergency teaching credentials. We found that while school type and schedule did not predict workplace retention, the qualifications of the teaching staff were significantly associated with school movement as well as role changing. Controlling for the priority status of the school as well as other covariates in the model, we discovered that if a Center X graduate were either going to stay or change schools but remain teaching, he or she is more likely to move to a different workplace to continue teaching or shift into another role in education the higher the percentage of teachers with emergency credentials at the current workplace. Figures 7.2a and b depict the estimated outcome category probabilities for two levels of percentage of teachers with emergency teaching credentials (0% and 50%) at the sample means for the other covariates.

We interpret these findings as powerful evidence that highly qualified urban teachers are motivated and able to stay teaching in schools where they are most needed – high-priority schools – especially if they are joined by others who are similarly prepared for the challenge. Our survey data further elucidate these findings by exploring teachers' motivations for remaining in teaching at a given school versus moving, changing roles, or leaving education all together. Based on tests of associations across all individuals and career year intervals, we found:

- Teachers were less likely to *change roles* between 2 consecutive years if they found their careers fulfilling and challenging, if they found their work flexible and conducive to parenting/family life and reported liking the school calendar

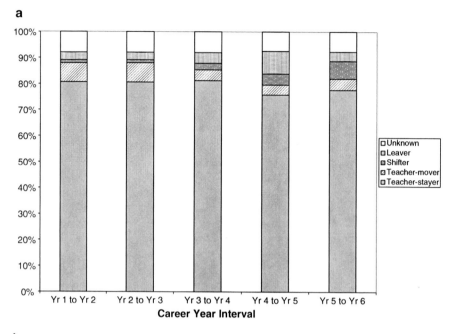

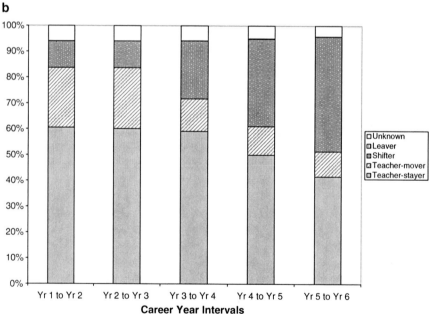

Fig. 7.2 (**a**) Model-estimated proportions for teachers in schools with 0% teachers with emergency credentials. (**b**) Model-estimated proportions for teachers in schools with 50% teachers with emergency credentials

and work hours, if they were pleased with opportunities for professional advancement, and if they were intellectually challenged by their daily work.

- Teachers were less likely to *move schools* if they were committed to working in a low-income community, and if they felt professionally respected by students and parents.
- Teachers were less likely to *move schools or change roles* if they reported a lot of autonomy in their jobs, if they reported strong administrative support and leadership, if they had good relationships with their colleagues, if they felt safe in their primary workplace, and if they felt professionally respected by colleagues.
- Teachers were less likely to *leave education* if they reported feeling respected by society as a whole.
- Teachers were less likely to *move schools*, *change roles*, or *leave* if they reported feeling hopeful that their school would improve over time.

Together, these survey findings contribute to the substantial body of research that articulates the working conditions associated with teacher retention. Teachers stay in urban schools where they feel professionally respected, challenged, and supported; where they have autonomy and voice; and where they feel they can make a difference in the lives of their students. How to create and sustain these schools is the challenge.

Part Two: Promising Policy Responses

The National Commission for Teaching and America's Future (NCTAF) has framed the key to solving the teacher retention crisis as "finding a way for school systems to organize the work of qualified teachers so they can collaborate with their colleagues in developing strong learning communities that will sustain them as they become more accomplished teachers" (NCTAF, 2003, p. 7). Our research confirms that such professional learning communities and collegial networks contribute to workplace retention. This long-term policy goal represents a broader professionalism movement that has deep roots in American education. As Zeichner (2003) describes, it is "the quest to establish a profession of teaching through the articulation of a knowledge base for teaching based on educational research and professional judgment" (p. 498). The professionalism movement integrates four policy arenas – targeted teacher recruitment, specialized preparation, induction, and career advancement – in its effort to secure a more stable, qualified workforce for the schools most in need of good teachers (Quartz et al., 2005). These policy arenas seek to create a professional culture of teaching and schools where learning is not packaged into stages or programs but instead is viewed as a continuum that lasts throughout a teacher's career. Instead of isolating, bureaucratic structures, schools are viewed as professional learning communities – sites where both students and teachers can grow and develop.

On one hand, this move to heighten teacher professionalism is a hopeful and far-reaching solution to the retention crisis. It seeks to elevate the status of teachers by setting up structures and regulations that ensure high-quality work supported by continual learning. With these structures and regulations come new programs and roles for educators, both within and outside the educational system. Specialized teacher education programs such as Center X are created. Induction coordinators are hired, trained, and supervised. Staff developers proliferate within districts and across a staggering array of educational organizations. Instructional coaches are recruited to facilitate school-wide reform. Organizations such as the National Board for Professional Teaching Standards are created to support teachers. Evaluators are brought in to gauge the success of new packages and programs. And the agency for all of this lies within an entity we call "the educational system." As Jiao observed, "in teaching, you're just a teacher," yet the larger system is ripe with opportunities for professional advancement. As described above, most of the attrition we studied was due to teachers' changing roles within education. Moreover, national work-force data reveals that these opportunities for role changing are on the rise.

Of pressing policy concern is the extent to which the professional benefits of role changing outweigh the direct costs of attrition to schools and students. One response to this concern is the new vision of teaching espoused by Darling-Hammond (1997) and others that includes "complementary hyphenated roles" for teachers, allowing them to grow and contribute professionally beyond the classroom but still spend part of their day or week teaching students. For example, these advocates recommend creating new leadership roles for teachers, facilitated by flexible administrative structures that allow teachers to take on new roles, such as preservice mentor, professional development coordinator, or university instructor without leaving the classroom entirely. This vision has gained momentum in several professional communities throughout the United States. The Teacher Leaders Network, for example represents a growing national community dedicated to supporting teachers' growth and development in research and advocacy roles that extend beyond the classroom without stripping teachers of their core identity and work as educators. Even teachers' unions have advocated for a fresh look at long-standing career and advancement structures.

Traditionally charged with protecting the interests of teachers, union activists are trying to reenvision what it means to support teachers and their profession. For example, Rochester's Career in Teaching program advocates for flexible structures that will allow teachers to have it all – career advancement tied to their core work as teachers. This program includes four stages of teacher development: intern, resident, professional, and lead teacher. Here, advancement does not mean leaving the class-room. Lead teachers, who are selected by a joint panel of teachers and administrators, take on leadership roles such as mentor, staff developer, and curriculum specialist, but continue their accomplished teaching at least half time. In return, lead teachers have the potential to earn more than administrators. As Urbanski and O'Connell (2003) explain, this staffing framework provides "an opportunity for exemplary teachers to inspire excellence in the profession, share their knowledge and expertise with others, and actively participate in instructional decision-making without leaving."

Based on these developments and the findings from our longitudinal retention study of Center X graduates, UCLA is currently partnering with the Los Angeles

Unified School District, the local teachers' union, and several community-based organizations to create retention-oriented staffing policies within a new urban public school, Bruin Community School.[2] These policies will include opportunities for teachers to develop hybrid careers, taking on complementary multiple roles simultaneously or sequentially. Many of the Center X teachers we studied assumed many roles at once – layering on responsibilities beyond the classroom using structures such as release time, summer vacation, and sometimes evenings and weekends. Others opted to move out of the classroom for short or extended periods, on special assignments or sabbaticals, and then return to their teaching posts renewed and enriched. Developing site-based structures to facilitate these hybrid careers requires extra resources and flexibility in addition to sustained professional development that supports teachers' learning over time. These are investments in human capital that Bruin Community School expects to translate into heightened teacher retention and quality. Staffed by Center X graduates and other highly qualified urban educators, UCLA is hoping to create a school that builds on the strong commitment of teachers to serve high-poverty urban students and communities over the long haul – rewarding their retention within a professional learning community that supports them to make a difference in the lives of urban students and communities.

Notes

1. Other members of this research group included Katherine Masyn, Kimberly Barraza Lyons, Brad Olsen, Lauren Anderson, and Andrew Thomas.
2. For more information about this school, see http://bruincommunityschool.gseis.ucla.edu.

References

Anderson, L. & Olsen, B. (2006). Investigating early career urban teachers' perspectives on and experiences in professional development. *Journal of Teacher Education* (September/ October).

Carroll, S. J., Reichardt, R. E., Guarino, C. M., & Mejia, A. (2000). *The distribution of teachers among California's school districts and schools.*

Cochran-Smith, M. (2003). The multiple meanings of multicultural teacher education: A conceptual framework. *Teacher Education Quarterly*, 30(2).

Darling-Hammond, L. (1997). *The right to learn: A blueprint for creating schools that work*, First edition. San Francisco, CA: Jossey-Bass.

Hanushek, E. A., Kain, J. F., & Rivkin, S. G. (2004). The revolving door. *Education Next*, 4(1), 76–82.

Horng, E. L. (2004). *Recruiting and retaining teachers at hard-to-staff schools: Examining the tradeoffs teachers make when choosing a school.* Unpublished dissertation, UCLA, Los Angeles.

Ingersoll, R. (2003a). *Is there really a teacher shortage?* Seattle, WA: Center for the Study of Teaching and Policy.

Ingersoll, R. (2003b). *Who controls teachers' work: Power and accountability in America's schools.* Cambridge, MA: Harvard University Press.

Johnson, S. M. & Birkeland, S. E. (2003). Pursuing a "sense of success": New teachers explain their career decisions. *American Educational Research Journal*, 40(3), 217–236.

Johnson, S. M., & The Project on the Next Generation of American Teachers. (2004). *Finders and keepers*. San Francisco, CA: Jossey-Bass.

Lankford, H., Loeb, S., & Wyckoff, J. (2002). Teacher sorting and the plight of urban schools: A descriptive analysis. *Educational Evaluation and Policy Analysis*, 24(1), 37–62.

Loeb, S., Darling-Hammond, L., & Luczac, J. (2005). How teaching conditions predict teacher turnover in California schools. *Peabody Journal of Education*, 80(3), 44–70.

Lyons, K. B. (2007). Preparing to stay: An examination of the effects of specialized preparation on urban teacher retention, Unpublished dissertation, University of California, Los Angeles, California.

Masyn, K., Quartz, K. H., & Lyons, K. B. (submitted) Why Do They Stay? Early Career Retention of Highly-Qualified Teachers in High-poverty Urban Schools.

National Commission on Teaching and America's Future. (2003). *No dream denied: A pledge to America's children*. Washington, DC: National Commission on Teaching and America's Future.

National Partnership for Excellence and Accountability in Teaching. (2000). Projects and activities. (http://www/web3.educ.msu.edu/projects.html#recr.)

Oakes, J. (1996). Making the rhetoric real: UCLA's struggle for teacher education that is multicultural and social reconstructionist. *National Association of Multicultural Education Journal*, 4(2), 4–10.

Oakes, J. & Lipton, M. (2003). *Teaching to change the world*, Second edition. Boston, MA: McGraw-Hill.

Olsen, B. & Anderson, L. (2007). Courses of action: A qualitative investigation in urban teacher retention and career development. *Urban Education*, 42(1).

Quartz, K. H., Priselac, J., & Franke, M. (in press). Transforming Public Schools: A Synthesis of Research Findings from UCLA's Center X. Equity and Excellence in Education.

Quartz, K. H. & TEP Research Group (2003). Too angry to leave: Supporting new teachers commitment to transform urban schools. *Journal of Teacher Education*, 54(2), 99–111.

Quartz, K. H., Lyons, K. B., & Thomas, A. (2005). Retaining teachers in high-poverty schools: A policy framework. In N. Bascia, A. Cumming, A. Datnow, K. Leithwood and D. Livingstone (Eds.), *International handbook of educational policy*. Dordrecht: Kluwer.

Quartz, K. H., Thomas, A., Anderson, L., Masyn, K., Lyons, K. B., & Olsen, B. (2008). Careers in motion: A longitudinal retention study of role changing patterns among urban educators. *Teachers College Record*, 110(6), 218–250.

Quartz, K. H., Olsen, B., Anderson, L. M., & Lyons, K. B. (2009). *Making a difference: career pathways in urban education*. Boulder, CO: Paradigm Publishers.

Thomas, A. (2005). *Social networks and career paths of urban teachers: Effects of career decision-related communication networks on teacher retention*. Unpublished dissertation, University of California, Los Angeles, California.

Thomas, A. (2007). Teacher attrition, social capital, and career advancement: An unwelcome message. *Research and Practice in the Social Sciences*, 3(1), 19–47.

Urbanski, A. & O'Connell, C. (2003). Transforming the profession of teaching: It starts at the beginning. Retrieved May 9, 2006, from http://www.nctaf.org/article/?g=0&c=3&sc=13&ssc=0&a=39.

Zeichner, K. M. (2003). The adequacies and inadequacies of three current strategies to recruit, prepare, and retain the best teachers for all students. *Teachers College Record*, 105(3), 490–519.

Chapter 8
Teacher Gender and Career Patterns

Mary Thornton and Patricia Bricheno

Introduction

In general, across the world, the career trajectories of men and women are clearly differentiated. There has been much research that demonstrates men and women tend to occupy different positions in the workplace and there is a clear gender divide between some occupational groups, with, for example, men predominant in engineering and women in nursing (horizontal segregation), and a gender divide within many occupations, where men disproportionately occupy senior positions and women disproportionately more junior ones (vertical segregation, Hakim, 1979). Such divisions have most recently been confirmed by the British Equality and Human Rights Commission (EHRC), which, in its annual report, 'Sex and Power: Who Runs Britain? (EHRC, 2008a), likened women's progress in the workplace to that of a snail, and recorded a 'worrying trend of reversal or stalled progress' in terms of 'women in top positions of power and influence across the public and private sectors'. Indeed, in the Commissions press release about the report, its chief executive, Nicola Brewer said:

> We always speak of a glass ceiling. These figures reveal that in some cases it appears to be made of reinforced concrete. (EHRC, 2008b)

The EHRCs concerns are illustrated through reference to there being fewer women, in 2007, holding top posts in 12 of the 25 categories surveyed, than there were in 2006. The proportion of women in top posts remained the same in five categories and increased in just 8 of them. One of those categories, the proportion of women in secondary headship increased from 30% to 34% between 2003 and 2006 (figures were not available for 2007). This corroborates the historic patterns for teachers' career trajectories that we discuss below, with increasing numbers of women obtaining headships and leadership roles in both primary and secondary schools in England and Wales. However, despite these increases, women remain under-represented in leadership roles while men remain disproportionately over-represented. The glass ceiling in education may have been raised a little but it has yet to be removed.

M. Bayer et al. (eds.), *Teachers' Career Trajectories and Work Lives,*
Professional Learning and Development in Schools and Higher Education 3,
© Springer Science + Business Media B.V. 2009

This chapter provides an overview of research into the relationship between gender and teachers' careers. As far as possible it identifies similarities and differences between the UK and other regions of the world, and seeks to relate both to the political, economic and social influences that can have a significant impact upon the differential gendering of teachers' careers in different social locations.

We will argue that going against social mores is always difficult, whether it be for men thinking of training to teach in primary schools in England, or for women in India or Afghanistan whose own education is often restricted, and for some of whom social/cultural traditions prevent them working outside the home.

We find that a sexual division of labour in teaching does exist, albeit manifesting itself in different shapes and forms, which link to social constructions of masculinity and femininity within the societies in which they live and work.

Gendered Careers in Teaching

> The divisions are not of caste-like rigidity, but the probabilities that the sexes will experience differential career lines and typical locations in school are striking enough to allow us to speak confidently of a sexual division of labour in teaching. (Acker, 1994: 76)

The sexual division of labour which Sandra Acker speaks of is not a purely European or Western phenomenon. It is a common feature of teaching across the world. Drudy (2008: 309) uses figures from the Organisation for Economic Cooperation and Development (OECD), the United Nations Educational, Scientific and Cultural Organization (UNESCO) and the European Union to suggest that

> the teaching profession is characterised by gender imbalances. Female predominance in school teaching is to be found in most countries throughout the world.

Figures from UNESCO (2006) confirm this global predominance of female teachers: For example, in 2004 the proportion of female teachers in primary education was 61% and in secondary education it was 52%.

However, there is considerable variation across the world and there are still many countries where females do not predominate: UNESCO figures for 2008 suggest that male teachers predominate in primary schools in approximately a fifth of the countries of the world, in secondary schools, in over a third of countries and in Higher Education over 80% of staff are male. These figures are approximate as data for some countries is not available every year.

In 2004 in North America and western Europe 84% of primary teachers were female (UNESCO, 2006). In contrast only 45% of teachers in sub-Saharan Africa and 44% in south and west Asia were women. In secondary education, similar trends were observed although proportions of female teachers were generally lower than at the primary level. In general, the higher the educational level, the lower is the proportion of women on the teaching staff.

To a degree, a distinction might be drawn between developed and developing countries based upon differences in cultural traditions and economic contexts. In more developed countries, teaching is traditionally an important source of employment for women looking to combine family and career. Yet the opposite tends to be true in the developing world (Wylie, 2000).

Gendered Career Patterns in Primary Teaching in England and Wales

Publicly available records show that, between 1900 and 2006 in England and Wales, the proportion of men in primary teaching has always been low (29% at its peak in 1938), and that their propensity to obtain headships of primary schools has always been disproportionate to their numbers (until 2000 at least 40% of all primary headteachers were male), as shown in Fig. 8.1. While male primary teachers are generally seen to be a scarce resource in the UK, especially at the chalk face – in the classroom, they do have a strong and continuing track record of being appointed to manage and lead primary schools.

However, some recent changes in trends for men in primary teaching are noteworthy. From 2000 to 2006 there has been a sharper than expected fall in the proportion of headteachers who are male, and of male teachers who are heads while

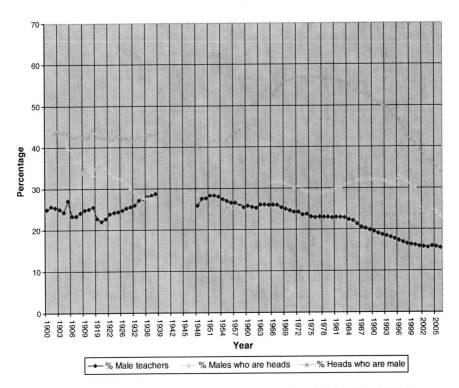

Fig. 8.1 Trends relating to male primary teachers in England and Wales 1900–2006 (Sources: Board of Education 1900–1944; Ministry of Education, 1944–1964; DES/DfEE 1964–2000; DfES 2000–2007)

at the same time the trend of falling numbers of male teachers overall has slowed considerably.

Despite these recent trends men still disproportionately acquire headships.

This gendered pattern of differentiated career trajectories for teachers is not unusual. Similar patterns can be found in other predominantly female professions, such as nursing, where men also disproportionately occupy senior posts (Finlayson & Nazroo, 1998), in other UK studies (Coleman, 2002), and in other countries such as France (Casassus, 2000), the USA (Acker, 1994), Scandinavia (Kauppinen-Toropainen & Lammi, 1993), Ireland (Drudy et al., 2005), and in Australia (Mills et al., 2004).

Coleman (2002) has found these gender patterns across different age ranges and phases in all the UK's different regions, while Goddard (2005: 1) points out that men disproportionately hold 85% of vice chancellorships or professorships in UK higher education, and 63% of research or senior lecturer posts, while women make up 40% of higher education staff overall.

Research by Powney et al. (2003) found that 69% of headteachers in state secondary schools in the UK were men yet 55% of secondary teachers were women. Lee and Slater (2005) found that in private co-education schools 95% of headteachers were men, again quite disproportionate to the numbers of male and female teachers teaching in such schools.

Data from our own studies (Thornton & Bricheno, 2006) confirm that while men may find it difficult to enter primary teaching, and to successfully complete their training courses, once qualified and in post their career trajectories are highly likely to be towards leadership and management positions and that their careers progress at a relatively quick pace when compared to women primary teachers.

Why might this be so?

> The research reveals that there are a complex set of interrelated economic, social and political factors that come into play when males and females consider embarking on education as a career. (Wallace, 2008: 2)

Political Factors

Historically in the UK there has been a strong interplay between political and economic factors regarding teaching as a career. The abolition of the 'marriage bar' in 1919, which prevented married women from taking or keeping teaching posts, was effectively reinstated during the Great Depression, when jobs for men were scarce. It was not until 1944 that the marriage bar was finally removed in practice and women were able to continue teaching after marrying and thus to pursue it as a viable career on a par with men.

The Equal Pay Act (1970) and the Sex Discrimination Act (1975) made discrimination against women teachers illegal, and may partially explain the decline in the proportion of male headteachers post-1975, as indicated in Fig. 8.1, although gaps in pay and promotion between male and female teachers still persist (an 11% pay differential was recorded by the Equal Opportunities Commission in 2005:

EOC, 2005). However, while the prospect of equal pay may have encouraged more women to enter teaching during this period, their increased availability may also have helped to depress teacher's salaries to levels more in line with a predominantly female profession (Chevalier & Dolton, 2004).

The Education Act of 1918, immediately after the First World War, which required all children to remain in school until the age of 14, also presaged the need for more teachers, a gap that was largely filled by men due to the marriage bar then in place. It was not until after the 1944 Education Act, which separated elementary schooling into primary and secondary age phases, that we began, in the 1950s to see a decline in the numbers of male teachers. Given the propensity for men to teach older children and the social perception that working with young children is 'natural' for women and 'odd' for men (see the section 'Social Factors' below) this age-phase division within compulsory schooling may well have acted as a deterrent for men to enter or remain in primary teaching.

After a period of relative stability between 1975 and 1985, the numbers of men in primary teaching again began to decline, noticeably sinking below 20% in 1990, just 2 years after another major piece of educational legislation, the Education Reform Act of 1988 (DES, 1989). This Act introduced a compulsory National Curriculum and Assessment regime in England and Wales, alongside national tests, league tables, school inspections and performance-related pay for teachers. Between 1991 and 2001, as the full impact of these changes percolated through the education system, the proportion of male primary headteachers also declined quite significantly, dropping from above 50% to below 40%. These declines in the proportions of men in teaching certainly took place against the backdrop of political reform of the education system, but it is not possible to causally relate the two. During much the same period and beyond, up until 2007, there was an increasing feeling of economic well-being, with unemployment low and standards of living generally rising, periods which historically have tended to show lower proportions of men in teaching.

It has been argued (Mahony et al., 2004; Arnot & Miles, 2005) that the changes in the structure and delivery of schooling brought about by the ERA have served to masculinize rather than feminize it, with care and nurture being replaced by formal hierarchical structures that control, manage, assess and monitor, in minute detail, teachers' work in schools.

> Women remain the front line workers in schools but why and for how long? As a so-called semi-profession teachers are deemed in need of control … and in the current situation this will be through centralised bureaucratic controls. Men in centrally powerful roles can manage this without needing to be physically at the chalk-face in schools and classrooms. (Thornton & Bricheno, 2006: 52)

Economic Factors

Figure 8.1 indicates two particular periods during which the proportion of male primary teachers increased in England and Wales. The first, between 1920 and 1938, covers the period of the 'Great Depression' following the First World War; the second, between 1945 and 1952, covers the period immediately after the Second World War. Both the periods reflect a time of great social and economic upheaval, with an unstable economy and high unemployment, particularly for men whose work then, if not now, was the main source of family income. Unemployment rose to 2.7 million during the 'Great Depression', and after the Second World War there was a concerted drive to reintegrate returning military personnel into the civilian workforce. The latter included the intensive recruitment of men onto emergency teacher training programmes. It is clear that there were economic drivers behind the increase in the proportions of men recruited to primary teaching in England and Wales during these periods.

By way of contrast, during periods of economic stability and growth the proportion of men in primary teaching has declined (notably post-1968), as has the proportion of male headteachers (notably post-1975). There has been something of a decline (just under 10%) in the proportion of male primary teachers who become headteachers between 1991 and 2001 but prior to that, between 1985 and 1990, while the number of male primary teachers was in decline, the proportion of men who became headteachers actually increased. Since 2003 the rate of decline in the numbers of men in teaching appears to have slowed, and more recently, the 'credit crunch' and fears of recession have seen a 34% rise in the numbers of men enquiring about teaching as a possible career (TDA, 2008a). The Training and Development Agency for Schools

> believes that this could be a sign that graduates and people looking to change careers are seeking more secure career paths in the wake of heightened economic concern. (TDA, 2008a)

Greece, in contrast to the UK and to most other western European countries has a relatively low proportion of women teachers: In 2006, 64% of primary teachers and 56% of secondary teachers were female. The relatively good salaries and the high levels of unemployment in Greece (Stylianidou et al., 2004) might go some way to explaining this anomaly.

Drudy's (2008: 310) international comparisons of the proportions of men and women in teaching also suggest an economic correlation, with the proportion of women teachers being at its lowest in the least developed countries, where the number of women is roughly equal to men in primary schools but considerably lower than for men in secondary schools. She suggests that

> the proportions of women in teaching in the different regions world-wide could reasonably be taken as indicators of the stage of economic development in various regions.

This view is, in part, supported by UNESCO (2006), which suggests that the economic contexts of more and less developed countries could be a basis for distinguishing the proportions of male and female teachers:

> In general, as the prestige of an occupation declines, the proportion of female workers tends to increase, which in turn corresponds to falling wages. ... As the salary rises, the proportion of female teachers falls. (p. 40)

One might conclude that in developing countries, and at times of economic stress in developed countries, there are likely to be more men in teaching, even though it is more usually a predominantly female profession.

Social Factors

Although globally female teachers predominate, there are some countries, both more and less economically developed, where male teachers are in the majority. The sexual division of labour that permeates teaching (Acker, 1994: 76) has social as well as economic antecedents. As individuals our career choices are based on a complex web of influences and underlying reasons relating to our past and current social and educational experiences. Our early socialization, family upbringing, friends, and partners all impact in some way upon the people we become and the career choices that we make. Those experiences and relationships are in turn influenced and shaped by our age, sex, race, ethnicity, religion, nationality, place of birth, and the culture and the politics of the society into which we are born and live. It is a complex mix that produces unique individuals making unique career choices but, whilst not determined by the social structures that frame us and our lives, as social beings we are influenced by them and patterns do emerge. Teachers are not divorced from their social location and it is this that can go some way to explaining the gendered nature of the profession.

The career choices that we make are

> an outcome of socially structured possibilities that partly reflect and result from gendered relationships of domination and subordination in society, from the differential distribution of power resources. (Thornton & Bricheno, 2006: 121)

Jensen (2008) suggests that where male teachers predominate this could be related to

> socio-cultural issues where women cannot go out of the house, or go far from the house. It's difficult in Pakistan or Afghanistan, for instance, to hire female teachers in remote rural areas because for a woman, to move from her home to the school is a challenge.

In India, where the cultural traditions and expectations for girl children are mirrored within the teaching force, women account for only 44% of all teachers at primary school level, and 34% of secondary teachers (UNESCO, 2008)

In one sense this is not surprising given the literacy rates recorded in India's 2001 census (54% women, 66% men). However, underpinning these gender differences in literacy are patriarchal traditions and customs that differentiate male/female 'access to education ... employment opportunities and social support systems' (Thornton & Iyer, 2009: 2), with

> unfriendly school environments and social sanctions. ... The non-availability of female teachers in many rural school, the absence of single sex schools, the location of many schools more than two kilometres from home, are all serious factors discouraging even progressive minded parents from sending their daughters to schools. (p. 4)
> [I]n India highly persistent cultural norms and values about the education of girls and the position of women remain strong ... the social value assigned to the girl child ... in India is frequently negative, and this has a devastating impact on their educational opportunities. (p. 9)

Women teachers are more often located in city rather than in rural areas. In rural areas in India men are in a substantial majority, and it is here that families of both teachers and pupils are more likely to maintain traditional cultural values and orientations that differentiate between appropriate and acceptable behaviours and occupations for men and women.

The sexual division of labour in teaching is also strongly linked to social constructions of masculinity and femininity within the UK and other societies, resulting in horizontal patterns of workplace segregation. For example, in the UK and elsewhere, teaching has long been seen, stereotypically, as a socially acceptable career for women, akin to mothering, a view observed in 1998 by Johnston, McKeown, and McEwan and still prevalent in 2005 amongst Drudy's sample of school pupils and student teachers in Ireland (Drudy, 2008). It involves children, whose nurture is often seen as 'natural' for women and 'unnatural' for men. As paid work the hours and holidays are thought helpful for women to combine with homemaking and family responsibilities, including raising their own children. Pay is considered good for a second household income rather than that of the main breadwinner, who is still usually thought of as male. Primary teaching especially is often not thought to be too intellectually stretching, or physically demanding, and working with children is generally considered low status (all of which is encapsulated in the then Minister of State for Education, John Patten's, suggestion of a 'Mums Army' of non-graduate early years teachers). More recently the introduction of Higher Level Teaching Assistants (HLTAs), of whom only 1% are male (Wilson et al., 2007), who need lower qualifications and receive lower pay than teachers, has reinforced this perception. Doug McAvoy (general secretary of the National Union of Teachers, at that time) said:

> [T]he proposals 'wouldn't be a mile away from the mum's army' scheme put forward under John Major's government a decade ago, which sought to put more unqualified helpers in the classroom. That was opposed by teachers' leaders as a 'dumbing down' of the profession. (Garner, 2002)

By way of contrast, dominant constructions of masculinity suggest that men should exhibit manly traits such as sporting prowess, good discipline, IT skills, leadership potential, a drive to succeed and an avoidance of activities deemed feminine, such as the care and nurture of children. Sargent (2001) notes that there is often strong pressure on men to emphasize, through their actions and choices, the characteristics of 'real men', while Mills et al. (2008) demonstrate how pressure 'to conform to traditional, or hegemonised, forms of masculinity' can lead to male teachers being labelled 'suspect'.

Men who exhibit feminine traits are thought unmanly and suspicion surrounds any such men who express a desire to work with children. Homophobia remains strong and works against men choosing teaching as a career, or following non-stereotypical pathways once in teaching, whatever their sexual orientation. Being thought of as a potential child abuser acts as a strong social deterrent to teaching for many men, particularly in the UK. At the very least, men choosing to teach primary-age children are often thought of as 'odd', not just by the public at large but also potentially by family members too. One of our male interviewees reported that his own grandmother had said 'men shouldn't be in primary classrooms' (Thornton, 1999b). Male teachers are clearly as equally 'burdened with gendered discourses that define them in certain ways and determine their roles' as are their female counterparts (Sabbe & Aelterman, 2007).

Teaching in most Western developed societies is largely a predominantly female occupation because it is thought to be low status, because it is increasingly seen as feminized, because it is deemed to be 'women's work' in the eyes of many, and because men who choose to teach are often perceived to be abnormal in some way, certainly suspicious, potentially dangerous, perhaps paedophile or gay (Skelton, 1991; Mills, 2004; Thornton & Bricheno, 2006; Wallace, 2008; Drudy, 2008). These perceptions impact negatively on men who might want to teach, making it quite difficult for them to challenge or go against them. That some can and do is proven, but it doesn't make it any easier. Going against social mores is always difficult, whether it be men in England or women in India or Afghanistan. It is particularly hard for inexperienced young men at school in England thinking about their career choice. They are more susceptible to peer pressure, homophobia and innuendo than their more mature, confident counterparts already with families of their own (thus confirming their heterosexuality) who go into teaching as career-changers rather than as a first choice occupation.

Teaching as a Career Choice

Teaching is rarely a first choice occupation for men in England (Reid & Thornton, 2000; Scott et al., 1998; Skelton, 1991). It is far rarer for men than women to say that they have always wanted to teach, that it is their lifetime goal. Instead it is often the case that men choose teaching when disappointed by their initial choice career, or they fail to get the necessary grades to study it in the first place (Thornton & Bricheno, 2006). However, it has been found that men entering teaching in this way have been successful and, according to Parry (2005), are equally committed to it as a career and are more likely to stay. This lends credence to the view that older men, with greater confidence in themselves, wider experience of the world, and families of their own, are better able to counter prevailing stereotypes, challenge sexual innuendo and aspire to a career that is seen socially stereotyped as female.

In a possible counter to growing speculation that men who want to teach are being disadvantaged by a social context that questions their motives and casts aspersions on their sexuality, a recent broadsheet headline stated: 'Prejudice isn't what keeps men out of nurseries' (Ellen, 2008: 13). This opinion piece suggests that it isn't fear of being seen as unmanly, suspicious, possibly paedophile or gay that puts men off teaching but the fact that they themselves see it as 'chick-work', where women predominate in low paid, low status, often arduous work involving children or care, and thus as an unsuitable career for them, as men. Ellen cites the exponential growth of celebrity chefs on our TV screens to illustrate that predominantly female occupations can become very attractive occupations for men if they are changed to represent glamour, power, wealth and high status. That, she suggests, is what many men are looking for in their careers. If so, whilst teaching as 'chick-work' may put men off entering, once inside, the potential to obtain power and high status through rapid promotion may be a significant draw.

Roles and Responsibilities

The sexual division of labour in teaching, and its links to social constructions of masculinity and femininity, also results in vertical patterns of segregation once men and women are in teaching. So-called manly traits, such as leadership, and a socially framed desire for, or expectations of, male power, status and success also play a part.

Men do, disproportionately 'get on' in teaching in England and Wales, as Fig. 8.1 demonstrates, in much the same way as described by EHRC (2008a) above for other occupations. Men predominate in senior leadership positions in a great many professions and occupations across our society. In teaching, because it is so predominantly female, this is less pronounced, and as noted above, there has been a rise in the proportion of women headteachers in secondary schools. Much the same has occurred in primary schools although not recorded in the EHRC report. However, despite currently declining rates, there can be little doubt that men still disproportionately occupy senior leadership positions in our schools and achieve disproportionate power and status vis-à-vis women. This has implications for all teachers, the students they teach and the learning that takes place in schools.

> A community of practice will be strongly affected by who is perceived to have power within it, and who is perceived to be an expert. ... Senior management is disproportionately male. Thus what is perceived as expertise by novices and outsiders is strongly influenced by gender ... senior management is in a position to influence practices within their schools ... such influence not only affects the practices of teaching, but also the perceptions of students about learning. (Griffiths, 2006: 397)

The power dividend for men in teaching occurs as much by chance as it does by choice, as a 'by product of circumstance' based on their sex. They are a 'prized commodity' whose valorization works 'to boost their employment opportunities relative to female teachers regardless of the men's pedagogic skills' (Mills et al., 2008: 73).

Social perceptions of sex-based traits frame and shape teachers careers in many ways regardless of their veracity. While individual teachers may not adhere to them, they nonetheless can inform others' views.

> [T]raits have become assigned by gender as they relate broadly to female and male. According to a male dominated culture men are aggressive, daring, rational, strong, objective, dominant, decisive and self-confident. Women on the other hand are portrayed in opposite terms, as passive, shy, intuitive, dependent, subjective, submissive, indecisive and nurturing. Kruse and Prettyman (2008: 454)

Family members, headteachers, school governors or pupils' parents may perceive male and female teachers, the roles for which they are suited within teaching, and their potential for promotion to leadership positions, from the perspective of a social framework that sees power and leadership as the natural attributes of men. Whatever its source the outcomes are clear and self-reinforcing: Men disproportionately achieve promotion and occupy positions where they manage the majority of the workforce who are women.

Bradley (1993) notes the internal demarcation that takes place within gendered occupations (such as men and women teachers differentially occupying different areas and responsibilities), and the differential distribution of higher status positions (such as headship and leadership roles). She suggests that men in predominantly female occupations may seek, or be encouraged by others to seek, career advancement. The educational research literature suggests that while some men really want to teach and remain in the classroom (Johnston et al., 1998; Sargent, 2001; Mills et al., 2008), others do expect rapid promotion to management positions (Thornton & Bricheno, 2000). Some are pushed towards, or supported for, promotion by others (perhaps a governor or older peer) simply because they are men. It is interesting to note that this teacher sex 'dividend' is rarely recognized by male teachers (Keamy, 2008), who, according to Powney et al.'s research (2003: vii), tend to see all teachers as being 'promoted according to their experience and ability', while their female peers believe that 'gender has affected their career progression'. Citing Klinck and Allard (1994), Keamy notes that if you are part of a privileged group you often cannot see the benefits that accrue to you. Despite this lack of recognition on the part of many male teachers, 'research has long acknowledged that men have greater access to social and interpersonal power regardless of their talent and skill set' (Kruse & Prettyman, 2008).

As a result, and as Bradley predicts, there is internal demarcation within teaching. The areas in which men disproportionately predominate are patterned according to the social mores and stereotypes indicated above. These help to shape the directions taken and choices made by men once in teaching, and they also help to shape the views taken of male teachers by others, both within and beyond the educational playing field. Appointment and promotion procedures may well be a case in point.

Constant and continuing appeals in the UK for more male teachers, as role models for children (TDA Press Release, 2008b), emphasize their rarity. This is not missed by male students in training, some of whom see it is an opportunity to progress more quickly up the pay scales. For example, two male final-year students in our research (Thornton & Bricheno, 2006: 109) said the following.

> Because there's a shortage of males ... schools are more likely to push you ahead ... in order to keep those males. But if you boost the amount of men in the profession then career prospects drop. (Tom)
>   I've also got another school chasing me already so I'm going to play two ends against each other and I'm going to see if I can't get some financial benefit. (Dick)

Nor is it missed by those in positions of power when it comes to making those appointments.

There is considerable evidence within the literature that men are encouraged and pushed towards promotion (Sargent, 2001), and that women seeking promotion perceive there is a bias against them and a preference for men (Coleman, 2002), especially when they are competing against 'rare' men. Coleman's large-scale study of secondary headteachers found that 63% of women teachers felt that interview and promotions panels were overly staffed by men and what they believed were 'sexist' governors, untrained in, or unaware of, equal opportunities legislation. Her study confirms our own earlier research (Thornton & Bricheno, 2000) which found that women applicants for promoted posts felt they were treated differently, and more negatively, than their male counterparts, by, for example, being asked questions about marriage plans and family responsibilities or, in one instance, for wearing trousers at an interview.

School governors in England and Wales have a significant amount of power when it comes to promotions, appointing staff and pay. They are drawn from local businesses, community organizations, parents and representatives of the Local Educational Authority (LEA). They sit on interview panels alongside senior mangers, who, like the governors, are drawn from populations that are almost always disproportionately male (parents being perhaps the main exception). The majority are lay governors, and are rarely trained in, or knowledgeable about, equal opportunities legislation (Bagley, 1993; Thornton, 2000) the main exception being the LEA advisers. The more laypeople involved in teacher appointments and promotions the more likely it is that 'traditional' attitudes about male and female roles and traits will come to the fore, such as men being needed for leadership roles, disciplining boys and 'balancing' the predominance of women in schools. The latter is an interesting point given the continuing belief that primary headships and deputy headships should be 'balanced' between men and women teachers – female head, male deputy, and vice versa. It may sound equal and fair but it directly contributes to the distortion in promoted positions when the majority of the workforce from which they are drawn are women.

> [A]ll things being equal they would choose the men, because the governors would want to choose a man because they wanted a man in their school. (Geoff, Headteacher: Thornton & Bricheno, 2006: 111)

The evidence suggests that as men become even rarer in our schools, such bias continues. But rarity is not the only male dividend in the career stakes. Those traditional social stereotypes that frame both lay and professional perspectives continue to suggest, when it comes to promotions, that men are the main breadwinners, that they are needed as role models especially for disaffected boys, that they are better at handling discipline, that they can sort out problems with technology, that male traits somehow better match the leadership needs of schools (Coleman, 2002).

Stereotypically, different areas within teaching are also patterned along sex lines. For example men are more likely

- To be found teaching older children (years 5 and 6 in primary schools; Powney et al., 2003; Thornton & Bricheno, 2006), which reflects the low status accorded to work with young children (Skelton, 1991)
- To be teaching examination years in secondary schools, which reflects the high status attached to public examinations and academic subject disciplines (Thornton, 1998)

- To be teaching in the larger schools, where there are more men, and which reflects the higher salaries on offer, increased availability of management positions and thus greater chance of promotion (Edwards & Lyons, 1996; Bricheno & Thornton, 2002; Thornton & Bricheno, 2006)
- To be taking responsibility for maths and science teaching, each perceived to be high status subjects, and difficult (Alexander, 1991; Thornton, 1996, 1998)

Despite their low numbers, men are frequently found, and disproportionately over-represented, in each of these areas of education. The processes by which this happens are complex, sometimes operating independently of the male teachers themselves, but the patterns are firmly established in the research literature.

Studies in the UK and the USA, such as Thornton and Bricheno's (2006), of men in teaching, Sargent's (2001) of male elementary teachers, Powney et al's (2003) of 'Teachers Careers', Coleman's (2002) of 'Women as Headteachers', and Alexander's (1991) of primary schools in Leeds, have all addressed issues relating to the sex of teachers and their teaching careers. Each maps out, in different ways, sex-based patterns in the allocation of teachers' roles and responsibilities, and in the expectations others place upon them, according to whether they are men or women.

There is an established hierarchy in terms of subject disciplines within education. The 'hard' natural sciences of physics, chemistry, biology, mathematics in information technology take precedence over the 'softer' human sciences of psychology, sociology, arts, humanities and media studies, as the annual media coverage of A-level passes constantly reminds us. The research undertaken by Alexander (1991) confirms that this hierarchy is also present in Leeds primary schools, albeit with slightly different subject labels attached. The English core National Curriculum subjects of English, maths and science take precedence over other subjects and there is a tendency to see English as lower ranking than the other two core subjects. The key issue is that this hierarchy, even in primary schools, maps fairly consistently against the sexual division of labour between primary school teachers, in terms of promotion and pay, with men disproportionately holding responsible posts in maths and science (Thornton, 1998; Thornton & Bricheno, 2000; Alexander, 1991).

Men in English primary schools do disproportionately take responsibility for maths, science and IT, and for teaching the oldest children in primary schools (Thornton, 1996; Thornton & Bricheno, 2000; Powney et al., 2003; Wallace, 2008). In our survey of nearly 400 schools in Hertfordshire (Thornton, 1999a) we also found that most of the women teachers (61%) were placed on the main pay scale while most of the men (65%) were receiving additional pay associated with additional responsibilities and management roles. Just 7% of the female sample were in headship positions while there were more than 33% of the male sample. More than 80% of men in that sample taught Key Stage 2 (8–11 years) or were headteachers.

The types of additional responsibilities also vary by teacher's sex, with women traditionally occupying special needs' posts, assessment, ones associated with pastoral care or a particular age-phase, or with arts and humanities subjects that rank lower in status (Bricheno & Thornton, 2002). Alexander's study of Leeds primary schools included information about the pay, status and sex of curriculum coordinators. He found that while women held most of the maths responsibility posts and were paid on the main salary grade, all the men who held responsibility for mathematics within a school were paid additional salary and allowances. In addition

> in only 3 of the 17 schools which had any male staff *at all* were women rather than men responsible for maths. (Alexander, 1991: 131, our emphasis)

Men are clearly associated with promoted posts and higher salaries, particularly with maths responsibility, and appear to be chosen for that role over and above women candidates, if men are available within the school, even if these are not their particular, codified areas of expertise. Our own research (Thornton & Bricheno, 2000) suggests that this outcome cannot be explained by differential subject expertise as evidenced by initial qualifications or Continuing Professional Development (CPD).

Career Expectations and Pathways

Our National Careers Survey (Thornton & Bricheno, 2000) indicated sex differences in teachers' career expectations. Some men clearly expressed their desire for leadership, in the ultimate form of headship as a logical career expectation, whilst others wanted to remain at the 'chalk-face', in the classroom, but experienced pressure from others to put themselves forward for promotion. Sargent (2001) similarly found that men, in his sample of elementary school teachers in America, were expected to move onwards and upwards in their careers fairly rapidly, by both male and female peers. Women teachers, on the other hand, tended to see more obstacles in their career pathways, such as dual responsibilities at home and at work, the interruption of work through childcare and the subsequent loss of career momentum, the need to have a supportive partner who could lighten the load of domestic responsibilities, and perhaps even a partner prepared to put his wife's teaching career ahead in importance of his own.

There is compelling evidence that the family responsibilities of women teachers correlate strongly with a relative lack of career progression in both the UK and elsewhere. Career breaks for child-rearing interrupt career development and make it likely that women teachers will be older than their male counterparts if and when they seek promotion to headship (You & Ko, 2004; Powney et al., 2003), with age then becoming an additional barrier to promotion. In addition, taking a career break in the UK puts women teachers at a significant financial disadvantage if they have already obtained promotion and achieved Teaching and Learning Responsibility (TLR) points. These salary points are lost unless, on their return to teaching, they can find a post advertised at their former level.

> As a consequence women teachers, having risen to the top of the ladder before a career break will often find themselves slipping down the snake when they seek to return, unless schools ... allow them to apply for promoted posts whilst not currently in employment. (McNamara et al., 2007: 6)

Powney et al. (2003) found that almost 33% of the disproportionately low number of female headteachers in their sample actually lived alone, without partners or children, whereas only 2% of male headteachers were without partners at home. For women teachers as for women in other occupations, careers and promotion may be more frequently sacrificed (by choice or under duress) in order to cope with family responsibilities. This is far less frequently the case for men. Women are also far more likely than men to be teaching part-time or working as supply staff, which not only hampers career progression but also affects their opportunity to participate in career development activities.

That women teachers are more likely to take career breaks to raise children, care for elderly relatives, manage family responsibilities, work part-time on their return or undertake supply teaching could suggest that they choose not to pursue promotion opportunities that might be equally available to them. Wallace (2008) suggests that dominant male norms may discourage women from seeking promoted positions in teaching. Powney et al. (2003: 18) report that

> [b]elow deputy and headteacher post, we find women are significantly more likely than men (at the 5% level) to report that they are not interested in promotion.

They also found that men were more likely to plan their careers while women tended to 'view personal circumstances as a career barrier' (pp. 39–40). Women teachers' 'personal circumstances' are compounded by the heavy workload currently afflicting UK teachers. It leaves little time for the additional family responsibilities that women continue to bear unequally alongside their male peers. As one of our respondent's commented (Thornton & Bricheno, 2006: 108):

> [I]t could be easier for a man; men can almost drift into things and are often not restricted by their families. (Gavin, male headteacher)

Unlike women teachers, men have virtually no career breaks. Whilst promoted men are more likely to have families than their female peers, they are far less likely to feel or be held back by them. The additional responsibilities of the home are much more frequently borne by female teachers than by male teachers.

There are some strong indications that men teachers are more likely than women to seek out promotion opportunities, go for them and get them, which echoes the confident, proactive male in those traditional social stereotypes. Indeed, Cubillo (1999) suggests that male applicants for the UK's National Programme for Qualified Head Teachers (NPQH) exhibit hyper-confidence in their abilities.

Some commentators have suggested that women lack similar motivation although many argue against that (Measor & Sikes, 1992; Coleman, 2002). Instead, women are thought to be considerably more cautious when considering promotion opportunities, wishing to make doubly sure that they have the right CPD experiences, knowledge and qualifications required for the post.

Mahony et al. (2004) found similar patterns of caution amongst women when applying to cross the pay scale threshold on to 'Expert Teacher' status.

Whether it be caution, lack of desire or actual discrimination, women teachers careers do generally progress more slowly than those of their male peers.

20% of male primary teachers with 5–9 years of service are already on the Leadership
Scale (in the UK) compared with 8.5% of women; 54% of male primary teachers with
19 years of service are on the Leadership Scale compared to 26% of women; 70% of men
are on the Leadership Scale/a promoted post after 20 years service compared with 40% of
women. The situation is similar in the secondary sector. (McNamara et al., 2007: 3)

Some of the stereotypical male and female traits cited above can be found in the
attributes frequently associated with male and female leadership styles. These
suggest that women in leadership positions are 'collaborative, caring, courageous
and reflective', 'task-oriented problem-solvers', having 'high expectations of
themselves and others' (Kruse & Prettyman, 2008: 453). However, women 'openly
seeking power' can be viewed as 'unbecoming' and 'forward' (Ibid, p461). The
traits associated with women leaders can also be disempowering in career terms,
resulting in them being seen as non-assertive, disinclined to lead from the front,
non-decision making and potentially emotional, traits which do not fit well with
dominant, masculinized models of leadership.

Conclusions

Economic, social and political factors intertwine to shape, form, constrain and
give direction to the different career choices and career trajectories of men
and women teachers. Whilst recognizing that there are some notable exceptions,
women teachers tend to predominate, in terms of overall numbers, in the more
economically developed societies, while men tend to be in the majority in the less
developed ones.

Within more developed societies, economic factors also influence trends in
teacher recruitment and teachers' careers. From Fig. 8.1 we see that in England
and Wales there appears to be an established pattern that more men are inclined to
become teachers in times of economic recession and high unemployment than they
are in times of high economic growth and stability. As economic recession deepens
and unemployment rises we are beginning to see in the UK a slowing of the historic decline in the numbers of male teachers in our primary schools and increasing expressions of interest from men about training to teach, probably because, in
times of economic turbulence, teaching is considered to be a relatively safe, secure,
reasonably well-paid occupation.

Again with some notable exceptions, male teachers usually predominate in
terms of overall numbers in societies where teaching is considered to be a relatively
high status occupation. They also tend to predominate in terms of overall numbers
in societies where women's education and employment opportunities are more
limited, and where the acceptable roles, behaviours and occupations of women are
more culturally bounded.

The slight improvement in the status and prestige of teachers, compared with
the situation in the early 1990s (Hargreaves et al., 2007), and the current economic
climate, may well see an expansion in the numbers of men in teaching, with schools

becoming slightly less predominantly female workplaces. That would be one small step towards greater gender equality in teaching as a career. On the other hand, more men in teaching may add to their over-representation in school leadership and management roles – one small step backwards!

It is difficult to access data from countries worldwide specifically about male and female career trajectories within teaching, but there is no reason to suppose that, once in, men are not also disproportionately represented in senior, high status positions and management roles in other countries. Whatever the social, cultural and economic context, men do appear to disproportionately rise to the top.

Appropriate legislation and educational policies are largely in place (such as equal pay and opportunities, UK; equal rights for women in India) but have yet to achieve the desired change to gender equality in teaching and career patterns, at least to the degree that is desirable. We can and should develop and implement more policies that facilitate greater equality within the teaching profession and which open up opportunities for those willing and able to take advantage of them, such as work experience in primary schools for men and leadership training for women. Their effect on gendered career patterns may be small and slow but they do open the door to those individuals, men and women teachers, who are willing to walk through it and who, in so doing, may begin to counter those pervasive social stereotypes.

Power within education inevitably flows from this sexual division of labour; hence it is worth remembering Bernstein's (1972) dictum: Schools cannot compensate for society. The political, economic, social and sexual stereotypes that frame our wider lives and understandings are not, and cannot easily be, left at the school gate, nor are they likely to be changed from within. Wider political, economic and social change is needed in order to change the gendered power structures and teaching careers that persist in all our schools, and whose role (conscious or unconscious, intended or unintended), in effect continues to be one of social reproduction.

References

Acker, S. (1994). *Gendered education*. Buckinghamshire: Oxford University Press.

Alexander, R. (1991). *Primary education in Leeds: Twelfth and final report from the primary needs independent evaluation project*. Leeds: University of Leeds.

Arnot, M. & Miles, P. (2005). A reconstruction of the gender agenda: The contradictory ender dimensions in New Labour's educational and economic policy. *Oxford Review of Education*, 31(1 Special Issue), 173–189.

Bernstein, B. (1972). Education cannot compensate for society. In D. Rubenstein and C. Stoneman (Eds.), *Education for democracy*. Harmondsworth: Penguin.

Bradley, H. (1993). Across the great divide: The entry of men into 'Women's Jobs'. In C. L. Williams (Ed.), *Doing 'women's work': Men in non-traditional occupations*, (pp. 11–27). London: Sage.

Bricheno, P. & Thornton, M. (2002). Staff gender balance in primary schools. *Research in Education*, 68, 57–64.

Casassus, (2000). Female staff call for state support. *Times Higher Education Supplement*, 18th August 2000, p. 10.

Chevalier, A. & Dolton, P. (2004). The labour market for teachers WP04/11, *Centre For Economic Research Working Paper Series*, May 2004, Department of Economics, University College, Dublin.

Coleman, M. (2002). *Women as head teachers: Striking the balance.* Stoke-on-Trent: Trentham Books.

Cubillo, L. (1999). Gender and leadership in the national professional qualification for head teachers: An opportunity lost? *Journal of In-Service Education*, 25(3), 545–556.

DES (1989). *The Education Reform Act 1988: The School Curriculum and Assessment, Circular No.5/89.* London: HMSO.

Drudy, S. (2008). Gender balance/gender bias: The teaching profession and the impact of feminisation. *Gender and Education*, 20(4), 309–323.

Drudy, S., Martin, M., Woods, M., & O'Flynn, J. (2005). *Men and the classroom: Gender imbalances in teaching.* London: RoutledgeFalmer.

Edwards, S. & Lyons, G. (1996). It's grim up north for female high flyers. *Times Educational Supplement, School Management Guide*, 10th May, 2.

EHRC (Equality and Human Rights Commission) (2008a). *Sex and power: Who runs Britain?* London: EHRC.

EHRC (Equality and Human Rights Commission) (2008b). *Sex and power report reveals fewer women in positions of power and influence.* Press Release http://www. equalityhumanrights.com/en/newsandcomment/Pages/CommissionsSexandPower reportrevealsfewerwomeninpositionsofpowerandinfluence.aspx accessed 5th September 2008.

Ellen, B. (2008). Prejudice isn't what keeps men out of nurseries. *The Observer*, Opinion, 21.09.08, p. 13.

Equal Opportunities Commission (2005). *Facts About Women and Men in Great Britain 2005*, January, EOC (ISBN 1 84206 126 7) available at www.eoc.org.uk.

Finlayson, L. R. & Nazroo, J. Y. (1998). *Gender inequalities in nursing careers.* London: Policy Studies Institute.

Garner, R. (2002). Unions protest at new role for classroom assistants. *The Independent*, 18 October 2002.

Goddard, A. (2005). Female heads big winners in pay stakes. *Times Higher Educational Supplement*, 25th February 2005, p. 1.

Griffiths, M. (2006). The feminization of teaching and the practices of teaching: Threat or opportunity? *Educational Theory*, 56(4), 387–405.

Hakim, C. (1979). *Occupational segregation: A comprehensive study of the degree and pattern of the differentiation between men and women's work in Britain, the United States and other countries*, Research Paper No. 9, London: Department of Employment.

Hargreaves, L., Cunningham, M., Everton, T., Hansen, A., Hopper, B., McIntyre, D., Oliver, C., Pell, T., Rouse, M., & Turner, P. (2007). *The Status of Teachers and the Teaching Profession in England: Views from Inside and Outside the Profession. Evidence Base for the Final Report of the Teacher Status Project*, DfES, Research Report RR831B, Nottingham: DfES Publications, 2007.

Jensen (2008). *VietNamNet Bridge* 14/07/2008 http://english.vietnamnet.vn/education/2008/07/ 793576/ accessed 01/11/2008.

Johnston, J., McKeown, E., & McEwan, A. (1998). *Gender factors in choosing primary school teaching.* Northern Ireland: Equal Opportunities Commission.

Kauppinen-Toropainen, K. & Lammi, J. (1993). Men in female dominated occupations: A cross-cultural comparison. In C. L. Williams (Ed.), *Doing 'women's work': Men in non-traditional occupations.* London: Sage.

Keamy, R. K. (2008). Crossing uncertain terrain: Messages from male academics. *Gender and Education*, 20(3), 267–279.

Klinck, P. & Allard, A. (1994). Neither frogs, nor princes: Changing models of leadership in academia. Paper presented at the *Australian Association of Researcher in Education* Conference, Newcastle, Australia.

Kruse, S. D. & Prettyman, S. S. (2008). Women, leadership, and power: Revisiting the wicked witch of the west. *Gender and Education.* 20(5), 451–464.

Lee, J. & Slater, J. (2005). Old boys' club of private headship. *Times Educational Supplement*, 14th January, p. 5.

Mahony, P., Hextall, I., & Menter, I. (2004). Threshold assessment and performance management: Modernizing or masculinizing teaching in England? *Gender and Education*, 16(2, June 2004), 131–149.

McNamara, O., Gunter, H., Onat-Stelma, Z., Howson, J., & Sprigade, A. (2007). Women teachers' careers, paper presented at *BERA, University of London Institute of Education*, September, 2007.

Measor, L. & Sikes, P. (1992). *Gender and schools*. London: Cassell.

Mills, M., Haase, M., & Charlton, E. (2008). Being the 'right' kind of male teacher: The disciplining of John. *Pedagogy, Culture & Society*, 16(1), 71–84.

Mills, M., Martino, W., & Lingard, B. (2004). Attracting, recruiting and retaining male teachers: Policy issues in the male teacher debate. *British Journal of Sociology of Education*, 25(3), 355–369.

Parry, (2005). Teach at first, but then move on. *Times Educational Supplement*, 8th July 2005, p. 13.

Powney, J., Wilson, V., Hall, S., Davidson, J., Kirk, S., & Edward, S., in conjunction with Mirza, H. S. (2003), *Teachers' careers: The impact of age, disability, ethnicity, gender and sexual orientation* (Research Report RR488). London: Department for Education and Skills.

Reid, I. & Thornton, M. (2000). *Students' reasons for choosing primary school teaching as a career*. Aldenham: University of Hertfordshire, Centre for Equality Issues in Education.

Sabbe, E. & Aelterman, A. (2007). Gender in teaching: a literature review. *Teachers and Teaching*, 13(5), 521–538.

Sargent, P. (2001). *Real men or real teachers? Contradictions in the lives of men elementary school teachers*. Harriman, TN: Men's Studies Press.

Scott, C., Cox, S., & Gray, A. (1998). *The state of the profession: An English study of teacher satisfaction, motivation and health*, a paper presented at the British Educational Research Association Annual Conference, Belfast.

Skelton, C. (1991) A study of the career perspectives of male teachers of young children. *Gender and Education*, 3(3), 278–289.

Stylianidou, F., Bagakis, G., & Stamovlasis, D. (2004). Country Background Report for Greece: Attracting, Developing and Retaining Effective Teachers. Education Research Centre (KEE). *Report for OECD Activity 'Attracting, Developing and Retaining Effective Teachers'* (http://www.oecd.org/dataoecd/24/20/30101431.pdf)

TDA (Training and Development Agency for Schools) (2008a). *Teacher training inquiries hit a million since credit crunch*, Press Releases 2008. http://www.tda.gov.uk/about/mediarelations/2008/180908.aspx Accessed 3/11/08.

TDA (Training and Development Agency for Schools) (2008b). *Male teachers crucial as role models*, Press Releases 2008, http://www.wired-gov.net/wg/wg-news-1.nsf/1fi/165850 Accessed 8/10/08.

Thornton, K. (2000). A new beginning. *Times Educational Supplement*, 20th October, p. 29.

Thornton, M. (1996). Subject specialism, gender and status: The example of primary school mathematics. *Education 3 to 13*, 24(3), 53–54.

Thornton, M. (1998). *Subject specialists – primary schools*, UCET Occasional Paper Number 10. London: Universities Council for the Education of Teachers.

Thornton, M. (1999a). Men into primary teaching: Who goes where? Dilemmas of entry, survival and career prospects. *Education 3 to 13*, 27(2), 50–55.

Thornton, M. (1999b). Reducing wastage among men student teachers in primary courses: A male club approach. *Journal of Education for Teaching*, 25(1), 41–53.

Thornton, M. & Bricheno, P. (2000). Primary teachers careers in England and Wales: The relationship between gender, role, position and promotion aspirations. *Pedagogy, Culture and Society*, 8(2), 187–206.

Thornton, M. & Bricheno, P. (2006). *Missing men in education*. Stoke-on-Trent: Trentham.

Thornton, M. & Iyer, P. (2009). Poor girls: A comparative analysis of their educational experiences in England and India. In G. Parameswaran & T. Kader (Ed.), *Educational Access and Social Justice: A global perspective*. New York: Rowman and Littlefield Publishing.

UNESCO (2006). *Teachers and educational quality: Monitoring global needs for 2015*, UNESCO Institute for Statistics, Montreal, 2006.

UNESCO (2008). *Statistics and indicators on women and men*, http://unstats.un.org/unsd/demographic/products/indwm/tab4e.htm, accessed 01/11/2008.

Wallace, J. (2008) *Questioning Assumptions about Male Teachers*, www.teachers.ab.ca/issues + in + education/diversity + and + human + rights/gend accessed 08.09.08.

Wilson, R., Sharp, C., Shuayb, M., Kendall, L., Wade, P., & Easton, C. (2007). *Research into the deployment and impact of support staff who have achieved HLTA status*, NFER 2007.

Wylie, C. (2000). *Trends in feminization of the teaching profession in OECD countries 1980–95* New Zealand Council for Educational Research International Labour Office Geneva March 2000 Accessed 01/11/2008 http://www.ilo.org/public/english/dialogue/sector/papers/feminize/wp-151.htm

You, M. H. & Ko, P. S. (2004). Gender and career development: An analysis of the promotion of elementary school principles in Taiwan. *Bulletin of Educational Research*, 50(4), 45–77.

Chapter 9
Regenerating Teachers

Corrie Stone-Johnson

Julie is in her eighth year of teaching at one of the top suburban high schools in the state of Massachusetts in the United States. She teaches history and psychology at both the general and Advanced Placement levels and has been at this same school since she began her career in teaching. Since the birth of her son more than 2 years ago she has been working a reduced schedule, which she hopes to continue into next year as well. Julie is in her mid-30s and teaching is her second career; prior to teaching she worked in political organizing.

Like many other teachers of her generation, Julie struggles with the balance between home and work life; with the types of changes she is being asked to make to her curriculum as a result of standardized testing regimes; and with her role as a teacher as she moves from being the new kid on the block to one of the more veteran teachers on her staff. She loves teaching but is considering a move into counseling, which would allow her to continue to work with students but perhaps offer something exciting and new in terms of her personal career development. She expresses little to no interest in being in administration, although she has held multiple leadership positions in her school over the course of her 8 years there.

Harrison is also a teacher in mid-career at a public school in the same state. In his late-30s, he works in an urban, underperforming school district. He has taught for 15 years and has changed schools multiple times. He currently teaches pre-algebra to students in the eighth grade. At his school, math is one of the most scrutinized subjects, as the school has not made Adequate Yearly Progress as required by No Child Left Behind (NCLB). Harrison's teaching is monitored tightly and he feels very little pedagogical freedom at present, a change that he feels undervalues him as a professional.

Harrison enjoys teaching but always keeps his eye on job listings for placements outside of his school. He would like to be an administrator but feels that his status as an African-American male works against him. He has applied for multiple administrative positions only to be turned away time and again. He feels he is well-compensated for his work and takes on extra opportunities to make more money, so he is not eager to leave the field entirely, especially within his district which, while challenging, pays well. He has a wife and small child at home, and until his wife goes back to work he feels obligated to stick it out.

M. Bayer et al. (eds.), *Teachers' Career Trajectories and Work Lives,*
Professional Learning and Development in Schools and Higher Education 3,
© Springer Science + Business Media B.V. 2009

These two teachers, on the surface, have a number of things in common: both are in mid-career, both are in their mid- to late-30s, both teach in secondary public schools in a state that has had high-stakes testing in place for several years. Both enjoy teaching and feel successful in their roles, both have young children, and both are slightly uncertain as to what the future holds in terms of their career growth and development. Both are part of Generation X, the generation known for supposedly trying to have it all and on their own terms. How will their careers unfold or progress? For the leaders who work with these teachers, what knowledge is necessary to keep them satisfied and effective in their work?

Generations are very much in the news. The *Boston Globe Magazine* (2008) dedicated an entire issue to the Baby Boomer Generation in July 2008, and William Safire (2008) devoted his "On Language" column in *The New York Times* to defining generations in November of the same year. Even as I began to organize my thoughts for this chapter, I could not help but think how much my generation defines me. I barely set foot in the library to retrieve books and articles to support my data; instead, I Googled the term "description of Generation X" to find out key sources, spent a fair amount of time on Wikipedia reading relevant articles, and searched my university's electronic journal archive for sources. I do not write by hand or even use a typewriter. Rather, I exclusively use a computer – a Macbook, of course. While I type, I keep several windows on my desktop open: Gmail, Facebook, and the *New York Times*. I cannot multitask as well as my younger peers, but I am wired in at all times. Like most of my peers, I am half of a household (one fourth, I suppose) with two working parents. I have the luxury of writing today because my husband has arranged his work schedule such that he stays home on Mondays so I can work. While I type away, he watches our infant son upstairs. Our toddler daughter is enrolled in a local Montessori school. When we made our childcare plans, we just worked under the assumption that each of our employers would accept this more flexible schedule. While one of Generation X's defining characteristics is its unwillingness to actually identify as part of a generation, I cannot help but see myself reflected in the literature I have read and stories I have heard about my generation.

This anecdote might seem unimportant, but I believe it is actually quite telling. I am a bona fide member of Generation X. I was born in 1973, which pretty much puts me right in the middle of my generation. We are a unique generation, sandwiched between the Boomer generation, known for its idealism, and Generation Y (also called Millennial), still working out its adult identity but currently seen as more engaged and defined as more productive than my generation, its predecessor. Even demographically speaking we are smaller: 46 million compared to 80 million (Boomer) and 78 million (Millennial) (Stephey, 2008). Nobody really has anything good to say about my generation. We are seen as cynical as slackers (Zemke et al., 2000) and as unable to commit to careers, marriage, or family life (Watters, 2004). In fact, we have married much later than our parents did and are having children later too. Our inability to commit is seen as a by-product, in some ways, of being latchkey children of the 1980s, left to fend for ourselves while our mothers entered the workforce unlike generations of women before them (Zemke et al., 2000; Lovely & Buffum, 2007). Our prospects are bleak – we may even be the first generation to not be as financially successful as the previous generation (Ellis, 2007).

And yet, in speaking to Generation Xers, specifically Generation X teachers, I have found something quite different from these standard stereotypes, something more promising and optimistic. What others see as slack, we see as flexible. What others see as entitled, we see as balanced. We want to work on our own terms, and we are willing to walk away from jobs that do not meet our needs (Zemke et al., 2000; Lancaster & Stillman, 2002). These differences play out not only in terms of family and work life generally, but specifically in terms of the careers of many of today's teachers. No matter how one looks at it, this is not our parents' teaching career, nor is it the career described by the Boomer generation writers who still dominate this literature and the portraits of that generation largely centered within it.

Through an analysis of the literature on generations, as well as interviews with 12 Generation X teachers, this chapter explores the generational differences of teachers and how understanding these differences is critical to understanding trends regarding the teaching career. The title "Regenerating Teachers" suggests two notions to keep in mind: First, that the way in which educational scholars understand teachers and their career trajectories may need to be reconsidered in light of generational differences among teachers and the academics who interpret their lives, and second, that this revised generational understanding may in fact help regenerate teachers' satisfaction and efficacy in their work and workplace.

This chapter is timely for several reasons. First, earlier work by such researchers as Huberman (1989) and Sikes et al. (1985) was conducted within systems and times with traditional career structures, where a new teacher might expect to enter teaching and remain for the duration of the career, or move after a period of time into leadership positions. In this structure, leadership meant leaving the classroom, and moving away from learning and instruction as a teacher. Teachers who did not progress to leadership but stayed in the classroom were most likely people who deliberately chose not to move up, or people who, by their own judgment or others', simply lacked the capacity to lead. Now, teachers have different leadership opportunities that do not necessarily take them away from the classroom. Leadership, and its relationship to teaching and learning, is positioned differently. Teachers are encouraged to take on more roles, and to take them earlier, than their predecessors (Bartlett, 2004). However, administrative roles are often shunned by people in this particular age group as they are viewed as taking teachers away from the very students whom they desire to serve (Donaldson, 2007). This study incorporates the changed understanding of teachers' roles regarding practice and leadership in a way that earlier studies, situated in a more traditional, linear career model, could not.

Second, this study fills several gaps in the literature on teachers' careers. Much of the literature in the field is primarily from the 1980s and early 1990s. Work in the current context of No Child Left Behind may provide different understandings of the career cycle. Additionally, the best-known work in the field, namely Huberman (1989) and Sikes et al. (1985), takes place outside of the American context. While these studies undoubtedly provide insight into the paths of teachers' careers, they do not address the unique American context, post-A Nation at Risk and up to and including No Child Left Behind. And last, the issues that face teachers in the other work on teachers' careers, such as generational mission (Goodson et al., 2006; Riseborough, 1981) and gendered patterns of mid-career choice, such as homemaking (Sikes et al., 1985) may no longer apply. This study will shed new light on the issues facing teachers in the present, post-millennium, American context.

Finally, this study will explore an area that has yet to be examined by researchers, that of generational identity of teachers, particularly those considered Generation X. Most teachers in mid-career now fall into this generational category, and the issues that face them as they progress through their careers differ to a great extent from those of the generations both before and after them. These differences warrant a new field of study, one that intersects both the study of teachers' careers and lives and the leadership issues that affect this new crop of mid-career teachers, both in terms of what type of leadership is needed to keep them engaged and involved in the classroom but also one that understands how they progress into newly defined leadership roles of their own.

Research Design

The empirical data that inform this study are part of a larger, mixed-methods study that is the basis for my dissertation. This particular chapter uses the qualitative data collected from semi-structured interviews (Merriam, 1998) of 12 participants with 7 to 20 years of teaching experience in secondary schools. These teachers are considered established and in the mature phase of their teaching (Burden, 1982, in Fessler, 1995; Sikes, 1992). For the purposes of the original study, which focuses on the impact of mandated change on teachers in mid-career, the sample was limited to secondary teachers primarily because change is notoriously difficult in secondary schools due to their size, bureaucratic complexity, subject traditions and identifications, and closeness to university selection (Goodson, 1983; Hargreaves, 2003; Louis & Miles, 1990; McLaughlin & Talbert, 2001). The limit regarding teaching experience is based on my understanding that a teacher who remains in the class after 7 years has committed significant emotional, physical, and financial resources to her career as a teacher and thus has a certain level of investment in – and identity with – her role as teacher (Sikes et al., 1985). The data are also limited to public school teachers, because I was interested in speaking with teachers regarding mandated change and in particular the state of Massachusetts' high-stakes test, MCAS. I did not limit the study to urban or suburban areas but instead allowed sampling to encompass either type of school.

Sampling for this study was purposive and relied on a snowball design to get participants (Merriam, 1998). I began by posting a message to a listserv for parents to which I belong, asking for teachers in a public school in a major subject area with 7 to 20 years of teaching experience. From this post, I found four participants. These teachers referred me to other teachers they know, thus expanding my sample. I also found participants through personal contacts in local schools.

With a snowball design, the sample is not randomized and this one may appear to be fairly homogeneous. However, demographic trends note that at this moment, the teaching force itself is fairly homogeneous; that is to say, female, White, and middle-class (Cochran-Smith et al., 2002; Goodwin, 2002). As it turned out, my sample included more men than women – atypical of the current teaching force that is predominantly female.

Participants

Twelve teachers from multiple school districts in the state of Massachusetts participated in the qualitative component of this study. The participants were from major subject areas in secondary public schools: English Language Arts, Science, Mathematics, and History/Social Studies. Special Education was also included, although teachers with this classification typically worked within the major subject areas. As the study design to gather participants was snowball, there was little consideration for factoring in how many teachers of a particular subject area participated. Also not factored in were gender and race, although members from minority groups in teaching – people of color and men – were randomly included in the sample.

Table 9.1 details the participants in the study:

Data Analysis

The interviews lasted between 45 min and 1 h. Each interview was digitally recorded and then fully transcribed. As each transcription was completed, I used line-by-line coding to ensure the most thorough reading of each interview (Strauss & Corbin, 1990). Constant memoing (Charmaz, 2006) was used to record themes and keep track of noticeable patterns and trends as well as thoughts for further study. I used the qualitative software package HyperResearch to keep track of my coding.

Generations

The use of the term "generation" in human population terms is thought to have originated with Karl Mannheim's publication of the essay "The Problem of Generations" in 1952 (Edmunds & Turner, 2002). According to Mannheim, a generation is shaped, held together by, and ultimately determined by common events that form its worldview. People within generations experience these events at the same time. Furthermore, generations follow observable historical patterns (Strauss & Howe, 1991). As generational theorist Jean Twenge observes, "The society that molds you when you are young stays with you the rest of your life" (Twenge, 2006, p. 2). Generational conflict arises because members of different generations experience these same events in different ways (Edmunds & Turner, 2002).

Table 9.1 Study participants

ID[a]	Subject	Year born	Years teaching	Gender	Race	Type of school
Harrison	Math	1968	15	Male	African-American	Urban middle, low performing
Alice	English Language Arts	1973	10	Female	White	Suburban high, high performing
Andrew	Physics	1973	9	Male	White	Urban high, high performing
Julie	History	1973	8	Female	White	Suburban high, high performing
Samantha	Special Education/ English Language Arts	1973	8	Female	White	Urban middle, low performing
Doug	History	1973	13	Male	White	Suburban high, high performing
Michelle	Special Education	1977	8	Female	White	Suburban middle, high performing
Jim	English Language Arts	1969	15	Male	White	Suburban high, high performing
Sarah	English Language Arts	1979	7	Female	White	Urban high, low performing
Bill	History	1974	8	Male	White	Suburban high, high performing
Mike	Math	1973	11	Male	White	Urban high, high performing
Max	Math and Science	1973	9	Male	White	Urban high, high performing

[a]All the names have been changed to protect the identities of the participants.

At present, there are five living generations (Strauss & Howe, 1991), four of which are in the workplace (The G.I. generation being the exception): G.I., Veterans/ Traditionalists, Boomers, Generation Xers, and Millennials. Table 9.2 describes the boundaries for each of these. Different scholars use different age boundaries to define each generation but the bulk of the age group is roughly the same (Zemke et al., 2000; Lancaster & Stillman, 2002; Lovely & Buffum, 2007). There are roughly 22 years between generations, shown below in Table 9.2 (Strauss & Howe, 1991).

Each of these generations has its own unique "peer personality" (Strauss & Howe, 1991) defined by a common age location, common beliefs and behavior, and perceived membership in a common generation (p. 64). Table 9.3 charts some of these personality characteristics.

While it is helpful to see the peer personalities of each of these generations, this chapter focuses largely on only the Boomer and Generation X generations.

Table 9.2 Living generations (Adapted from Strauss & Howe, 1991)

Generation	Born	Age in 2008
G.I.	1901–1924	84 to 107
Silent/Veteran	1925–1942	66 to 83
Boomer	1943–1960	48 to 65
13er/Generation X	1961–1981	27 to 47
Millennial	1982–present	0 to 26

Table 9.3 Unique characteristics of each generation (Adapted from Zemke et al., 2000)

Veterans	**Baby boomers**
Dedication/sacrifice	Optimism
Hard work	Team orientation
Conformity	Personal gratification
Law and order	Health and wellness
Respect for authority	Personal growth
Patience	Youth
Delayed reward	Work
Duty before pleasure	Involvement
Adherence to rules	
Honor	
Generation X	**Millennials**
Diversity	Optimism
Thinking globally	Civic duty
Balance	Confidence
Technoliteracy	Achievement
Fun	Sociability
Informality	Morality
Self-reliance	Street smarts
Pragmatism	Diversity

The forces that shaped the Boomers and Generation X respectively clearly influenced the worldviews of each group (Strauss & Howe, 1991). The Boomers' parents raised them with the wisdom of child expert Dr. Benjamin Spock, who advocated affection and permissiveness with children (Wikipedia, 2008a). The launch of Sputnik revolutionized their education, moving a more traditional curriculum to focus on science and math to ensure American students could keep up with their global peers. As teenagers and young adults, Boomers participated in the Summer of Love, in peace rallies around the country, in Woodstock, and in protests at Kent State. They were feminists and civil rights pioneers who advocated equal rights for all. As young adults they were hippies who believed in peace and love; as they aged they became yuppies who espoused more materialistic goals. Boomers were the first generation to have access to legal abortions through *Roe v. Wade* and were the first to be able to prevent pregnancy with the use of birth control pills.

The children of the Boomers became Generation X, and the legacy of the Boom generation is clear (Wikipedia, 2008b). Literally and metaphorically speaking, this was the first generation whose parents chose to have them – or not to have them – because of their abortion and birth-control freedoms. They were latchkey children left at home while both parents worked. Generation X views themselves as "survivors": They survived skyrocketing divorce rates, stock market crashes, and outsourcing. Lovely and Buffum (2007) suggest that this survivor mentality is what shapes their view of work: They have lower expectations of what jobs can offer and lower trust in authority figures as a result of their difficult upbringing.

Generations in the Workplace

The peer personalities of each generation affect many aspects of their lives, including attitudes toward family and community (Strauss & Howe, 1991; Watters, 2004). Similarly affected are a generation's attitudes toward work and behavior in the workplace. Table 9.4 describes the "generational footprint" of each group in the workplace.

Not only are each group's beliefs about work and the workplace different; in fact, their very understandings of career differ sharply, and this too affects their work lives in terms of dedication to their job and to their career. Lancaster and Stillman (2002) argue that the two older generations in the workplace, Traditionalists/Veterans and Boomers, who came of age in an era of American productivity, are motivated by "job security" (p. 53). Job security is staying with one company, working one's way up, and protecting oneself on a track record of high performance and stability. Younger generations, however, operate under a "career security" model (p. 54). Career security is premised on creating a varied set of skills and experiences that will make a person marketable in a variety of circumstances. To obtain these skills and experiences, those seeking career security may change jobs several times. Generation Xers, who came of age as American job stability waned, are more likely to seek career instead of job security. Table 9.5 describes generational differences around career goals.

Generations and the Teaching Career

Each of the generations views just about everything differently, including careers in general and also teaching in particular. Generational research suggests that a new teacher entering the field today need not have the same career path and patterns as a teacher 30 years her senior (Strauss & Howe, 1991; Johnson, 2004). Johnson and her colleagues' work in Massachusetts demonstrates how today's new teachers are very different from their predecessors. They may not have entered teaching through traditional routes such as education schools or education majors in undergraduate institutions; they may be more likely to be men, to be different races, to speak different languages. These insights into how new teachers differ from veteran teachers as they begin their careers touches on the different types of knowledge we will need to have to understand the concerns of "new" teachers as they move up through the ranks.

Table 9.4 The generational footprint of a workplace (From Lovely & Buffum, 2007, and adapted from Lancaster & Stillman, 2002; Raines, 2003; Zemke et al., 2000)

Generation	How they perform on the job	How they integrate on teams	How they lead others
Veterans	Driven by rules and order Strive to uphold culture and traditions Able to leave work at work Need more time for orientation Find technology intimidating	Are okay with the power of collective action, as long as a central leader is in charge Respect experience Want to know where they stand and what's expected of them Eager to conform to group roles	Value dedication and loyalty Equate age with status/power Impose top-down structures Make most decisions themselves Keep work and personal life separate View change as disruptive and undesirable
Baby boomers	Have a strong need to prove themselves to others May manipulate rules to meet own needs Deferential to authority Focus on product outcomes Can become political animals if turf is threatened Work long hours	Enjoy and value teamwork Expect group to stick to the schedule and agenda Willing to go the extra mile Good at building rapport and solving problems Embrace equity and equality Want credit and respect for accomplishments	Shy away from conflict Tend to lead through consensus Generally apply a participatory approach, but may struggle with delegation and empathy Embrace leadership trends and personal development Expect people to put in their time Less flexible with change
Generation X	Strive for balance, freedom and flexibility Strong dislike for corporate politics, fancy titles or rigid structures Expect to have fun at work Prefer independence and minimal supervision Good at multitasking Value process over product	Like to work on teams with informal roles and freedom to complete tasks their own way Do well on projects calling for technical competence and creativity Work best with teammates of their own choosing Detest being taken advantage of Struggle to build rapport with other group members	Drawn to leadership for altruistic reasons – not power or prestige Casual and laid-back Try to create an environment that is functional and efficient May lack tact and diplomacy Able to create and support alternative workplace structures Willing to challenge higher-ups Adapt easily to change

(continued)

Table 9.4 (continued)

Generation	How they perform on the job	How they integrate on teams	How they lead others
Millennials	Anxious to fit in Respectful of authority, but unafraid to approach their boss with concerns Value continuing education Exceptional at multitasking Drawn to organizations with career ladders and standardized pay/benefits	Accepting of group diversity Determined to achieve team goals Respond well to mentoring Enjoy working with idealistic people Expect to be included in decisions Need a bit more supervision and structure than other groups	Open to new ideas Able to work with varying employee styles and needs Prefer flattened hierarchy Hopeful and resilient Display more decorum and professionalism than Xers Lack experience handling conflict and difficult people

Table 9.5 Clashpoint around career goals (From Lancaster & Stillman, 2002, p. 55)

Traditionalists	"Build a legacy"
Baby Boomers	"Build a stellar career"
Generation Xers	"Build a portable career"
Millennials	"Build parallel careers"

Strauss and Howe (1991) have written extensively on the topic of generations and argue that generations occur in cycles. Specifically, they argue that there are four generational types that recur in cyclical patterns over time. Each generation has a personality type and reacts to social changes in predictable ways – although different from each generation to the next. They urge researchers to think of aging using train and station metaphors. As they describe it, most people, when studying aging, focus on "stations." Every train goes through the same stations; every generation in this metaphor represents a different train. So, if stations are childhood, youth, midlife, old age, etc., each generational train passes through each station. The trains are fairly identical using this metaphor. What Howe and Strauss argue, in contrast, is that generations need to be framed as trains and that each train should be viewed differently although they pass through the same stations.

Stretching this metaphor, we can view teacher generations as "trains" as well. The current generation of teachers in mid-career is what Howe and Strauss call "thirteen-ers" and what others commonly understand as Generation X (Twenge, 2006). These teachers were born between the years 1961 and 1981 and are now in their late 20s to late 40s. Most of the research on aging teachers, however, has focused on teachers of the previous generation, what Howe and Strauss call the "boom" generation, born between 1943 and 1960, and an emerging body on the new "boom" of Millennials.

The current generation of new teachers, called "Millennials," have yet another set of concerns that differ from their predecessors and that will indeed differ from future generations, but the work of Johnson and her colleagues (2004) in relation to this new generation that is now entering the workforce in large numbers to replace their retiring Boomer colleagues focuses largely on how this "next generation" of teachers will fare in today's classrooms, not on the issues facing teachers presently in mid-career. This chapter focuses on the middle generation of Generation X teachers currently in classrooms, not just as a "generation" of teachers but as a "generation" of adults different from those both before and after them.

Findings

When I began my research, I started with the idea that perhaps a teacher's generation, more than the conditions in which she works, might speak volumes about her desire to remain in teaching as a career. I based this hypothesis on my own abbreviated experience as a classroom teacher in a struggling urban school and on my friends' and colleagues' similar experiences. All of us felt that teaching was something we wanted to try, but when we felt either not good enough at it, or too overwhelmed by the micropolitics (Schempp et al., 1993; Blase & Anderson, 1995) of the school in which we worked, or we wanted to stay home with our children and find a way to still keep one foot in the world of education, we reshaped our careers to fit our desires. How very Generation X of us! We wanted to have our cake and eat it, too. While others (older generations) looked at our choices and felt we gave up or gave in too early, or that we were slackers who could not handle being adults with professional responsibilities, we saw it as within our right to make the choices that best suited ourselves and our families. If this was true of my peers, could it be generalized to speak of Generation X as teachers *writ large*?

Johnson and her colleagues (2004) touch on the idea that the new generation of teachers is different from its predecessors in that they entered the job market in different conditions and have different expectations about how their jobs should be performed. I hold this to be true but take it one step further: We are different from our predecessors not merely because of the context in which we enter into and remain in teaching, but by the very way in which we understand the world.

Not too long ago, research by others on the topic of who stays in and who leaves teaching focused on teacher recruitment strategies, as a looming teacher shortage seemed imminent due to the "graying" of the teacher workforce (*Teacher Magazine*, 1995; Murphy et al., 2003). Current work suggests that maintaining teacher supply is not an issue of recruitment but one of retention. Scholars of teacher retention focus on the conditions that affect teachers' retention and suggest strategies not just to bring teachers into the field but instead to ensure that those already in the field do not leave (Shen, 1997; Weiss, 1999; Ingersoll, 2001; Johnson, 2004).

I argue that teachers' career trajectories need to be reconsidered, revisioned, and indeed regenerated, to ensure that the people who are in today's classrooms remain engaged and sustained in their work. To me, the issue is not simply one of teacher retention. The teachers with whom I spoke do not plan to leave education, although many are looking to teach in different schools. They are dedicated to their students, their jobs, their colleagues, and their schools, and their level of commitment, in their own words, is tremendous. In comparison to the research on retention, what I found is that while these teachers are staying in their careers, their career trajectories are speeded up in comparison to earlier generations. Today's middle career teachers – those with 7 to 20 years in the classroom – are experimenting less in their own classrooms, burning out earlier, and generally resigning themselves to viewing teaching as something done during school hours instead of as an around-the-clock job at a younger age and at an earlier stage than teachers before them. The reasons for this acceleration are numerous and include the standardization of teaching due to No Child Left Behind and its focus on high-stakes testing and the desire for flexible work that allows a greater work–family balance. Whatever the reasons, though, careful consideration of the ways in which Generation X teachers view their work and their careers is necessary to keep them sustained in their work. While they might not be planning to leave, they are disengaging from their work much earlier than their predecessors.

The data presented here point to the ways in which today's mid-career teachers see their career trajectories compared to previous generations. The starting point for my argument lies with Huberman's influential writing on teachers' careers (1989). Huberman identified trends in the empirical literature on the phases of teachers' careers: *survival and discovery*, in which new teachers adjust to the shock of a new career and stumble to find their footing as novices; *stabilization*, in which teachers make a commitment to teaching as a career and gain more professional freedoms as they increase their experience; *experimentation/activism*, in which teachers attempt to increase their impact through experimenting with a variety of teaching techniques and taking on new roles, all the while bumping up against institutional barriers that seek to limit that impact; *taking stock*, in which teachers face a "mid-career crisis" and struggle to stay or leave the profession; *serenity*, in which teachers begin to distances themselves from their students and experience a slow deceleration; *conservatism*, in which teachers, finding themselves so much older than their students, begin to resist innovation and feel nostalgic for the way things were; and finally *disengagement*, in which teachers transfer their energies to pursuits other than work.

Each of these stages roughly corresponds with years teaching in the field. Figure 9.1, taken from Huberman's article, lays out a schematic model of these predictable stages.

Using this model as a starting point, and continuing with my own qualitative analysis of interviews with 12 teachers in Massachusetts, I found the following trends regarding the form and shape of teachers' career trajectories.

- The experimentation/activism phase is interrupted and/or stunted.
- Serenity and conservatism begin much earlier.
- Teachers begin the process of disengagement at an earlier point in time.
- The nature of teachers' career trajectories is no longer linear.

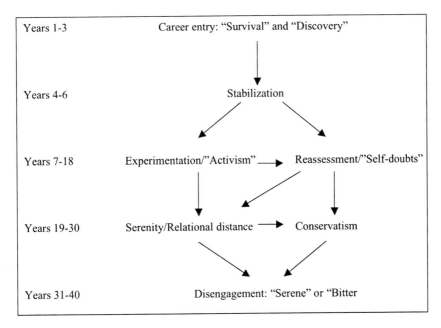

Fig. 9.1 Successive themes of the teacher career cycle: schematic model (From Huberman, 1989)

Experimentation/Activism

In Huberman's model, teachers, after passing through the early years of their new teaching careers, begin to settle in, find their sea legs and grow more confident in their abilities as teachers. Around this time, between 7 to 18 years, teachers enter a phase he calls *experimentation/activism*. Teachers start to experiment with new techniques in their classrooms, which is now possible due to their increased feelings of success and capacity as more seasoned teachers. During this time teachers may also begin to take on small leadership roles. At the same time that teachers feel increased feelings of efficacy, what stands out to Huberman during this time are also the initial stirrings of concern about growing "stale" in the profession.

For Boomer teachers, the progression from novice to growing expert was a logical and linear progression. To be a new teacher was to understand the limits of one's skills and capacities, and as one grew into one's own it made sense to become more confident, adventurous, even activist.

For Generation X teachers, however, the story has unfolded a little differently. There are both environmental and generational factors at play that influence this divergent path. First, the context in which today's middle career teachers – those in Huberman's group of 7 to 18 years – has changed dramatically. The field of teaching in the United States has become increasingly standardized (Hargreaves, 1994, 2003). While advocates of standardization argue that standards define what is to be taught and what kind of performance is expected, that they are necessary for equality of opportunity, and that they supply accurate information to students, parents, teachers, employers, and colleges (Ravitch, 1995), others argue that standardization deskills teachers (McNeil, 2000) by limiting curricular content and the teacher's control over what is taught, as well as intensifying teachers' work so that in practice they have less rather than more time to access the expertise and support of their colleagues (Hargreaves, 2003). Teachers, in this standardized and politically intensified environment, are not encouraged to think proactively and reflectively but instead think reactively in defense of their material needs (their jobs, curricular materials). They cannot take professional risks that may help them grow but instead must work to maintain their status quo. Schools, particularly urban schools that struggle with student achievement, are urged to adopt Comprehensive Reform models that are scientifically proven (Lytle, 2000; Datnow et al., 2002; U.S. Department of Education, 2002). These models often come with scripted teachers' guides and activities for students that minimize individual teachers' contributions to the curriculum and the learning of their students while simultaneously increasing the monitoring necessary for assessment and accountability, which are more strictly checked and more closely tied to the evaluation of the school (Hargreaves, 2003).

Thus, the necessary step in a novice teacher's career growth – experimentation – is complicated by simultaneously feeling more skilled while having fewer opportunities to demonstrate such development. In Massachusetts, this change is driven by the state's high-stakes test, the MCAS. After the implementation of MCAS, in combination with the pressures of achieving Adequate Yearly Progress under *No Child Left Behind*, Harrison, whose career path I described at the beginning, said:

> I feel like they have more and more layers of administration now. Whereas before they just didn't have the bodies to closely supervise you to the point that they wanted to, now they do. And now these people have nothing else to do other than sit around and think of things for you to do. And they just give you more than is humanly possible. And I think you still have the budgetary pressures to get people at the low end of the salary scale in place to save money and they are easier to control. They're not permanent teachers, they're provisionals. A lot of them aren't even certified so you give them the scripted curriculum and they do it. It's probably the best thing for them; they don't know how to teach so you may as well. But for somebody who has a professional license, who has a degree and who has been in the business a while, it's insulting, it's just crazy.

Mike, who teaches in one of Boston's pilot schools, expressed a similar sentiment:

> I work at a Boston Public School and within the Boston System group of schools called Pilot Schools which have some autonomies, that are separate from the rest of Boston System. Autonomies around budget, hiring, curriculum, calendar, there's another autonomy somewhere but the big one for me is about curriculum and as a teacher I think that's the big difference in teaching in a pilot school versus teaching in another school. So at my school, other schools in Boston there's a set teaching guide, there's a set textbook, set curriculum for a math teacher and at my school, because of the pilot school autonomy and also because of how the leadership of my school delegates that responsibility to the teachers, I have a lot of control over what I teach, how I teach it, when I teach it. So when I originally started I kind of could do whatever I want in whatever order I wanted. That was a really exciting but sometimes frustrating thing about being a teacher. MCAS in my department has meant that we are much more obligated to follow a certain path, a certain sequence of

events. While we still have that autonomy, while our headmaster still delegates that level of responsibility to the teachers, I feel like we're much more in line with what you would see in another school in Boston or another school in the state.

The second confounding factor is a generational difference regarding the desire to become leaders. While many teachers in previous generations moved from the classroom into administration, many Generation X teachers express a clear disdain for leadership roles, specifically high-level roles such as principal but also roles such as department chair or curriculum or testing coordinator that take them out of their classrooms and away from their students (Donaldson, 2007). Of the teachers with whom I spoke, 67% (8 out of 12) said they did not want a leadership role. Of those, a handful said they would take leadership roles that allowed them to stay in the classroom, or that they would take leadership roles in the future but not now. These teachers viewed administrative roles as taking them away from the students. Julie said:

> I'm not cut out to be an administrator. I'm not interested in organizing within schools. I'm interested in being part of the organization and part of making change but not administering it or working really primarily with adults in the building. My focus is really on kids.

Similarly, Sarah said:

> Every administrator I know is unhappy. Because unlike I think a lot of people, my interests didn't change. My interests still remain first and foremost English and second children. And you don't get to do that as an administrator and I've had people ask me why don't you and why won't you. I don't want the stress. I don't want to end up hating the kids. I don't want to end up hating; I don't want to have the teachers hate me.

The result of these two factors is that teachers are not experimenting and not taking on different roles.

Serenity and Conservatism

One typically views a move toward conservatism as a natural part of the aging process (Riseborough, 1981; Evans, 1996; Hargreaves, 2005). As teachers age, their focus often shifts from concerns at work to concerns at home. Instead of spending energy planning for the workday, older teachers begin to think about the future, about retirement, and about life after work. As such, they are less able to invest in changes or reforms occurring in their schools. This phase in Huberman's model begins after a long career in teaching, typically between 19 and 30 years.

Huberman's model both hits the nail on the head for the teachers with whom I spoke but also misses the mark. How can this be possible? Huberman suggests that in this phase of serenity moving toward conservatism, teachers experience a gradual decrease in energy that is made up for by a great sense of pride in themselves and their work over their careers. Thus, because they feel good about the work they have done and continue to do, they can begin to relax a bit and turn their energies elsewhere. This phenomenon is certainly true for the teachers in my study – but they have been teaching only between 7 and 15 years!

For those participants with families, teachers reported that their energies have turned away from school and toward home life. They no longer view their students as "their kids" as they have children of their own. Where they used to coach sports, direct plays and stay up nights working on curriculum and lesson plans, these teachers now do the minimum necessary to do their jobs well. Jim remarked:

> It's changed it an awful lot. Before I got married I was at school all the time. I was going to the dances, I was going to games, I had kids hanging out in my classroom just talking until 5:00 in the afternoon and none of that mattered. I just gave my whole life to the school. When I started dating my wife I was [head] of the drama club and so I was in the middle of the Crucible, which will henceforth be known as that damn play. And because it was taking time away from my girlfriend. So after that year, dumped the play, we got married and my time at school dropped. I don't go to dances anymore unless I have to. I do very little extra-curricular stuff that keeps me out at night. When my son was born four years ago I dropped even more. On the other hand it also made me very isolated at school because every free minute I had at school was dedicated to grading and prep work. I wanted to do as little as possible at home. So that meant no more socializing at lunch, leaving the teachers' room, hiding in my room for the grading. So that was difficult.

Mike expressed a similar sentiment:

> A lot of it is about when and how I do the work so that used to be my motto was stay in the building until 5:00, 5:30, 6:00, be as available as possible to students at every hour and go in early and stay late and now it's just not really a possibility to do it that way. You know, and then also the part that I bring home is much smaller. I used to come home and after dinner work for another two or three hours making beautiful worksheets, making beautiful curriculum. I don't know. And now I'm much more satisfied to do the best I can in a given amount of time which isn't always great but I feel like I have enough experience and enough other skills that kind of balance that out.

Sarah felt, after only 4 or 5 years, that she was able to "disconnect":

> The first day of school I put my phone number on the board and say, you never have any excuse, call me, if I don't answer the phone leave me a message, you know, like, not doing your homework isn't an option because you can call me and tell me why you can't do it, you can call me and ask me for help. Spent hundreds of dollars on books. You know, my kids like supplies, you know, pencils, putting white boards up in my room. It's just, you know, worrying, worrying about these students who … they're not, now I know, they're not mine. But it … over committed. It stressed me out … and I got to a place where I could disconnect but only after four, five years maybe and still, my husband would get so frustrated because the phone would ring, you know, eight times a night and these kids don't have phone manners. And, you know, it was just, I need help or I just called to, I mean, I had surgery and I remember when I had surgery, like, three hours afterwards the phone was ringing and my husband said, she can't talk right now. Just calling to say hi. So very committed.

It is perhaps Julie, though, who summed up the generational difference most succinctly.

> I started as an enthusiastic, dedicated teacher. Dedicated to figuring it out. And I was pretty successful early on. I could not recognize that at the time. Which I think many early teachers can't. And then I started taking on leadership roles in the school, to some extent, nothing administrative. But some leadership roles. And then I had a baby and … and I'm definitely figuring out still how to balance it and I'm kind of accepting that right now it's, while I'm there I do the best job I can do for the most part but it turns often into a totally

different energy than it used to. But sometimes that scares me a little bit, and I think oh God, I'm slacking, I'm turning into this teacher I really don't want to be. But in some ways I think there are parts of it that are healthy. The healthiest part being that I used to call my students my kids. And they were to an extent. But now they're really not. And I still love them and develop good relationships with them etc. but they are someone else's kids. Which is a good thing.

This does not mean that they have checked out of their jobs; indeed, they still say they are highly committed. However, the hours and mental energies directed toward their work have markedly decreased.

There is also both an environmental and a generational component to this expedited process of serenity moving into conservatism. The environmental difference between the generations of teachers is a change in the scope of teachers' work. Teachers are encouraged to take on more roles, and to take them earlier, than their predecessors (Bartlett, 2004). Teachers are urged to become more collaborative (McLaughlin & Talbert, 2001) and to take on leadership roles not just in their classrooms but also in their schools (Lieberman & Miller, 1999). This expanded view of the teaching role is more likely to include responsibilities outside the classroom, such as teacher involvement in directing the school's curricular, pedagogical, and assessment programs.

The teachers with whom I spoke have begun to move away from taking these once prized roles. While they used to direct plays and run student government, they now leave at the closing bell. They also took on these roles earlier in their careers, and have come to appreciate their roles as simply classroom teachers and not teacher leaders.

Generationally speaking, one of the defining characteristics of Generation X is a trend toward later marriage and family life as well as more job shifts than generations prior. Teachers used to enter the field after graduating college and begin their families earlier. A teacher with 19 years of experience might have been close to the age of 40. Today's middle career teachers, however, have often come to teaching from other lines of work and are thus older "earlier" in their career trajectories. A teacher who is 40 may have only been teaching 10 or 12 years, or even fewer. If the trend toward conservatism is a function of one's age, then it makes sense that today's mid-career teachers' trajectories more closely resemble later stage teachers' career trajectories from the prior generations.

A New Trajectory

The differences in the phases of teachers' careers as described above have both generational as well as environmental components. The context in which teachers work today is different than in past generations, largely due to the current focus on standardization and high-stakes testing. These differences are not necessarily permanent, though – educational change is a continuous process and the experiences that teachers have in their classrooms over time undoubtedly change with the times. What *is* permanently different is the generational makeup of teachers as time progresses. No matter what happens, new generations of teachers will enter into, work in, and leave teaching. These teachers will have different worldviews and understandings about life and careers than the generation before them, and understanding these varying viewpoints is a necessary step in understanding how teachers approach their work.

At present, perhaps the greatest generational difference that I found is the shape of the teaching career. Today's middle career teachers, largely members of Generation X, view work very differently from their predecessors and even from their successors. Huberman's model suggests that teachers' careers are shaped in a predictable and almost linear pattern. While Huberman's schematic does have differing pathways for teachers depending on their classroom experiences, there is a clear entry point, a clear departure point, and a fairly predictable middle section.

I found several differences in this pattern with the teachers with whom I spoke. First, the path is not as linear as it was in the past. Generation Xers do not view careers in a linear fashion: many of the teachers began their careers in other fields, many planned to leave the classroom for other jobs in education, and several were out of the workplace or only working part-time so that they could raise their families. Max raised this point in his conversation with me:

> I think that we think of our work differently but not necessarily in terms of privilege. I think we think of it differently because of the way that things work. I think it used to be the case that it was sort of expected and companies or organizations would sort of want you to come and stay and help build an organization or help build a company and now the incentive is not necessarily to stay. There's more incentive I think to jump around quite often because there's nothing really built in to help people build ownership and build, build up more value as they build time in a certain job.

Second, as I touched on above, the path is speeded up. This change is partly generational but also partly societal. Generation X had to grow up early, with their parents off at work and being left home after school to fend for themselves, and it appears that they are aging early as well. When asked about their generational identity, teachers even said that they felt older than their peers. Doug said, when asked about his generational identity:

> I feel like I'm right on the cusp to some extent, there's some Gen-X stuff but I also feel like I'm a little bit older. So there's a certain traditionalism. I don't know what you call the generation before Generation X but I feel like it's a mix ... I feel like a lot of my political opinions and a lot of how I make my own decisions are based on older issues. So, for example, a point of comparison for me is Viet Nam. Even though I'm not old enough to remember Viet Nam, because my parents were so impacted by it I feel like that's sort of my foundational point of comparison.

Max said: "I think I'm too old to be Generation X." Jim, too, felt older than his peers:

> I would've been comfortable in a classroom maybe 40 years ago. The level of expectations I have for my students, the level of work I give them, not the old fashioned way of teaching but definitely the expectations for student learning are, I think, very much out of step with the direction education is going these days.

Gleick (2000) writes that our society's understanding of time, as a concept, has shifted, and that is because of our increased education levels and wealth, we have a sense that we do not have enough time and this feeling causes tension. Time, as Gleick points out, is seen as a "negative status symbol": The more a person has, the less important he or she must be (p. 155). The very way we exist has speeded up; we buy pre-washed blue jeans because we do not have the patience to let them fade on their own. The door close button on the elevator is the most worn out, as we do not even have 10 extra seconds to spare to wait for the doors to close by themselves. This phenomenon of accelerated time is clearly present in the changed view of the teaching career as well. The teachers with whom I spoke are throwing themselves full-speed into their careers at an early stage, but they are burning out faster as well.

Particularly in an era of mandated reform and standardization, where expectations are raised for teachers in terms of performance and accountability, stress on teachers can lead to burnout (Smylie, 1999). Teachers may also burn out because they believe that teaching is a moral job; they take on more and more roles that they cannot handle because they feel that not doing so would let their students down (Bartlett, 2004).

Burnout theory suggests that teachers who burn out try to do well and "attempt desperately to succeed against all odds, risking their physical health and neglecting their personal lives to maximize the probability of professional success" (Farber, 1981, p. 328). Such teachers will not let their practice slide, and they leave teaching rather than allowing it to do so. Farber (1981, p. 328) also suggests that a separate phenomenon may be at play; teachers are worn out, not burned out – "Instead of burning out from overwork, they turn off to the job and stop attempting to succeed in situations that appear hopeless." These worn out teachers have experienced blows to their self-esteem, and have lost their desire to maintain the highest levels of performance; they do not necessarily leave the classroom, however.

Sarah talked about feeling burned out:

> Yes. I mean, if I wouldn't have had her (daughter), well, I would've taught I just couldn't stay where I was. It was just too dysfunctional. Too, I mean, it was like I was walking in to school every day and my analogy was like, I was just walking in, just trying to get in my classroom so I could help the kids and it was, like, different people were just, like, throwing things at me trying to stop me from getting there. It was just so hard. I was fighting so many things that weren't my job. You know, it didn't seem worth it anymore. So I would've gone to a different school but I would've bagged groceries before I would've gone back there. And I loved the kids, loved the kids.

Mike also spoke about the phenomenon of burning out:

> I always felt like education is such a demanding field that I could burn out really, really quickly and I've always left myself open to that possibility so I think that I could but I don't like to look too far ahead. I think my level of energy for the work has changed. The pace of how I do it has changed but I still feel energized by the teaching part.

It is clear to me in speaking with these teachers that something very different is happening in their careers, something that is on the one hand burning them out early yet at the same time keeping them in the classrooms. These teachers are going through the same stations, as Strauss and Howe (1991) suggest, that other teachers in the past have gone through, only they are on bullet trains, not steam locomotives. The ways in which school leaders and teacher education programs attend to this difference is critical to finding ways to keep these teachers satisfied as they remain in the workplace.

Leadership and Preparation for a New Generation of Teachers

The teachers in my study do not dislike teaching. In fact, they quite enjoy being around their students and feel great pride that they are finally reaching a great number of students and doing a fairly good job of doing so. Even so, they express a sense of early disengagement with their careers. They work less hard, in part because they are more experienced but also in part because they are just tired.

There are two issues facing this unique generation of teachers. The first is one of leadership. Of the teachers who plan to remain in teaching, many do not plan to become administrators. This situation creates a twofold problem. One, there is a certain level of disdain for administrators, who are viewed as out of touch with the students. Two, there will be a significant leadership gap when the Boomer-generation leaders leave and no one with experience in classrooms is there to fill their positions. This problem is one of both leadership and preparation, and it must be addressed to ensure that today's mid-career teachers can stay happy in their present roles but also progress in a productive way to leadership. Given what I have learned in speaking with teachers, I make the following suggestions.

First, generational research suggests that Generation X teachers are driven to leadership roles by altruistic reasons, not the desire for power (Zemke et al., 2000; Lancaster & Stillman, 2002; Raines, 2003; Lovely & Buffum, 2007). Distributed leadership that empowers teachers to lead and allows them to feel they are directly helping their students while not necessarily taking them out of their classrooms would both put teachers in positions of power and give them a sense that they are not losing time with their students (Harris & Muijs, 2004; Spillane et al., 2001). The type of leadership that teachers seem to disdain is the top-down kind, the kind that has one person at the top making every decision, a more power-based position than an altruistic one. Teachers also said they did not want to get bogged down in the politics of the school but instead wanted to be closely involved in the learning. While these two (politics and learning) are not by nature mutually exclusive, any moves to bring them closer together in ways that teachers view as helpful would bring experienced teachers into leadership roles.

Second, recent research on teacher leadership suggests that the teachers who remain the most engaged are those who are paid well for the work they do which they consider above and beyond their job descriptions (Bartlett, 2004). Extra pay for extra work is one avenue, as is giving teachers fewer classes to teach as they take on additional roles. Several of the teachers I talked to said they would consider leadership roles that allowed them to spend most of their time in the classroom and not in the front office. One perception of Generation X is that they want to have their cake and eat it, too. By giving them the opportunity to experience leadership while continuing to teach, school leaders might be able to bring a greater number of these teachers into leadership roles.

Of course, the general reluctance of teachers to move to administration is still a concern. Even with distributed leadership, the fact remains that many Generation X teachers simply do not want to be principals. They will assume leadership roles but not the general leadership of a school, or for that matter, a school district. For these teachers, a fundamental shift in how administration is viewed may be the only way to move experienced teachers into principalships. Distributed leadership can both allow teachers to share in the administration of school while remaining in their classrooms and allow them, if they become leaders, to keep a foothold in the more routine aspects of leadership instead of wholly immersing them in the more political aspects of the school.

The second issue facing this generation of teachers is one of sustainability. Generation X teachers will remain in their careers, but what can be done, both by the teachers themselves and by the leaders who work with them, to ensure that they remain engaged in their careers, especially if they do not plan to move into leadership positions? Generation X teachers appear to be burning out years before the generations of teachers before them, but they are not necessarily leaving teaching. In order to keep teachers sustained in their work, school leaders need to consider several factors. First, do these teachers need new types of work to stimulate their careers? Can they be given new courses to teach, or new groups of students? Teachers in mid-career are finally feeling good about the work they can do after years of learning the ropes. There is a fine balance to be achieved between asking teachers to take on new work that stimulates them, asking them to give up what they feel effective doing, and being mindful not to overload them. For teachers who are already beginning to experience burnout, taking on new work might seem not to be a stimulus but instead to be a drain. Asking teachers directly where their interests lie and working with them to create change in their work would be an ideal first step in this process.

Equally important, especially to Generation X teachers, is flexibility. This generation of teachers is highly dedicated to their students but also strongly family-oriented. They want the ability to keep their jobs while making time to spend with their own children. Several of the teachers I talked to were either currently out of the classroom to raise their children, working reduced schedules to accommodate family concerns, or consciously holding off on making moves either to different schools or to leadership roles while raising their families. This was true of both men and women. School leaders must be mindful that this generation, having been raised as latchkey children, is conscious of wanting to spend more time with their children, and their career trajectories may not be linear as in previous generations. Allowing teachers the flexibility to shift their careers in ways that best suit their needs is a critical component of keeping these teachers in the classroom. Generation X teachers, already prepared to leave any job that does not conform to their desires, may be better able to commit to staying in their jobs if they are reassured that their job will be there if they take time off for family. Departments may look different as teachers cycle in and out of positions, and strong leadership involves building strong teams with multiple strengths to accommodate these shifts.

Concluding Thoughts

This chapter examines the career trajectories of Generation X teachers using both a review of the literature on generations and in-depth qualitative interviews with 12 teachers. The analysis reveals several interesting points about how the career trajectories of these teachers are different than those of past generations. First, while teachers appear to be going through the same phases, the times at which they do so are different. Second, the shape of the trajectory is itself different. What used to seem a simple, straightforward and linear path from entry into the classroom to retirement is now more fluid.

Understanding these two points is important for at least two reasons. First is the notion of regenerating teachers. The way we see teachers needs to be "regenerated" so that we can meet their different needs and ensure that they stay and remain engaged in their careers and their work. Prior work about teachers' careers was conducted both by and about a different generation of teachers, and in order to understand how today's teachers differ it is necessary to view them and understand them differently.

Second is sustaining teachers. If teachers are committed to staying in their classrooms, then it is crucial to ensure that they do not burn out too soon. Generation X teachers in mid-career are already beginning to feel the early stages of burn-out. Working with them to meet their needs is a critical component of making sure that they remain pleased with the work they are presently doing and the work they hope to do.

By taking a generational approach to viewing teachers' career trajectories, this chapter opens up a new avenue of understanding the teaching career. While further research is necessary, it is an initial step in regenerating our knowledge about who is teaching and why they do or do not remain in the classroom and for what reasons. As the next generation of teachers, the Millennials/Generation Y, enters the teaching force, it will certainly be interesting to see how they view their careers and work as well.

References

Bartlett, L. (2004). Expanding teacher work roles: A resource for retention or a recipe for overwork? *Journal of Education Policy*, 19(5), 565–582.

Blase, J. & Anderson, G. (1995). *The micropolitics of educational leadership: From control to empowerment*. New York: Teachers College Press.

Burden, P. R. (1982, February). *Developmental supervision: Reducing teacher stress at different career stages*. Paper presented at the annual conference of the Association of Teacher Educators, Phoenix, AZ.

Charmaz, K. (2006). *Constructing grounded theory: A practical guide through qualitative analysis*. London: Sage.

Cochran-Smith, M., Davis, D., & Fries, M. K. (2002). Multicultural teacher education research, practice, and policy. In J. A. Banks & C. M. Banks (Ed.), *The handbook of research on multicultural education*, Second edition. San Francisco, CA: Jossey Bass.

Datnow, A., Hubbard, L., & Mehan, H. (2002). *Extending educational reform: From one school to many*. London/New York: RoutledgeFalmer.

Donaldson, M. (2007). To lead or not to lead? A quandary for newly tenured teachers. In R. H. Ackerman and S. V. Mackenzie (Eds.), *Uncovering teacher leadership* (pp. 259–272). Thousand Oaks, CA: Corwin Press.

Edmunds, J. & Turner, B. S. (2002). Generational consciousness, narrative, and politics. In J. Edmunds and B. S. Turner (Eds.), *Generational consciousness, narrative and politics* (pp. 1–12). Lanham, MD: Rowman & Littlefield.

Ellis, D. (2007, May 25). Making less than dad did. *CNN Money*. Retrieved November 30, 2008, from http://money.cnn.com/2007/05/25/pf/mobility_study/index.htm?cnn = yes.

Evans, R. (1996). *The human side of school change*. San Francisco, CA: Jossey-Bass.

Farber, B. A. (1981). Teacher burnout: Assumptions, myths, and issues. *Teachers College Record*, 86(2), 321–338.

Fessler, R. (1995). Dynamics of teacher career stages. In T. R. Guskey and M. Huberman (Eds.), *Professional development in education: New paradigms and practices* (pp. 171–192). New York: Teachers College Press.

Gleick, J. (2000). *Faster*. New York: Vintage Books.

Goodson, I. F. (1983). *School subjects and curriculum change*. London: Croom Helm.

Goodson, I., Moore, S., & Hargreaves, A. (2006). Teacher nostalgia and the sustainability of reform: The generation and degeneration of teachers' missions, memory, and meaning. *Educational Administration Quarterly*, 42(1), 42–61.

Goodwin, A. L. (2002). Teacher preparation and the education of immigrant children. *Education and Urban Society*, 34(2), 156–172.

Hargreaves, A. (1994). *Changing teachers, changing times: Teachers' work and culture in the postmodern age*. New York: Teachers College Press.

Hargreaves, A. (2003). *Teaching in the knowledge society*. New York: Teachers College Press.

Hargreaves, A. (2005). Educational change takes ages: Life, career and generational factors in teachers' emotional responses to educational change. *Teaching and Teacher Education*, 21(8), 967–983.

Harris, A. & Muijs, D. (2004). *Improving schools through teacher leadership*. London: Open University Press.

Huberman, M. (1989). The professional life cycle of teachers. *Teachers College Record*, 91(1), 31–57.

Ingersoll, R. M. (2001). Teacher turnover and teacher shortages: An organizational analysis. *American Educational Research Journal*, 38(3), 499–534.

Johnson, S. M. (2004). *Finders and keepers: Helping new teachers survive and thrive in our schools*. San Francisco, CA: Wiley.

Lancaster, L. C. & Stillman, D. (2002). *When generations collide*. New York: Collins Business. Laying a foundation for the future of teaching. *Teacher Magazine*, 6(4). 8–9.

Lieberman, A. & Miller, L. (1999). *Teachers transforming their world and their work*. New York: Teachers College Press.

Louis, K. S. & Miles, M. B. (1990). *Improving the urban high school: What works and why*. New York: Teachers College Press.

Lovely, S. & Buffum, A. G. (2007). *Generations at school: Building an age-friendly learning community*. Thousand Oaks, CA: Corwin Press.

Lytle, J. H. (2000). Teacher education at the millennium: A view from the cafeteria. *Journal of Teacher Education*, 51(3), 174–179.

McLaughlin, M. W. & Talbert, J. E. (2001). *Professional communities and the work of high school teaching*. Chicago: University of Chicago Press.

McNeil, L. M. (2000). *Contradictions of school reform: Educational costs of standardized testing*. New York: Routledge.

Merriam, S. B. (1998). *Qualitative research and case study applications in education*. San Francisco, CA: Wiley.

Murphy, P., DeArmond, M., & Guin, K. (2003). A national crisis or localized problems? Getting perspective on the scope and scale of the teacher shortage. *Educational Policy Analysis Archives*, 11(23). Retrieved 26.03.2009 from http://epaa.asu.edu/epaa/v11n23/.

Raines, C. (2003). *Connecting generations: The sourcebook for a new workplace.* Berkeley, CA: Crisp.

Ravitch, D. (1995). *National standards in American education: A citizen's guide.* Washington, DC: Brookings Institution Press.

Riseborough, G. F. (1981). Teachers' careers and comprehensive schooling: An empirical study. *Sociology,* 15, 325–381.

Safire, W. (2008). Generation what? *The New York Times.* Retrieved November 30, 2008, from http://www.nytimes.com/2008/11/30/magazine/30wwln-safire-t.html?ref = magazine.

Schempp, P. G., Sparkes, A. C., & Templin, T. J. (1993). The micropolitics of teacher induction. *American Educational Research Journal,* 30(3), 447–472.

Shen, J. (1997). Teacher retention and attrition in public schools: Evidence for SASS91. *Journal of Educational Research,* 91(2), 81–88.

Sikes, P. (1992). Imposed change and the experienced teacher. In M. Fullan and A. Hargreaves (Eds.), *Teacher development and educational change* (pp. 36–55). London: The Falmer Press.

Sikes, P., Measor, L., & Woods, P. (1985). *Teacher careers: Crises and continuities.* London: Falmer Press.

Smylie, M. (1999). Teacher stress in a time of reform. In R. Vandenberghe & M. Huberman (Eds.), *Understanding and preventing teacher burnout* (pp. 59–84). Cambridge: Cambridge University Press.

Spillane, J., Halverson, R., & Diamond, J. (2001). *Towards a theory of leadership practice: A distributed perspective.* Northwestern University, institute for Policy Research, working article.

Stephey, M. J. (2008, April 16). Gen-X: The ignored generation? *Time.* Retrieved November 30, 2008, from http://www.time.com/time/arts/article/0,8599,1731528,00.html.

Strauss, A. & Corbin, J. (1990). *Basics of qualitative research: Grounded theory procedures and techniques.* Newbury Park, California: Sage Publications.

Strauss, W. & Howe, N. (1991). *Generations: The history of America's future, 1584 to 2069.* New York: William Morrow.

The Boston Globe Magazine. (2008, July 27). The Boomers Issue.

Twenge, J. (2006). *Generation me.* New York: Simon & Schuster.

U.S. Department of Education. (2002). *No Child Left Behind: A desktop reference.* Washington, DC: Office of Elementary and Secondary Education.

Watters, E. (2004). *Urban tribes: Are friends the new family?* New York: Bloomsbury Publishing.

Weiss, E. M. (1999). Perceived workplace conditions and first-year teachers' morale, career choice commitment, and planned retention: A secondary analysis. *Teaching and Teacher Education,* 15, 861–879.

Wikipedia. (2008a). Baby boomer. In *Wikipedia, the free encyclopedia.* Retrieved November 30, 2008, from http://en.wikipedia.org/wiki/Baby_boomer.

Wikipedia. (2008b). Generation X. In *Wikipedia, the free encyclopedia.* Retrieved November 30, 2008, from http://en.wikipedia.org/wiki/Generation_X.

Zemke, R., Raines, C., & Filipczak, B. (2000). *Generations at work: Managing the clash of veterans, boomers, Xers and Nexters in your workplace.* New York: AMACOM.

Chapter 10
Listening to Professional Life Stories: Some Cross-Professional Perspectives

Ivor Goodson

In pursuing an understanding of teachers' lives and careers I have focused on an individual life story to highlight some contemporary themes. A number of these themes have been recently elucidated in the Professional Network Report (2008) covering eight European countries. These themes can be easily uncovered in a wide range of places and in all of the caring professions of the public services. In the past few years, I have had the opportunity to travel extensively and to interview a varied set of professional workers.

It is important to situate one's understanding of teachers' lives and careers in a general context of professional settings. Often these life narrative insights are a cross-professional phenomenon common not just to teachers but to most public service workers.

A few vignettes might provide a confirmation of the general nature of the responses that the teachers later epitomize. A group of young British nurses talking to me at great length about how the new focus on targets and league tables for hospitals takes them away from the vocation they entered nursing for:

> I came into nursing because, all my life – well since I can remember – I have wanted to look after people and care for them. It's something I grew up with in my family: my grandma was a midwife and my mum a part-time orderly. So you could say it was in the blood. I'm not a squeamish person and blood and vomit and poo have never put me off, if I can get to care for the person who is in the frontline of pain, namely the patient. Some fools in the Health Trusts now call them 'clients' – bloody silly if you ask me! But for me, looking after patients and talking to them, treating them and making them comfortable – sort of respecting their dignity – that's what I came into nursing for.

This testimony would, I think, be recognized by generations of nurses: it is part of the caring professional. The source of vocation, which has underpinned their commitment and their lifework, is nursing. So how do the reforms react to this precious ecology of commitment? One nurse describes her response to health reforms focusing on performativity:

> My whole life is nursing: my whole sense of purpose is flattened by the web of bureaucratic bullshit in which I find myself. Instead of being at the bedside caring for patients, talking to patients, watching and observing them carefully; instead of working as a team of nurses who have these skills and build a community of caring, I end up doing other stuff altogether.

M. Bayer et al. (eds.), *Teachers' Career Trajectories and Work Lives*, Professional Learning and Development in Schools and Higher Education 3, © Springer Science + Business Media B.V. 2009

If you watched me, you'd be amazed, bloody amazed. A lot of the time now, I don't go anywhere near a bed, let alone a patient. What am I doing? I am sitting alone in front of a computer – filling in forms, compiling data, fiddling about with figures – actually fiddling is the word [laughs and laughs]. But really, is this what I'm here for – a young woman in the prime of life? I reckon I have so much to offer in terms of love and compassion for those people in need and I can't get near them. It makes me sick: still at least I'll fit in here if I become sick!

These views about the affect of performance criteria-based reforms on these young nurses were shared by all the women I talked to. Perhaps the most powerful confirmation came from a much older nurse.

The job has changed so much and I and my friends (we're all about the same age, I guess around 50) … we try to hold on to our old world in the face of these silly targets and tables. In my ward we still put the patient first, and we continue as a team of dedicated, experienced nurses to do this. It means we skimp on the paperwork, fill in the minimum, skip as many sections as we can. We sometimes get ticked off by the managers, and so on, but they know us and nothing ever happens. But it's a funny world where you have to make excuses for being a proper nurse – I sometimes wonder what is going on. Do they really want the NHS (National Health Service) to succeed, or something else?

These nurses – the younger and the older – were both in the same hospital and I was able to spend a day observing them at work. In the past 20 years, I have spent a good deal of my time observing professionals at work. So it was fascinating to see the differences they had talked about really did exist in this practice.

An incidental realization came when I negotiated entry. The nurses preferred that I came in a personal capacity, rather than as an official visitor. This is because of what Frank Furudi calls the 'culture of fear', which prevails in many professional workplaces, because of the obsessive micromanagement of public services. Hence the nurses, even the experienced older ones, preferred that I kept them anonymous, and our meetings and my observations almost seemed covert at times.

My day in the hospital fully confirmed the different visions that the two cohorts of nurses presented. The younger nurses' wards were often empty of nursing carers, as patients lay alone. For long periods of the day, I found the nurses congregated in a long back room, entering data into their computers. Occasionally, one or two would pop into the wards, often in response to a bleeper. But the clear centre of gravity of their professional life was the computer room. The difference, as I present it, seems almost too stark and polarized to be believable, but this was exactly how it was on these wards. In the older nurses' wards, it was a far more traditional pattern: nurses talking to patients, arranging beds, interacting with visitors, coping with emergency medical situations. But, above all, they were present in the ward and in the intimate caring relationship to their patients. The younger nurses' ward was simply far less hands-on; there was less of a presence throughout the day. Visits were occasional and felt minimal. They seemed to be dealing with clients, rather than servicing their patients, and we have seen when they described their nursing that this led to a strong sense of frustration. They had ended up in a very different relationship with those they were hoping to care for than they had envisaged.

One nurse who was willing to talk about these changes, and go public with her views, was Bernadette Murphy, a 38-year-old community staff nurse from Sutton in London. She said:

> Nursing is struggling to recruit people now because women's attitudes have changed so much. When I started my training in 1984, women weren't expected to go out and have a career. Today, nearly all my friends work. It's not surprising that people don't want to come into a profession like nursing when there are so many other more glamorous and better paid careers out there.
>
> It is possible to earn a quite decent living from nursing, but to do so you have to really strive to get up the career ladder. And then that leaves you in a situation whereby you are no longer having that one-on-one contact with the patients, which is why you came into the profession in the first place. You get stuck doing administration and mountains of paperwork. (Doward & Reilly, 2003: 7)

These nurses' commentaries on the effects of public service are similar to the cases of teachers, and to reports from a wide range of agencies and professional workers. There is also the question raised by one of them about just what the reforms are really about if they are so manifestly counterproductive. The nurse who raises the question 'Do they really want the National Health Service?' is following a line pursued by other professionals. The 'culture of fear' and of 'blaming and shaming' underperforming hospitals through league tables and performance indicators is a strange strategy to employ. If it were so successful, why don't the much emulated business managements employ such regulatory frameworks? In business, as we have said, the emphasis seems to be more on 'free markets', free action and deregulation. Indeed, the promise is held out that the high performing hospitals will themselves be freed from micromanagement and obsessive regulation. We face here a conundrum which is plainly baffling, not only to the workers but also the professional elites in the health service. Again they are beginning to wonder, like the nurse: 'Do they really want the National Health Service?', or would some in government prefer a handover of this public service to private agencies, as has happened in so many other cases, such as the railways?

In a recent study of NHS nurses, the levels of disenchantment and dysfunction were clearly evident. Kim Catcheside found that patterns of professionalism were being transformed by the reforms. She states of the NHS:

> Modern nurses are a health hazard, the old-fashioned TLC-trained ['tender, loving, care' – a summariser for a caring professional vocation] ones have all retired or resigned and the new lot, badly trained and poorly motivated, could not care less and are as likely in their ignorance to kill as to cure. (Arnold, 2001: 12)

Behind this dysfunctionality, produced above all by the reforms, a growing body of opinion is emerging, calling into question the rationale of these reform initiatives. Professional leaders in the august and moderate body, the British Medical Association, have stated that the government reforms are 'changing the character of the NHS by turning it from an organisation that treats patients into a purchaser of services provided by private contractors' (Carvel, 2003: 2). Here, there are echoes of the frontline concerns expressed by nurses who see a changed relationship to patients being inflicted upon them to the detriment of both the carers and the cared for.

Mr. James Johnson, chairman of the British Medical Association, said that the first sign of the government's long-term plans for the health service was the proposal to transfer 250,000 operations from the National Health Service to 'private treatment centres run by multi-national health corporations'. These transfer deals were worth £2 billion. Johnson argued that it was 'inevitable' that the centres would perform the simplest operations on the fittest patients, leaving more complex work to the NHS. This is, in fact, a remarkable echo of the private schools that take the best-equipped students, teach them with better facilities and higher teacher/pupil ratios, and then conspire with the user that state schools are failing. Johnson, therefore, concludes that these changes in the health service are bound to lead to accusations that the cost of an NHS operation was greater. In a very insightful comment, he states that 'it is almost as if the NHS is being set up to fail' (ibid.).

The response of the young nurses to health reforms has been dramatically repeated by young teachers who have spoken out against the education reforms. Many teachers reiterate the same litany of complaints. One such teacher, Carmel Fitzsimons, qualified successfully as a teacher but decided, after watching the reforms in action during her training year, that she could not face becoming a teacher. Her sense of mission and dedication was to a view of teaching as a creative and compassionate caring profession – the vision, in fact, of generations of women (and men) who have entered the teacher profession. These people have had an overriding sense of 'vocation' that has allowed them to tolerate low pay and low status for the sake of their 'dream' of contributing to society and to students' lives. The reforms do unimaginable violence to these high hopes and vivid visions.

In the event, she determined not to follow her dream and go into teaching. She went further, writing an article on why 'I Quit' for one of the leading education newspapers in Britain. It was a very public and extremely articulate protest. She wrote: 'I don't think teachers are uncreative but creativity is being crushed out of them by the grinding cogs of bureaucracy and filing' (Fitzsimons, 2001: 2). What is interesting is her vision that teaching of the sort she wanted to practise should be a creative, innovative, intellectually invigorating profession. In this sense, she represents precisely the vanguard of creative and adventurous professionals which could carry teaching forward in these challenging times. As I shall argue later, this vanguard is a crucial element in the revitalization of any profession, so the loss of such a bright young woman is of more than singular significance.

She goes on to describe precisely what bureaucracy and reformist initiative led to her decision:

> To give you a glimpse: for every lesson a teacher is supposed to prepare assessment sheets from the previous lesson: they must then reflect upon the issues the assessment throws up. Then they must prepare a lesson plan – based on long-term, medium-term and short-term objectives from the curriculum; and having delivered the lesson, they must write up an evaluation of how the lesson went and then individually assess the progression of each child's learning. This can mean five sheets of written paper per lesson for each of the five lessons a day. Add the individual record of each child, the reading records and the collection of money for the school trip and you start to wonder whether there is any time left for getting your coat on before legging it across the playground. (ibid.)

Jim Roberts is a teacher in his early 40s who works in a comprehensive in Sussex on the South Coast of England. I have been spending a good deal of time interviewing him and indeed just talking to him over the past year. He is known as a highly gifted teacher, a master of his craft. He is bright (has a Ph.D. in Education) and ambitious. In short, he is just the kind of teacher to make up the 'vanguard' of a caring profession aiming to deliver high standards of education.

Early on in our talks he admits that his teaching work 'is his life'. In his early years in the 1980s and early 1990s, he was very close to the pupils he taught:

> I got to know them; got to know their parents; just fitted into that community really and absolutely loved it. Basically, I did everything I could and it didn't seem like work – it felt more like I looked forward to being in the community really – and then things started to change.

He continues:

> [W]hilst there was a degree of openness in the late eighties and early nineties – now, the landscape is more sinister in my view.

I ask what he means. At first he talks about his own physical response:

> Fatigue comes to mind; initiative after initiative ... that is so hard to actually name. I had sleepless nights over this because I was so intensely angry.

The general echoes of change, 'cascading from the centre' without consultation, had worn him down:

> I've been a bit down on it really because, you know, I came to the conclusion that all I was doing was supporting the system I was trying to challenge, or subvert. You end up in a mode of support for it. I don't mean that I've been turned into someone who can't think for themselves, who can't step outside, who can't find alternatives, but the fact that I'm working within that context and for that group of people that are aiming to do this work is ultimately self-defeating because it's too powerful. It's got a singular mind; it's got a singular view ... what many people describe as technical rationalism. How can we measure it, how can we implement it? There is a disregard for teachers, as far as I can tell, and obviously I've looked at the face of it and I've seen disregard for teachers, disregard for – not kids, because they think they're doing it on behalf of the kids; they think they're doing it on behalf of the 'client'. (We are supposed to be calling them clients at these meetings, which I find abhorrent.) And so this whole thing about marketisation of education is staring me in the face and no matter what I say or what I do, or which group I work with, all we can keep doing is articulating that voice, which stands up against markets.

This depression and demoralization has progressively undermined Jim's sense of his professionalism, his sense of his life mission. Above all, he has watched how other colleagues have been treated (or mistreated) and how they have reacted. At times, he is moved to tears by what he says in the following section from one of our interviews:

> It's the casualties along the way that get you down. It's the faces of the people that you've worked with who just can't take it anymore. It's the stories of illness, the stories of people leaving the profession who are good – it's not people that you would think would leave. It's the stories of people in my own department, my colleagues who want to find an alternative way to live their lives. For example, I've only been at my new place – this is my third year – and a colleague who's a sculptor was really down on the school. He was down on the initiatives, he was down on the reforms, he was down on performance management. In my first meeting with him, we sat down and I asked him: 'What objectives are you setting?' He goes, 'Jim, I don't want to do this anymore, I don't want to set objectives, I don't want to do performance management and I don't work here next September, so the school can stick it'.

What age is he?
He's over 40 – 43 – 44. I said, 'Phil, I'm with you mate, one hundred percent behind you on this. If you're going to be here, what are we going to do? Can we look at this idea that you're an arts educator in-residence'. All this stuff about 'let's get a so-called 'artist-in-residence'. Well we discussed the possibility that we could suspend his timetable for a while and he could be … along with his sort of career as an artist, he could have some time as an artist-in-residence in the timetable. And I put it to the Head and she said, 'I'm interested, I want these ideas. How much is it going to cost me? What's the effect on the staff going to be? How's it going to appear to them? How are we going to present it if we go through with it?' And so we worked on it, and we worked on it, and she was for it – she's a great woman in many ways: she has got humanistic values at the end of the day. So I basically had a package to offer him which I hoped would re-energise him, and he decided to go part-time and he, you know, I mean he was really grateful for the work that we put into getting this together.

But, basically, he's pulled out?
Basically, he's put one foot out. He's now doing three days a week. Basically, what he's doing – he looks at the week like this – two days on, two days off, two days on, because he works through the weekend on his own. He's got a workshop that's just been built. He's had three exhibitions; he's now working in St Ives and he's full of the joy of being an artist.

What does that look like to you? How does that…?
I'm pretty jealous, because I see someone who's now finding his feet again; who is doing, in a way, a better job in the classroom because he's happier within himself, and he's engaging with people outside who enjoy looking at his artwork and enjoy planning with him. He's looking at next year already to get his next exhibition now … it's not sorted out; he's doing little publications for his own work. Now, you know, it's not the kind of work that I do, but I've talked to you and you've talked to me about the kind of work I would like to do, so … but I see that he's found something that he wants to do and he can do it. He's running life-drawing classes on Frid. … When I left here tonight, he was running a life-drawing class which he could not be bothered to do two years ago because he was just burnt out – you know, he'd just had enough of it all, he wanted to get home, be with his wife.

And what has happened there, what sorts of freedoms have re-energised him? And what has he escaped from? What has changed him?
What he feels like is that he's into the part-time culture, because the part-time culture is very different. He doesn't have a tutor group; he doesn't have to pass stupid bits of paper around all morning. His responsibilities have changed. He's not now expected to pass other bits of paper around which tell us what our target, benchmarks and targets should be for our Year 10 classes.

In reflecting on 'escape stories' like this one from a close friend, Jim also finds himself reluctantly, very reluctantly, questioning his own capacity to continue: 'I mean, I'm going home and I'm thinking can I carry on like this? Can I do this anymore?' Jim seems to be moving, much against his own expectations, towards a decision; a hugely emotional decision and one which, towards the end of our long sequence of talks, I really push him hard to confront: 'I've come to that decision. I don't like working in that school anymore. I don't like working in a Secondary school'.

Because?
Because I get really upset. I get really upset by good teachers leaving – you know? … I see people destroyed. You know … (pause, clearly emotional).

I know, it's an emotional thing …
Yeah.

I mean, if it …? Who else have you seen being destroyed, I mean …?
Long-term illnesses. People coming back, trying to cope; crying in the morning because they can't do a cover lesson (which probably wouldn't bother them on another day)

because they've got so much work to do. … People fighting with each other that wouldn't fight normally. Teachers taking it out on each other. Teachers taking it out on kids. Kids being unhappy because the curriculum doesn't speak to them.

Can we … I mean, the question that comes to mind there, Jim, is whether this is endemic to teaching, which is a stressful up-front profession, or the extent to which these teachers (are) being destroyed – which makes you tearful as we talk – is a result of the new conditions of change and reform? That's the question I'm trying …

It's alienation. It's a divorce; they're divorced from what matters. Because the things that are being cascaded down … don't really matter to them – they don't own them, they don't make them, they don't have a role in creating them or adapting them.

But is it that that's destroying them?
It's that. … Yeah, it is that. Connected to and part of the reconstruction of the teacher – the notion that the teacher is being re-made through target setting; objectives; looking at performance management – that is a shambles, an absolute shambles! Teachers cannot cope with it as they don't own it, they don't know what it's about, they know it's just another form of appraisal. The management team in the schools can't manage it because they don't understand it! They don't understand … In the end, I find Jim caught between this sense of impending crisis and desperation and a continuing sense of hope. He himself is suffering the same physical symptoms that he has seen so many others confront. This, remember, is a young fit man full of professional wisdom, experience and compassion. A person who could offer so much in a wisely administered system of public education. I think it's getting to the point where my health won't hold out. If I do what I'm doing, at the pace I'm doing it now, with the health problems I've had in the last couple of years – and I was fit and strong – I mean, don't forget I was telling you that I worked at the school every night; I played table tennis in a league with some of the students, and I was at school the next day bright as a button.

And now?
And now really, at times, with the migraines, with the sickness, with the stomach ailments, with the anxiety; keeping up with the bureaucracy and keeping ahead of it in many ways, so that it doesn't beat you or it doesn't get you colonised, you know, it's taking its toll, and if I carry on the way I'm going, I don't think I can make it for another twenty years. At the end of the last interview, Jim tries to summarise his feelings of frustration and enduring hope in the face of ill-conceived reforms and centrally prescribed initiatives which transform his worthy contributions and undercut his professional mission. I ask him, does he have any concluding comment? He replies, 'I think I've cried enough now – I didn't realise that I was going to get so emotional!'

It's interesting, isn't it?
Yeah.

Why do you think that is?
Because when you're reflecting in a room like this, with someone I can get on with, I see the faces and I can't kind of tell you all the stories, but I can picture the hurt and anger, and the anxiety and the pressure and the frustration. And that's not just the teachers; it's coming out in the way the kids behave to each other and to us, you know? And, we've got to fight mate! We've got to keep the fight going, because it's just crap!

Even now, Jim knows what a noble calling teaching could be and why he so much wants to endure, to outlast the mindless machine of targets, tests and tables to live to fight another day.

There is a purpose to education, which I don't want to see destroyed. There's some fantastic teachers, some fantastic students who do fantastic work and I want them to have choice, mission, opportunity, social mobility, a sense of participating in their community – a sense that they own the culture of this land. And it has given my life meaning, if you take an existentialist point of view on it. We find and create meaning for our lives, and education is hope.

References

Arnold, S. (2001). Savage Angels. *Observer Review*, 4 February, p. 12.
Carvel, J. (2003). BMA warns of threat to future of NHS. *The Guardian*, 10 October, p. 2.
Doward, J. & Reilly, T. (2003). Shameful pay makes British women worst off in Europe. *The Observer*, 12 October, p. 7.
Fitzsimons, C. (2001). I Quit. *The Guardian Education*, 9 January, pp. 2–3.
Professional Network Report (2008). For Professional Knowledge in Education and Health (PROFKNOW): Restructuring Work and Life Between State and Citizens in Europe (2002–2007) a Collaboration. University of Brighton, University of Gothenburg, National and Kopodistorian University of Athens, University of Joensuu, University of Barcelona, University of the Azores, St. Patrick's College Dublin City University & University of Stockholm.

Epilogue: Teaching Professions in Restructuring Contexts

Sverker Lindblad

Introduction

The teaching profession has been in focus for a number of studies of quite different genres. Here I will present some research carried out in the European research project 'Professional knowledge under restructuring in education and health care' (Profknow).[1] This is a seven-nation research consortium that has published a number of reports, articles and other texts.

I will start with a presentation and discussion of an extensive review of research dealing with the intersection of studies on the teaching profession and on educational restructuring. The discussion is based on the idea that we need to consider the contexts of research in order to understand research problematics and progress. After a short presentation on the research problematics in focus I will end with a summary of conclusions concerning the teaching profession in different contexts based on a set of empirical studies.

Theoretical Frameworks and Geopolitical Contexts

From the general point of view that context matters in research I will shortly comment on two aspects of studies on the teaching professions based on the extensive and very interesting research reviews carried out by the research teams in Profknow (Norrie & Goodson, 2005). These reviews are of importance for the research progress as well as for conclusions from the Profknow research (Goodson & Lindblad, 2008). I will present different frameworks for the profession studies that could be identified in the review. After that I will comment on the geographical locations of research identified. The reason for this emphasis on contexts is that it will clarify the studies done, the discursive position and the research questions that were put forward.

To begin with research frameworks, one way of dealing with teachers in research is to put them into a profession theory framework: Are teachers professionals or are they on their way to obtain the characteristics of a profession? Here we can

M. Bayer et al. (eds.), *Teachers' Career Trajectories and Work Lives,*
Professional Learning and Development in Schools and Higher Education 3,
© Springer Science + Business Media B.V. 2009

go back to classical profession theories, e.g. referring to Talcott Parsons (1939), Amitai Etzioni (1969) as well as Dan C. Lortie (1975), dealing with professions as an exclusive as well as an excluding social category. We can also identify more modern approaches of this genre in terms of an alternative logic to the market and the bureaucracy as developed by Eliot Friedson (2001), or based on notions of power/knowledge, where professionalism is linked to the disciplinarization of professions by, for example, Valerie Fournier (1999), and their governing by reason and trust (Foss Lindblad & Lindblad, 2009).

A second framework is dealing with institutions and education systems, since the history of the teaching professions is intimately linked to the history of the school as an institution as presented by, for example, John W. Meyer et al. (1992) as a world movement, by Lindblad and Popkewitz (2004) in relation to travelling ideas and by Stephen J. Ball (1990) in terms of policymaking. Ivor F. Goodson et al.'s (2006) work on the long waves of school reform is an example of relations between institutional change and teachers' work and life. So is Andy Hargreaves' (1994) penetration of teaching under the post-modern condition.

A third research framework is to put teachers' work and life in relation to more general arguments concerning social and historical changes as put forward by Benedict Anderson (2002), Pierre Bourdieu (1988) and Anthony Giddens (1988). In such arguments we find examples or possibilities to develop notions on education as a societal phenomenon in transition. We can link that to more specific ways of conceptualizing schooling and teaching, for instance in terms of governance, as pointed out by Michel Foucault (1977), which also open up for different ways of analysing schooling and teaching.

And fourth, there is a mass of literature presenting and elaborating different perspectives on teachers' work and professional knowledge in relation to studies on teaching as presented in handbooks such as those edited by Merlin Wittrock (1986) or in books on professional communities, e.g. Milbrey McLaughlin and Joan Talbert (2001), or teachers as reflective practitioners referring to Donald Schön (1983) or their education as dealt with by Judith Warren Little (1993) and Marilyn Cochran-Smith and Mary Kim Fries (2001).

From these brief exemplifications of different frameworks or ways of conceptualizing the teaching profession under restructuring follows that research in this field is fragmented in and over research traditions, research foci, as well as discursive positions. Thus, there is a lack of internal consistency and stability in this field of research, which opens up for the working of external factors in the construction of specific research approaches and interests.

Such a *collage* of research is actually what could be expected when entering the intersection between institutional change and professional work as is done in Profknow. However, considering the fragmentation concluded from the research review this specific focus did not imply that the research consortium had a tightly defined epistemic object. Instead, it opened up for various ways of dealing with the teaching professions under restructuring. This also implied that it opened up for a large contextual sensitivity in the progress of work. A technique to reflect on this sensitivity is to analyse the referencing to research made by the seven national research teams in the Profknow research review. I will use that technique here.

Looking at the way the extensive literatures were dealt with by the research teams we made two main observations. First, there was a large amount of references – more than half of the total sum – that was only mentioned by one and only one of the national research teams. To some extent these singular references were referring to specific national sources of information such as parliament bills, but still a main conclusion is that the research field was fragmented in the research consortium. Second, looking at the impact of references derived from the different national contexts, publications presented outside the Anglo-Saxon had little influence on the conclusions of the review, even if those texts were published in English. In sum, just a little more than 10% of non-Anglo-Saxon publications were referred to here. This latter finding is further underlined by the fact that the literatures found in search engines such as the ISI Web of Science were to a very high extent found in the Anglo-Saxon domain.

In sum, we got a fragmented research field constructed by the national teams, which in turn was covered by an Anglo-Saxon domination in the review conclusions. To me, these results point to the importance of considering different research cultures at work in international research cooperation and to find measures to integrate research from different parts of, for instance, Europe in research cooperation.

Research Problematics on the Teaching Professions Under Restructuring

The empirical studies in the Profknow project were based on an elaborated research proposal, a research review and case studies (edited by Beach, 2005), plus a number of meetings in the consortium. Based on the research review focusing on the intersection between the teaching professions and institutional restructuring presented above, three broad hypotheses could be put forward. I will here concentrate on these hypotheses in order to obtain a concise presentation of our work in this respect.[2]

The first hypothesis is about restructuring and *innovation*. It is summarized as follows:

- Restructuring is producing innovative institutions, by means of deregulation, increased autonomy, and marketization so that schools and hospitals will communicate more with their environments and will increase their possibilities to improve performances.

The second hypothesis is about *dissolution*:

- Restructuring is building an iron cage around institutions such as health care and education, decreasing their space for action. A number of technologies, such as league tables, quality indicators and audits, are used to regulate and discipline work processes in health care and education.

These two hypotheses are not quite contrary. In both cases they put forward the making of communicative systems. However, the working of these systems is going in different directions. The innovative hypothesis underlines the possibility to learn by inputs, e.g. from comparisons of performances or markets mechanisms. From the dissolutive hypothesis position restructuring is considered as a collapsing of institutional norms and virtues when opening the doors for market forces and commercialism.

In sum, for both hypotheses on education restructuring there is an assumption that there is a transition in the communication system and that this change is causing an impact on education and health care.

• Given this working of communication systems in relation to restructuring we have to put forward a null hypothesis as well, stating that the causal processes of communication are not working – not functioning, or blocked or reworked or ignored in different ways. Assuming that restructuring is functioning we can summarize this hypothesis in terms of organizational *decoupling*. This means here that restructuring measures are not translated all over the organization but are being isolated in relation to work processes.

When focusing on the teaching professionals we put forward three main hypotheses as well:

• *Professionalization*: Restructuring will improve the position and expertise of the professionals and their organizations. The professional autonomy at the workplaces will increase as well as the professional authority and legitimation vis-à-vis clients. This is based on communication of expertise at work producing expected and valued outcomes.
• *Deprofessionalization*: This is a contrary process built on the same dimensions concerning autonomy, authority and legitimation. The main tendency it that restructuring implies a deprofessionalization of teachers in terms of responsibility, intensification and control.
• *Professional reconfiguration*: This is an alternative hypothesis focusing on changing qualities in professional definitions implying that patterns in terms of professional governance are in transition. A main idea is that we would notice 'new' workings of professions related to restructuring.

In the first two hypotheses we are focusing on the professionals with the notions on social positions and professional closure in mind. In order to investigate into the dimensions of professionalization and deprofessionalization we focus on the organizing of work on one side and on the interaction with clients on the other side. What are then the causalities at work here? In a word, it concerns asymmetries in communication. Under the professionalization hypothesis it is on one hand opportunities to closure from the professionals' point of view, and on the other hand having an impact on organizational decisions as well as on acceptance and trust from the side of the clients. Given the statement that expertise excludes (Nowotny, 2000), we can state that increasing asymmetries in communication with clients and increasing participation in organizational decision-making are basic under professionalization processes. In the same way, decreasing asymmetries is basic in de-professionalization as well as increasing participation in organizational decision-making. Tendencies concerning autonomy and authority are indications of outcomes of such processes.

The third hypothesis is twisting the notions of professionalization–deprofessionalization a bit. The point is that restructuring implies differences in institutional working and institutional relations. Given this, we might expect that the structure of professional characteristics might change as well. Thus, the classical notions of closure, expertise and asymmetries might be turned around in other ways. Indications on this are the 1960s notion concerning 'a profession for everyone' (Wilensky, 1964) and analyses of the expansion of the profession concept during the last decades as pointed out by Fournier (1999).

The first two hypotheses are focusing on positions and interaction. They are contrary in their workings, and we could also assume an outcome in between professionalization and deprofessionalization. The scale is the same but the position on the scale is changing. The third hypothesis is pointing towards new constellations of professional work and life. This means that we need to identify such eventual constellations and their structural relations.

Researching the Teaching Professions

Going back to the Profknow research review (Norrie & Goodson, op. cit.) little research was devoted to the fact that restructuring is part and parcel of professional work life carried out by actors such as teachers and nurses with their orientations and experiences based on previous actions, interactions under given preconditions and boundaries. Thus, we focused our studies on the professionals and their ways of organizing work in interaction with their clients. For such reasons, this turned out to be the focus of the Profknow project.

With this focus – and its limits – we learn about professions and restructuring from a specific point of view, which is based on the information that professionals' provide us regarding their experiences and strategies when dealing with work life in change. We also learn about the meaning of restructuring from these actors' perspective and their conceptions of how restructuring is working. What we get are narratives of restructuring from the perspectives of the professional actors. The ambition here is that restructuring processes are dealt with as part and parcel of professional work life, where other aspects are integrated into the set of processes, resources and events that make up this work life. Stated otherwise, with this contextualizing research strategy we had the ambition to capture ongoing processes of institutional restructuring in their lived working, as experienced by central actors in these institutions.

On the other hand, such research is interactive for obvious reasons – being implications of our frameworks in constructing instruments and a mutual construction of data in communication with the teachers that were in focus of our studies.

In a set of studies we did ethnographies and life histories in seven European multicultural contexts working with primary school teachers summarized by Müller et al. (2007), surveys of 4,400 teachers in four countries, as presented by Sohlberg et al. (2007) plus document analyses concerning educational politics and reform edited by Beach (2005). These studies are presented, including current publications, by Lindblad (2007) and reflected upon by Hernandez et al. (2008).

Findings from Research

Two first findings were based on the national case studies with a focus on policy discourses and nationally based narratives on periodizations and educational change. We noted – not unexpectedly – that such system narratives were quite differently organized (see Goodson & Lindblad, op. cit., p. 298) having their basis in the fight against dictatorships, in the (re)construction of welfare states, or in the introduction of neo-liberal measures. Stated otherwise, the system narratives were presenting quite different preconditions for educational reform. But we also noted an increasing homogenization at the end – in terms of similar agendas. In sum, we find quite different trajectories into the current states.

The Profknow research approach had as a distinct characteristic that a bottom-up strategy was used, with a focus on teachers' and nurses' experiences, perspectives and strategies. Such an approach has distinct constraints and opportunities by studying professional work life as codified by the professionals at work in the periphery of welfare state institutions. Within the theoretical and methodological framework used, the studies resulted in a number of distinct findings. An example of this was the rejection of the generation concept as an organizing concept, based on the works of de Lima et al. (2008).

It has to be underlined that large numbers of the professionals are experiencing a work life that is characterized by a combination of individual conceptions of control over work *and* on the other side by lack of participation in organized decision-making at the workplaces of these individuals. Thus, we have a combination of statements about individual professional autonomy and control *and* exclusion from decisions on resources, development of strategies and so forth. The individual professional autonomy is exemplified in Table 1, based on the survey studies (Sohlberg et al., 2007):

Concerning *teachers' life histories*, Müller et al. (2007, p. 3) put forward common themes as well as distinct differences over national contexts:

- Literally all teachers reported the difficulties they face through a more and more heterogeneous student population involving students with disabilities, immigrant students, or simply students with different learning needs.
- Teachers also reported their students to be more rebellious, harder to control and indisciplined.
- All teachers across the countries were distressed with a loss of prestige and respect of their profession. Loss of class barriers, a consumerist attitude towards education, or public blaming of teachers (in mass media) for the 'failures' of the younger generation all contributed to a sense of status loss.

In contrast to these commonalties between the cases, teachers expressed themselves very differently on their *working conditions* in their professional work life histories.

Table 1 How much are different factors conceived of having an impact on the professional work life of teachers?[a] Percent that state that the respective factor has large or very large influence

Factor	Sweden	Finland	Ireland
My own conception of how work should be done	61	74	80
Control of supervisors	2	1	4
Demands of documenting work	15	4	25
Competition with other institutions	2	2	4
Evaluation of work	6	5	21
Planning will colleagues	16	13	19
Opinions of clients/students	25	8	14
Risk of being sued	2	5	10
Mass media coverage	2	2	6

[a]Question: How much would you say that following factors *influence* your everyday work as a teacher? ($N = 3.300$ with a response ratio = 68.3). See Sohlberg et al. (2007, p. 39) for further technical information.

- Virtually all the teachers talked about an increase in terms of documentation and paper work they had to fulfil. However, the real impact in terms of accountability and evaluation was very diverse and ranged from 'control by the educational authorities coupled to consequences' to simply 'formal compliance and paper work'.
- Educational, state-initiated reforms occurred in all participating countries; however, their effect and impact on teachers were very diverse. No simple, one-dimensional process of professionalization or de-professionalization can be described. What appears to be common between the cases is rather a certain 'tiredness' of educational reform by teachers.
- Very different levels of infrastructure (equipment, building) were found and described in all cases as 'improvable'. The most decisive factor for working conditions, however, remains tied to class size and competent, professionally committed staff. The entry into the profession was reported by most teachers as being especially difficult and unstable due to the precarious types of temporary contracts.

What Müller et al. (op. cit.) present on the common thematics is a picture supporting notions of teachers' work and life as preoccupied by their everyday interactions with clients – similar to so-called street-level bureaucrats. Furthermore, what is noted in a number of work life narratives is the increase of tasks in the teaching profession – such as documentation and evaluation – implying a change in content of professional work life.

However, when considering differences in working conditions, these seem to be varying over contexts. In the survey studies, northern European teachers (Finland and Sweden) present themselves as more autonomous with less of external control compared to western Island Europe (Ireland), a fact that also corresponds to the work life histories.

With these findings as a background I will present conclusions from the studies carried out in relation to the general hypotheses presented previously concerning work life restructuring and the teaching professions.

The Innovation Hypothesis

Frequent in the introduction of restructuring measures were statements that such measures in different forms would produce a more dynamic and innovative educational system. For instance, deregulation and autonomous schools were expected to increase variation in ways of working in these schools in combination with distinct estimates of success, which in turn would lead to renewals in education (e.g. Chubb & Moe, 1990; Papagiannis et al., 1992). However, our studies showed no signs of such innovative dynamics. What mattered for teachers was instead to deal with everyday work life, with its encounters. This is often done in combination with a lack of resources and a bit more problematic relations to clients. An eventual source to more innovative work could be found in increased teamwork and increasing demands on documentation. But we found little evidence that could make us accept this hypothesis in ethnographies and in teachers' work life histories in Müller et al. (2007) as well as in the survey studies by Sohlberg et al. (2007).

The Dissolution Hypothesis

In a number of critical studies on restructuring in education and health care distinctively summarized by Beach (2005) it is expected that restructuring would be translated into a number of technologies – league tables and information systems for consumer choice as well as quality indicators and audits – technologies in use that would increase tight disciplinarization and regulation of professional work life. The same picture is also presented in the research reviews. Though our results differ over national contexts, one main tendency is that professional work life experiences are focused on what is going on in the interaction with clients within preconditions of work that is demanding in different ways – time pressure, conflicting demands, intensification and so on – in combination with changes in relations to their clients.

A number of observations in different contexts point in the direction that consumer choice, or management supervision and evaluation are not experienced as being of vital concern from the professionals' point of view. Thus, on the basis of work life narratives educational restructuring measures or rationales are not the main thing in 'professional work life under restructuring'. Given the current bottom-up approach, a rejection of the dissolution hypothesis would fit best with professional work life narratives.

Thus, we got a seemingly contradictory combination of system narratives pointing towards a thorough restructuring shown in policy discourse analyses *and* work life narratives pointing in another direction that these measures do not matter much according to teachers' work life histories and analyses of survey results. In order to deal with this combination we are going over to the decoupling hypothesis.

The Decoupling Hypothesis

A starting point is the combination of system narratives of restructuring welfare state institutions and work live narratives rejecting the impact of such restructuring. How do we understand this seemingly inconsistent finding?

A first answer – based on, for instance, theories on policy implementation from a Weberian point of view – is that restructuring measures have failed since the professionals do not experience or behave in a way that corresponds to the prescriptions put forward in restructuring measures, for instance adjust themselves to market demands.

However, as pointed out by, for example, Meyer and Rowan (1977), it is reasonable to expect that there is a difference between technical activities (such as teaching or nursing) in an organization and its proclaimed institutional rules (such as adjusting to markets and parental choice or quality indicator improvement) and that this difference is more or less inherent in institutional change due to conflicts between rules, demands to solve tasks at hand in specific and unique situations and so forth. Such differences are dealt with in a number of decoupling issues such as professional delegation, ambiguous goals, ceremonialization of evaluation and inspection and so forth, making organizations work *and* correspond to institutional rules introduced. Meyer and Rowan (op. cit., p. 357) state:

> The advantages of decoupling are clear. The assumption that formal structures are really working is buffered from the inconsistencies and anomalies involved in technical activities. Also, because integration is avoided disputes and conflicts are minimized, and an organisation can mobilize support from a broader range of external constituents.

Based on such understandings of organizational change it is possible to claim that decoupling is what is expected to happen – that the celebration of restructuring rules is living side by side with autonomous professional activities in a way that makes the organization of work more flexible and sustainable. This, in turn, is consistent with studies on the stability of schooling as an institution, such as those by Cuban (1993).

The hypotheses of innovation and dissolution were constructed on the basis of communication – that restructuring measures are being implemented, making a difference in teachers' and nurses' professional work life. The decoupling hypothesis is questioning such an implementation, stating that boundaries are at work making professional autonomy possible and at the same time facilitating the introduction of institutional restructuring. This is also a way of reformulating relations between system narratives and work life narratives as parallel stories. It is also a way to understand how teachers and schools can deal with contradictory tasks as well as the stability in schools' way of working.

Professionalization, De-professionalization or Professional Reconfiguration

When considering the professions and their positions under restructuring, the Profknow research presented a number of findings. Thus, Müller et al. (2007) noted a loss of prestige and respect for teachers, which can be read as an indication for de-professionalization. Similarly, Sohlberg et al. (op. cit.) point to increasing demands on teachers to explain what they mean to students and parents and to listen more to students' opinions in their work, indicating decreasing asymmetries in the relation between professional and client, as exemplified in Table 1 above.

Given such findings in combination with other analyses in the Profknow research we would like to abandon the professionalization–deprofessionalization argument as such. Instead we would like to put forward a professional reconfiguration hypothesis, arguing that the professional positions are in transition. Thus, Foss Lindblad and Lindblad (2009) state that professional distinctions as such (autonomy, knowledge base, monopoly, etc.) are in change in general, and that notions of self-disciplinarization and trust (see also Fournier, 1999 and Harvey, 1989) are put forward in organizations that are becoming more flexible. This they relate to issues of accountability and deregulation with a focus on the teaching profession. So far our studies point in similar directions for the nursing profession, as noted by Kosonen and Houtsonen (2007). Given such notions of reconfiguration, current professionalization discourses – referring to professional traits and functions and re- or de-professionalization – can be considered as somewhat outdated as a research problematic.

Actually, though we have put forward a decoupling stance above, we noted some changes experienced by the professionals pointing in a reconfiguring direction, for instance increasing demands on documentation, more of collegial teamwork and communicative interaction with clients. Thus, there are quite a few indicators that are possible to interpret in terms of reconfiguration of the nursing and teaching profession.

In this short presentation of findings we have learned about professional work in the intersection between the welfare state schools and citizens in societies in transitions in terms of demography and social structures as well as authority relations. In the Profknow project we compared work life over national contexts as well as over generations and we have tried to capture ongoing institutional changes in relation to professional strategies and organization of experiences. In our work notions of knowledge have been frequent – in terms of knowledge distinctions and different demands on professional expertise. Quite a few of our studies (such as Foss Lindblad & Lindblad, 2007) have dealt with professional work life in a knowledge society (Stehr, 1994) and changing demands on education and lifelong learning.

Concluding Comments

In this final chapter we have put forward a number of findings concerning professional work life under restructuring. They can also be summarized in the following preliminary theses to be further discussed and explored:

National differences turning into harmonization: Welfare state restructuring in different European national contexts is based on qualitatively different trajectories moving into similar policy and reform characteristics today. Such a variation implies that preconditions for educational restructuring differ over national contexts. Thus, it is important in research cooperation to consider and preserve such differences when working with research problematics in a comparative way.

System narratives differ from professional work life narratives: Policy discourses on welfare state restructuring correspond to some extent with professional work life experiences. This conclusion is of vital importance when doing, for example, policy ethnographies. What the political is in the politics of schooling, for instance, is then important to identify.

Institutional restructuring is combined with professional decoupling: Differences between system narratives and work life narratives are possible to understand in a fruitful way as organizational decoupling makes professional work life autonomous and conflicting rules in restructuring workable, given the often-changing preconditions at work.

Reconfiguration of professions: The teaching and nursing professions are not being one-dimensionally professionalized or deprofessionalized. Instead we are noting indications of professional reconfiguration in terms of autonomy, client interaction and governance.

To end, given these preliminary conclusions a reconfiguration of the teaching profession can be a highly interesting comparative research problematic, especially when combined with organizational decoupling and professional work life in restructuring schools.

Notes

1. This text is based on research carried out in the Profknow research project supported by the European Commission. Project no. CIT2-CT-2004-506493. The following researchers carried out studies in this project. Without their work the current text could not have been written: Ari Antikainen, Jorge Ávila de Lima, Dennis Beach, Amalia Creus, Magdalena Czaplicka, Nasia Dakopoulou, Maeve Dupont, Rita Foss-Lindblad, Xavier Giró, Ivor Goodson, Fernando Hernández, Jarmo Houtsonen, Toni Kosonen, Verónica Larrain, Jörg Müller, Max Muntadas, Caroline Norrie, Helder Pereira, Ewa Pilhammar Andersson, Constantina Safiliou-Rothschild, Juana M. Sancho, Giannis Skalkidis, Peter Sohlberg, Areti Stavropoulou, Ciaran Sugrue, Dimitra Thoma, Evie Zambeta, and Gun-Britt Wärvik.
2. Here I am using the final report from Profknow. For further elaboration, see Goodson and Lindblad (2008, pp. 7ff and 296–310)

References

Andersen, B. (2002). *Imagined Communities: Reflections on the Origin and Spread of Nationalism.* London: Verso.

Ball, S. J. (1990). *Politics and Policymaking in Education.* London: Routledge.

Beach, D. (Ed.) (2005). Welfare State Restructuring in Education and Health Care: Implications for the Teaching and Nursing Professions and their Professional Knowledge. Report No 2 from the Profknow project. www.profknow.net

Bourdieu, P. (1988). The 'Globalisation' Myth and the European Welfare State. In P. Bourdieu, & R. Nice (Eds.), *Acts of Resistance: Against the New Myths of Our Time.* New York: The New Press.

Chubb, J. & Moe, T. (1990). *Politics, Markets and America's Schools.* Washington, DC: Brookings.

Cochran-Smith, M. & Fries, M. K. (2001). Sticks, Stones, and Ideology: The Discourse of Reform in Teacher Education. *Educational Researcher*, 30(8), 3–15.

Cuban, L. (1993). *How Teachers Taught: Constancy and Change in American Classrooms, 1890–1980.* New York: Longman.

De Lima, J.Á., Houtsonen, J. & Antikainen, A. (2008). *Teachers' Experiences of Restructuring: Problems and Possibilities of a Generational Approach.* www.profknow.net

Foss Lindblad, R. & Lindblad, S. (2009). The politics of professionalising talk on teaching. In M. Simons, M. Olssen & M. Peters (Eds.) *Re-reading Education Policies: Studying the Policy Agenda of the 21st Century.* Rotterdam: Sense Publishers. (In print)

Foucault, M. (1977). *Discipline and Punish: The Birth of the Penitentiary.* London: Tavistock.

Fournier, V. (1999). The Appeal to 'Professionalism' as a Disciplinary Mechanism. *Social Review*, 47(2), 280–307.

Friedson, E. (2001). *Professionalism, the Third Logic: On the Practice of Knowledge.* Chicago: University of Chicago Press.

Giddens, A. (1988). *The Third Way: The Renewal of Social Democracy.* Oxford: Polity Press.

Goodson, I. & Lindblad, S. (Eds.) (2008). *Crossprofessional Studies on Nursing and Teaching in Europe.* Report No 6 from the Profknow project. www.profknow.net

Goodson, I., Moore, S., & Hargreaves, A. (2006). Teacher Nostalgia and the Sustainability of Reform: The Generation and Degeneration of Teachers' Missions, Memory and Meaning. *Educational Administration Quarterly*, 42(1), 42–61.

Hargreaves, A. (1994). *Changing Teachers, Changing Times: Teachers' Work and Culture in the Postmodern Age.* London: Cassell.

Harvey, D. (1989). *The Condition of Postmodernity.* Cambridge, MA: Blackwell.

Kosonen, T. & Houtsonen, J. (Eds.) (2007). University of Joensuu: European Nurses' Life and Work Under Restructuring: Professional Experiences, Knowledge and Expertise in Changing Contexts. Report No 5 from the Profknow project.

Lindblad, M. (2007). Analysis of Work-Controlling Factors for Street-Level Bureaucrats. A comparative analysis of teachers and nurses over generations. Revised C-thesis in Statistics at Uppsala University, Sweden.

Lindblad, S. & Popkewitz, T. S. (2004). *Educational Restructuring: International Perspectives on Travelling Policies.* Information Age Publ.

Lortie, D. (1975). *Schoolteacher: A Sociological Study.* Chicago, IL: University of Chicago Press.

McLaughlin, M. & Talbert, J. (2001). *Professional Communities and the Work of High School Teaching.* Chicago, IL: University of Chicago Press.

Meyer, J. E. & Rowan, B. (1977). Institutionalized organisations: Formal Structure as Myth and Ceremony. *American Journal of Sociology*, 83, 340–363.

Meyer, J. W., Ramirez, F. O., & Soysal, Y. N. (1992). World Expansion of Mass Education, 1870–1980. *Sociology of Education*, 65(2), 128–149.

Müller, J., Hernández, F., Sancho, J., Creus, A., Muntadas, M., Larrain, V. & Giro, X. (Eds.) (2007). European Schoolteachers work and life under restructuring: *Professional Experiences, Knowledge and Expertise in Changing Context*. Report No 4 from the Profknow Project. www. profknow.net

Norrie, C. & Goodson, I. (Eds.) (2005). A literature review of welfare state restructuring in education and health care in European contexts. Report 1 from the Profknow project.

Nowotny, H. (2000). Transgressive Competence: The Narrative of Expertise. *European Journal of Social Theory* 3 (1), 5–21

Papagiannis, G. J., Easton, P. A. & Owens, J. T. (1992). *The School Restructuring Movement in the USA: An Analysis of Major Issues and Policy Implications*. Paris: UNESCO.

Parsons, T. (1939). The Professions and Social Structure. *Social Forces* 17, 457–467.

Schön, D. A. (1983). *The Reflective Practitioner: How Professionals Think in Action*. New York: Basic Books.

Sohlberg, P., Czaplicka, M., Lindblad, S., Houtsonen, J., Müller, J., Morgan, M., Wärvik, G., Dupont, M. & Kitching, K. (2007). *Professional Expertise Under Restructuring: Comparative Studies of Education and Health Care*. Report No 3 from the PROFKNOW project.

Stehr, N. (1994). *Knowledge Societies*. London: Sage.

Warren Little, J. (1993). Teachers' Professional Development in a Climate of Educational Reform. *Educational Evaluation and Policy Analysis*, 15(2), 129–151.

Wilensky, H. (1964). The Professionalization of Everyone. *American Journal of Sociology*, 70, 137–158.

Wittrock, M. (Ed.) (1986). *Handbook of Research on Teaching*, Third edition. New York: Macmillan.

Author Index

A

Abbott, A., 75
Achinstein, B., 40, 86, 87, 89
Acker, S., 6, 57, 117, 127, 160, 162, 165
Aelterman, A., 167
Alexander, R., 171, 172
Allard, A., 169
Anderson, G., 189
Anderson, L., 145, 150, 151, 157
Apple, N., 118
Archer, M.S., 75, 81, 90
Arnold, S., 205
Arnot, M., 163
Atkinson, P., 120

B

Bagley, C., 170
Ballet, K., 30, 40
Ball, S., 3
Ball, S.J., 68, 117, 131, 212
Barnard, N., 132
Bartlett, D., 130
Bartlett, L., 181, 195, 197, 198
Bayer, M., 1–8, 15, 16, 21, 93–115
Becker, H., 120, 121
Benard, B., 63
Berger, P., 31
Berger, P.L., 128
Bernstein, B., 49, 94, 95, 175
Bertaux, D., 72
Birkeland, S.E., 151
Blase, J., 189
Blumer, H., 10, 31
Borman, G.D., 71
Bourdieu, P., 72, 73, 76, 80–82, 85–88, 212
Boyd, D., 85, 86
Bradley, H., 169
Brewer, N., 159
Bricheno, P., 6, 19, 159–175

Brinkkjær, U., 1–8, 15, 16, 21, 93–115
Broadfoot, P., 122
Brown, M., 118, 131
Bryk, A.S., 62
Buffum, A.G., 180, 184, 186, 187, 198
Burden, P.R., 182

C

Campbell, R.J., 118, 123
Carney, S., 3
Carroll, S.J., 152
Carter, K., 30, 37, 43
Carvel, J., 205
Casassus, B., 162
Casey, K., 31
Castells, M., 57
Catcheside, K., 205
Charmaz, K., 183
Cheng, Y.C., 62
Cherniss, C., 117, 130
Chevalier, A., 163
Christensen, J., 1, 10, 12, 17, 18, 20, 93, 115
Clandinin, D., 31
Clark, C., 31
Cochran-Smith, M., 31, 144, 183
Coleman, M., 162, 169–171, 173
Connelly, F., 31
Convery, A., 121
Cooley, C.H., 10
Cooper, C.L., 118–120, 128
Corbin, J., 183
Craig, E., 85
Crosswell, L., 62
Cubillo, L., 173

D

Dainton, S., 119
Darling-Hammond, L., 156

Datnow, A., 192
Day, C., 4, 9–13, 16, 17, 20–26, 49–66, 71, 93
Deketelaere, A., 43, 44
Densmore, K., 118
Denzin, N., 32
Dinham, S.K., 118, 120
Dolton, P., 163
Donaldson, M., 181, 193
Doug, M., 166, 196
Doward, J., 205
Dowling, N.M., 71
Doyle, W., 30, 43
Drudy, S., 160, 162, 164, 166, 167
Due, J., 107

E
Ebmeier, J., 62
Edmunds, J., 183
Edwards, S., 171
Elbaz, F., 25
Elkins, T., 50
Ellen, B., 167
Elliott, B., 62
Elliott, J., 50
Ellis, D., 180
Evans, R., 193
Evetts, J., 50, 117, 127

F
Farber, B.A., 197
Fenstermacher, G., 40
Fessler, R., 1, 9–13, 17–20, 23–26, 93, 115, 182
Filipp, S.-H., 32
Finlayson, L.R., 162
Firestone, W.A., 62
Fitzsimons, C., 206
Ford, M.E., 131
Franke, M., 143
Fransson, G., 15
Fries, M.K., 212
Furudi, F., 204

G
Gardner, J.A., 118
Garner, R., 166
Geoff, T., 5, 22, 117–132, 137–141
Gergen, K., 31
Gergen, M., 31
Gewirtz, S., 50
Giddens, A., 120, 121, 131
Glaser, B.G., 120
Gleick, J., 197

Goddard, A., 162
Goffman, E., 121, 125
Goodson, I., 7, 30, 37, 57, 72, 203–210
Goodson, I.F., 117, 181, 182
Goodwin, A.L., 183
Goss, S., 50
Griffiths, M., 168
Gudmundsdottir, S., 31
Gu, Q., 4, 49–66

H
Hakim, C., 159
Hammersley, M., 120, 132
Hanushek, E.A., 152
Hargreaves, A., 3, 40, 49, 50, 57, 118, 123,
    182, 191–193
Hargreaves, L., 174
Harris, A., 29, 198
Healy, G., 129
Henderson, N., 63
Hess, F.M., 86
Higgins, G., 63
Hobbs, D., 119
Hodkinson, H., 50
Hodkinson, P., 50
Horng, E.L., 153
Howard, G.R., 89
Howe, N., 183–186, 188, 197
Howson, J., 119
Huberman, M., 1, 9–26, 32, 53, 61, 93, 99,
    110, 117, 118, 121, 125, 126, 181, 190,
    191, 193, 196

I
Ingersoll, R.M., 50, 71, 143, 147, 189
Iyer, P., 165

J
James-Wilson, S., 57
Jeffrey, B., 122, 127, 131, 132
Jensen, V., 165
Johnson, J., 205–206
Johnson, S.M., 150, 151, 186, 189
Johnston, J., 166, 169
Judith, C.C., 10
Judith, W., 212

K
Kauppinen-Toropainen, K., 162
Keamy, R.K., 169

Kelchtermans, G., 2, 3, 29–44, 50, 57, 120
Kington, A., 4, 49–66
Klinck, P., 169
Ko, P.S., 172
Krüger, H.-H., 30
Kruse, S.D., 168, 169, 174
Kushman, J.W., 62
Kyriacou, C., 5, 21, 22, 50

L
Lammi, J., 162
Lancaster, L.C., 181, 184, 186–188, 198
Lankford, H., 152
Lawn, M., 118
Lazarus, R.S., 121
Lee, J., 162
Leithwood, K.A., 118
Levinson, D.J., 12
Lieberman, A., 195
Lindblad, S., 7, 211–221
Lipton, M., 144
Loeb, S., 153
Lortie, D., 1, 2, 25, 106
Louis, K.S., 62, 182
Lovely, S., 180, 184, 186, 187, 198
Luckmann, T., 31
Lundgren, U.P., 99
Lyons, G., 171
Lyons, K.B., 144–147, 157
Lytle, J.H., 192
Lytle, S. L., 31

M
Maclean, R., 117
Macleod, D., 119
Macnicol, J., 130
Madsen, J.S., 107
Mahony, P., 163, 173
Mannheim, K., 183
Markus, H., 31
Marotzki, W., 30
Mary, T., 159–175
Maslach, C., 5
Masyn, K., 145, 157
Maxwell, J.A., 81
McAvoy, D., 166
McCormack, A., 15
McEwan, A., 166
McKenzie, P., 117
McKeown, E., 166
McLaughlin, M., 50
McLaughlin, M.W., 182, 195
McNamara, O., 172, 174

McNeil, L.M., 192
McNess, E., 50
Mead, G., 10, 31
Measor, L., 13, 14, 32, 102, 173
Menter, I., 118, 119
Merriam, S.B., 182
Miles, M.B., 182
Miles, P., 163
Miller, L., 195
Mills, M., 162, 166–169
Milstein, M.M., 63
Morberg, Å., 15
Muijs, D., 89, 198
Murphy, B., 204
Murphy, P., 189

N
Nash, P., 50
Nazroo, J.Y., 162
Neill, S.R., 118, 123
Nias, J., 38, 39, 40, 43, 61, 62, 117, 118, 123,
      126, 128, 129
Nicklaus, H., 62

O
Oakes, J., 143, 144
O'Connell, C., 156
Ogawa, R., 40
Olsen, B., 145, 150, 151, 157
Osborn, M., 122
Oser, F., 40
Oswald, A.J., 118

P
Park, R..E., 10
Parry, L., 167
Passeron, J-Cl, 72
Patricia, B., 6
Patten, J., 166
Peter, 5, 22, 117–132, 137–141
Peterson, P., 31
Placier, P., 31, 43
Plauborg, H., 1–8, 9–26
Polkinghorne, D., 31
Pollard, A., 122, 123
Powney, J., 162, 169–173
Prettyman, S.S., 168, 169, 174
Priselac, J., 143

Q
Quartz, K.H., 6, 143–157

R

Raines, C., 187, 198
Ralph, S., 118, 131
Ravitch, D., 192
Reay, D., 72
Reid, I., 167
Reilly, T., 205
Relf, S., 119
Reynolds, D., 89
Richardson, L., 120
Richardson, V., 43
Riddell, S., 6
Riehl, C., 62
Riseborough, G.F., 121, 181, 193
Roberts, J., 206–207, 209
Robertson, S.L., 75
Rolls, S., 1–8, 9–26
Rosenholtz, S., 132

S

Sabbe, E., 167
Sachs, J., 16, 49
Safire, W., 180
Sammons, P., 4, 49–66
Sargent, P., 166, 169, 171, 172
Sayer, A., 81
Schein, E., 31
Schempp, P.G., 189
Scott, C., 118, 120, 167
Sennett, R., 130
Shen, J., 189
Sikes, P., 32, 93, 117, 120, 121, 173,
        181, 182
Sikes, P.J., 1, 9–13, 17–20, 24–26
Sipple, J.W., 62
Skelton, C., 167, 170
Slater, J., 162
Smylie, M., 29, 118, 197
Spillane, J., 198
Spock, B., 185
Steensen, J., 71–90
Stephey, M.J., 180
Stillman, D., 181, 184, 186–188, 198
Stobart, G., 4, 49–66
Stone-Johnson, C., 6, 7, 179–200
Strauss, A., 183
Strauss, A.L., 117, 120, 132
Strauss, W., 183–186, 188, 197
Stylianidou, F., 164
Susan, 77, 87, 129, 130
Sutcliffe, J., 5
Sutherland, S., 119

T

Talbert, J.E., 50, 182, 195
Tatto, M.T., 49
Tett, L., 6
Thomas, A., 145, 151, 157
Thornton, K., 170
Thornton, M., 6, 19, 159–175
Tickle, L., 14, 15, 115
Travers, C.J., 118–120, 128
Tripp, D., 14
Troman, G., 5, 22, 25, 50, 117–132
Tschannen-Moran, M., 50
Tsui, K.T., 62
Turner, B.S., 183
Twenge, J., 183, 188

U

Urbanski, A., 156

V

Vandenberghe, R., 30, 32, 57, 118

W

Wallace, J., 162, 167, 171, 173
Watters, E., 180, 186
Weiss, E.M., 189
Werner, E., 50
Wideen, M., 31
Wilhelm, K., 21
William, 126
Wilson, R., 166
Woodhead, C., 131
Woods, P., 5, 22, 25, 50, 117–132
Wragg, E.C., 120
Wurf, E., 31
Wylie, C., 161

Y

You, M.H., 172
Young, S., 119

Z

Zeichner, K., 74
Zeichner, K.M., 155
Zemke, R., 180, 181, 184, 185, 187, 198
Znaniecki, F., 72
Znaniecki, W.I.T., 72
Zumwalt, K., 85

Subject Index

A

Adaptation, 5, 67, 117–132, 137–141
Attrition, 21, 51, 62, 71, 88, 89, 123, 124, 144, 146–148, 150–153, 156, 190, 196

B

Burnout, 5, 40, 62, 123, 139, 197, 199

C

Career expectations, 172–174
Career patterns, 6, 26, 159–175
Career stages, 7, 10, 13, 24, 25, 32, 138
Center X, 143–153, 156, 157
Commitment, 10, 12, 16–20, 23, 24, 33–37, 40, 41, 49, 50, 52–67, 88, 107, 109, 111, 112, 117, 122, 126, 128–130, 132, 137, 138, 141, 143, 157, 190, 203
Continuing professional development (CPD), 10, 16, 18, 25, 29, 30, 35, 38, 43, 44, 53, 55, 66, 106, 143, 151, 156, 157, 172
Critical incidents, 13, 14, 23, 26, 30, 32, 33, 35, 37, 38, 59, 120, 121
Cross professional perspective(s), 7, 25, 203–210

D

Dispositions, 4, 63, 71–90

E

Economic factors, 162–164, 174
Educational policy, 1, 7, 29, 138
Educational reform, 3, 20, 137, 216, 217
Effectiveness, 3–4, 9, 11, 17, 49–68, 71

E

Efficacy, 12, 17, 50, 53–55, 57–59, 62, 67, 181, 191
Emotional identity(ies), 49, 57, 65
Entering the profession, 5, 6, 11–16, 21, 26, 93, 94, 100, 150

G

Generation(s), 4–7, 130, 150, 179–191, 193, 195, 196, 198–200, 203, 206, 216, 220
Generational identity, 182, 196
Generation X, 7, 180–182, 184–186, 188–191, 193, 195, 196, 198–200

H

Habitus, 4, 71–90

J

Job motivation, 34, 39, 40, 43

L

Longitudinal study, 6, 11, 21, 143–157

M

Mid-career, 13, 16–22, 26, 63, 179–182, 188–190, 195, 198, 200

N

Newly qualified teachers, 11, 12, 14, 15, 21, 94, 97–101, 105, 106, 109, 111, 112, 114, 120
Nurse(s), 7, 25, 78, 96, 118, 203–206, 215, 216, 219

P

Performativity, 3, 4, 14, 39, 49, 52, 57, 62, 64, 67, 101, 105, 108, 137, 138, 153, 186, 192, 197, 203–205, 213, 214

Personal interpretative framework, 30, 38–43

Political factors, 162–163, 174

Primary/elementary teachers, 22, 57, 150, 153, 171, 172, 215

Professionalism, 3, 5, 88, 138, 155, 205, 206, 212

Professional identity, 15, 57, 59, 62, 66, 87, 145

Professional learning, 5, 32, 38, 43, 66, 93–115, 146, 151–155, 157

Professional learning communities, 146, 151–155

Profknow, 7, 25, 211–213, 215, 216, 220, 221

R

Recruitment, 4–6, 51, 85, 118, 119, 139, 155, 164, 174, 189

Resilience, 49, 50, 53, 58, 59, 61–67

Restructuring contexts, 7, 211–221

Retention, 1, 4–6, 9, 16, 49, 51, 52, 64, 66, 67, 71, 88, 118, 139, 145–153, 155–157, 189, 190

S

Secondary teachers, 51, 56, 58, 60, 74, 162, 164, 165, 182

Self-esteem, 36, 37, 39, 40, 43, 44, 57, 197

Self-image, 39

Social factors, 6, 163, 165–167

Socio-economic background, 72, 73, 75, 85, 89

Standard(s), 20, 49, 51, 52, 56, 61, 66, 67, 80, 89, 118, 119, 137, 156, 163, 181, 191, 207

Stress, 5, 12, 21, 22, 32, 33, 37, 38, 42, 55, 67, 73, 76, 80, 85, 117–132, 137–141, 164, 197

Subjective educational theory, 38, 41–43, 45

T

Teacher training, 11, 14, 21, 26, 27, 36, 71, 72, 74, 84, 88, 89, 95, 96, 101, 164

Teaching and gender, 6, 159–175, 181, 183, 184

Teacher narratives, 2, 7, 29–44, 73, 76, 77, 83, 139, 203–210, 215–219, 221

Teachers' personal lives, 2, 4, 6, 9, 10, 13, 24–26, 30–32, 40, 44, 49–68, 106, 218, 219

Teachers' professional lives, 10, 11, 17, 49, 52–56, 58, 59, 62, 63, 65, 66, 118, 203–210

U

Urban school(s), 6, 85, 143, 147, 148, 150, 155, 189, 192

V

VITAE project, 4, 10, 11, 13, 21, 23, 26, 51, 67, 71

W

Workplace curriculum, 5, 93–115

Printed in the United States
154009LV00003B/26/P

9 789048 123575